Connecting lives and learning

Connecting lives and learning: renewing pedagogy in the middle years

edited by Brenton Prosser, Bill Lucas and Alan Reid

Wakefield
Press

Wakefield Press
1 The Parade West
Kent Town
South Australia 5067
www.wakefieldpress.com.au

First published 2010

Cover design by UniSA Document Services, cover photography by
   Sam Noonan, Noonan Photography
Book designed and typset by Paul Wallace

National Library of Australia Cataloguing-in-Publication entry

Title: Connecting lives and learning: renewing pedagogy in the middle
                  years/edited by Brenton Prosser, Bill Lucas and Alan Reid.
ISBN: 978 1 86254 892 3 (pbk.).
Subjects: Learning – Social aspects.
                  Teaching – Social aspects.
                  Effective teaching.
Other Authors/Contributors:
                  Prosser, Brenton James, 1970–   .
                  Lucas, Bill, 1956–   .
                  Reid, Alan (Alan D.).
Dewey Number: 370.1523

University of South Australia | Hawke Research Institute

Government of South Australia

Arts SA

fox creek wines

The Hawke Intersections series of books
aims to foster the sustainability and social
justice goals of the Hawke Research Institute
at the University of South Australia.

Contents

Foreword

Every fortnight 70 small children leave the confines of Rufford Nursery and Infant School in Bulwell, Nottingham, to walk along the banks of the River Leen. Once the dirtiest river in the county, it is now one of the cleanest and clearest in the country. If the children are very lucky, they might spot one of the otters that have returned to this inland stream, or catch sight of the elusive voles – now on the official vulnerable species list. But this walk is not simply an enjoyable muddy day out; it is the basis of a two-year multi-disciplinary study of 'my place'.

Rufford head teacher Judy Berry and her staff conceived this curriculum project out of frustration with a nationally funded regeneration project slowly taking shape in the surrounding estate, one of the poorest postcodes outside of London. Judy and her colleagues were angry that an explanation of regeneration inevitably proceeded as if the area was uniformly desperate, had few if any community values or practices, and was comprised of broken families (with dependent, antisocial behaviour and a damaging lack of aspiration for their children). As a long-term resident, Judy knew this to be untrue.

The school's counter move to the deficit representations of the regeneration initiative was *The Generations Project*. This is a planned sequence of activities that aims to help local children to understand the history of their place, its people and their built and natural environments.

In the first year of the project the children walked the length of the river upstream, through disused cotton mills, dye factories, potteries, locks and lace factories, to the wellspring in Newstead Abbey, former home of the infamous Lord Byron, where they enjoyed a picnic in full Victorian regalia. The second year of the project saw them walking through more industrial areas, then suburbs populated by the city's Asian peoples, followed by the city itself and ending at the River Trent. Judy is confident that the project will build important foundational, experiential understandings of the histories and contemporary manifestations of the diversity of local labour and leisure activities, patterned by class, gender and race. It will also teach the importance of water as a sustainable natural resource.

The Rufford refusal to go along with simplistic and demonising explanations of their local place, and determination to recognise and value its distinctive assets, histories and narratives, has much in common with the motivations and the work of researchers in this volume. In particular, the two projects share a:

- 'sufficient' view of children living in neighbourhoods made poor
- commitment to teachers as knowledge-producing professionals
- concern for the politics of place in globalising times.

I want to briefly address each of these in turn to show how the projects undertaken by teacher-researchers in this book, like that of Judy and her staff, are not a parochial whimsy, but an important intervention which speaks to much larger national and international concerns.

All Western educational systems are concerned to improve educational outcomes for children and young people who live in neighbourhoods suffering variously from de-industrialisation, rural decline, low levels of income support, and the imposition of marketised public services. However this endeavour is invariably framed in, and by, public policy as a discourse of lack and need. This is a deficit view where children and their families are known for their deficiencies and inadequacies, rather than for their assets and capacities. In this view, the job of public services, and the many professions that work within them, is to address flaws and weaknesses. This approach actively denies opportunity to local residents, not only to say what it is that they think needs to be done in their area, but also to take a meaningful part in the renewal process.

In reality, urban regeneration usually means reducing the proportion of people in the population mix who are living in poverty (Cameron 2003; Taylor 2000) rather than seeking ways to build on community strengths and potentials (Meegan & Mitchell 2001). This common definition of renewal is what I call an insufficient approach to working-class communities – it sees local people as having insufficient resources and therefore capabilities, and on that basis what is offered is insufficient to make meaningful change in their interests. This insufficient 'deficit thinking' (Valencia 1997) is also manifest in schooling in particular ways. In urban schools, children from communities such as Rufford are assessed for what they do *not* know rather than what they do know, and all of their interactions with the formal and informal curriculum are predicated on their insufficiency.

Running counter to this prevailing story of shortcomings is a view of children, young people and families as possessing 'assets'

(McKnight 1995) and 'funds of knowledge' (Gonzalez, Moll & Amanti 2005), which might, if recognised, form the basis of a different way of developing communities and designing and delivering key public services such as formal schooling. Educators who take up this contrary line of thought, seek ways to open children's 'virtual school bags' (Thomson 2002), rather than accept the given view, and to use it not only as the basis for connecting to the mandated curriculum, but also to work towards changing what is regarded as important and valuable knowledge.

The search for a pedagogical practice based on a view of children and young people as 'sufficient' is not confined to any one country. This South Australian edited collection shows what can be accomplished when teachers in schools and universities work together to make a difference for schools in neighbourhoods and communities that are the object of much government intervention, but are much less often the subjects of, and in, their own reform program.

Such an endeavour is not necessarily easy at a time when the very same public policy discourse, which renders entire regions as faulty and inferior, also situates public servants in general, and teachers in particular, as both the problem and the solution. The policy concern to 'lift the bar and close the gap' has been accompanied by a search for culprits to blame for poor performance. Hence, in addition to the shortcomings of marginalised children and families, it is the teaching profession that is seen to have failed. The policy remedy is to provide teachers with expert solutions and tighter prescriptions and to monitor their performance.

While this approach has been more heavy-handed in England and in parts of the United States, there is little doubt that the culture of teacher censure, with its accompanying de-professionalising and de-skilling practices, is also manifest in Australia (Smyth et al. 2000). Those represented in this book take a different view. Here, while teachers are seen as integral to redressing inequitable schooling outcomes and unjust practices, it is their individual and collective know-how – that combination of critical capabilities, reflection, skills and knowledge production that constitutes professional expertise – rather than their incapacity that is promoted, supported and (individually and collectively) developed.

The combination of a 'sufficient' view of children, families and their communities, and a productive view of teachers as knowledge-producing professionals is especially critical now. At a time when globalisation is stripping meaning from many local communities, we need a new (g)localism that supports diverse acts of resistance to globalisation and allows young people to stay in their home communities rather than leave them (Gruenewald & Smith 2008). We need an education that helps to materially, socially, and semiotically renew local communities (Sobel 2004). Gruenewald and Smith (2008: xvi) called this a place-based curriculum. They suggested that this requires:

a community-based effort to reconnect the process of education, encul-
turation, and human development to the well-being of community life.
Place-based or place-conscious education introduces children and youth to
the skills and dispositions needed to regenerate and sustain communities.

By connecting students with different people in their local neighbour-hoods, teachers and students are folded into everyday lives which are not simply here and now, but are also embedded in now and then 'stretched-out' relations, practices and narratives (Childress 2000; Davies 2000; Massey 1994). Place-based projects are thus inevitably historical and geographical. Foregrounding difference and particularity, community and place are seen as both a relationship to be strengthened, and as a text to be read (Sorenson 2008). They draw on different kinds of knowledge from those which are abstracted and distantiated in national curricula and in commercial textbooks.

Place-based and *life-world* projects are also social and cultural. A place-based curriculum forges new social bonds: it offers opportunities for schools to explicitly and critically foster identity work through events and tasks that allow students and their teachers to encounter embedded social practices and agents that they would normally avoid. Eschewing a narrow, insular and potentially inequitable localism (Gruenewald 2003), teachers create opportunities for students to engage with difference(s) and to critically engage with contemporary and popular cultures; and to question the relationship of people and nature, and the histories of oppression of indigenous peoples (Bowers 2005). Students have the space, time and support to stage events and produce texts in which they describe or inscribe themselves, those with whom they are in dialogue, and their mutual place in the world (Smith 2002).

The *Redesigning Pedagogies in The North* (RPiN) project is a fine example of *place-based* and *life-world* affirming curriculum development. Situated in schools that serve some of the poorest postcodes in Australia, it seeks to build learning experiences that are literally grounded in students' everyday lives. Like the Rufford Nursery and Infant School Generations Project in Nottingham, South Australian university and schoolteacher researchers involved in the RPiN project are committed to doing what they can, where they can, to ensure the rights of children and young people to an education which is not only meaningful and relevant, but which also enhances their life opportunities. Taking time and care to work reflectively through cycles of curriculum development, the teachers who contributed to this volume demonstrate that it is possible to 'do school' differently.

Working counter to dominant and taken-for-granted ways of working, teaching and learning is not only time consuming, but also intellectually and emotionally demanding. In the absence of a policy agenda which recognises and rewards this kind of effort, we readers must acknowledge this dimension of the professional labour of writers in this book and of the children and young people with whom they worked. We must also thank them for holding out the possibility for, and demonstrating the practicality of, combining socially just intentions with ethical pedagogical practices.

Pat Thomson
Nottingham, December 2009

References

Anyon J, 2005, *Radical possibilities. Public policy, urban education and a new social movement.* Routledge, New York.

Bennett K, Beynon H & Hudson R, 2000, *Coalfields regeneration: Dealing with the consequences of industrial decline.* The Policy Press, Bristol.

Bowers CA, 2005, *The false promises of constructivist theories of learning. A global and ecological critique.* Peter Lang, New York.

Cameron S, 2003, 'Gentrification, housing redifferentiation and urban regeneration: "Going for growth" in Newcastle upon Tyne', *Urban Studies,* 40(12), 2367–2382.

Childress H, 2000, *Landscapes of betrayal, landscapes of joy. Curtisville in the lives of its teenagers.* State University of New York Press, New York.

Davies B, 2000, *(In)Scribing body/landscape relations.* Alta Mira Press, Walnut Creek, CA.

Gold E, Simon E & Brown C, 2005, 'A new conception of parent engagement.

Community organising for school reform', in F English (ed.), *The SAGE handbook of educational leadership: Advances in theory, research and practice.* Sage, Thousand Oaks, CA, pp 237–268.

Gonzalez N, Moll L & Amanti C (eds), 2005, *Funds of knowledge: Theorizing Practices in Households, Communities and Classrooms.* Lawrence Erlbaum, Mahwah, New Jersey.

Gruenewald DA, 2003, 'The Best of Both Worlds: A Critical Pedagogy of Place', *Educational Researcher,* 32(4), 3–12.

Gruenewald DA & Smith G, 2008, 'Making room for the local', in DA Gruenewald & G Smith (eds), *Place-based education in the global age: Local diversity.* Lawrence Erlbaum, Mahwah, New Jersey, pp xiii–xxiii.

McKnight J, 1995, *The careless society. Community and its counterfeits.* Basic Books, New York.

Massey D, 1994, *Space, place and gender.* University of Minnesota Press, Minneapolis.

Meegan R & Mitchell A, 2001, '"It's not community round here, it's neighbourhood": Neighbourhood and cohesion in urban regeneration projects', *Urban Studies,* 38(12), 2167–2194.

Smith G, 2002, 'Place-based education: Learning to be where we are', *Phi Delta Kappan,* 83(8), 584–594.

Smyth J, Dow A, Hattam R, Reid A & Shacklock G, 2000, *Teachers' work in a globalizing economy.* Falmer, London.

Sobel D, 2004, *Place-based education: connecting classrooms and communities.* The Orion Society, Greater Barrington, MA.

Sorenson M, 2008, 'STAR. Service to all relations' in DA Gruenewald & G Smith (eds), *Place-based education in the global age: Local Diversity.* Lawrence Erlbaum, Majwah, New Jersey, pp 49–64.

Taylor M, 2000, 'Maintaining community involvement in regeneration: what are the issues?', *Local Economy,* 15(3), 251–255.

Thomson P, 2002, *Schooling the rustbelt kids: making the difference in changing times.* Allen & Unwin, Crows Nest, NSW.

Valencia R (ed), 1997, *The evolution of deficit thinking. Educational thought and practice.* Falmer, London.

Preface

It was with great pleasure that we accepted an invitation to edit a book in the social sustainability series co-published by Wakefield Press and the Hawke Research Institute (HRI). It has been a privilege to work and write with colleagues in education who are committed to more sustainable practices for this and future generations. Our collaborative research work has demonstrated that the contribution of educators to social sustainability is much more than just teaching young people how to earn and consume responsibly.

As co-researchers in a research institute committed to pursuing social sustainability, it is our belief that sustainability will only be achieved through an interdisciplinary effort. This is not a new idea. Those familiar with the development of historical discourses of social sustainability will recognise this commitment to interdisciplinarity through concepts such as the triple bottom line, or more recently in Australia, mutual considerations of economics, science, technology, environmental systems, social sciences, climate change and wellbeing. Further, the growing emphasis on cross-institutional and interdisciplinary research to secure funding in increasingly competitive grants processes has added to the impetus and interest in social sustainability research. Hence, one of our hopes for this book is that, through its documentation of research by educators, it will provide new insights for social sustainability debate and will foster new conceptual developments, both within and across disciplines.

However, as career educators and researchers, we also see in our everyday practice the embodiment of many of the core principles of social sustainability. For instance, in the use of what educationalists would call 'transdisciplinary' or 'integrative' approaches in the classroom, teaching can embody efforts to develop solutions to complex real life challenges, rather than dictate old answers from the established disciplines. Inherently a holistic view of knowledge production and learning, such approaches stress that the issues facing this and future generations will not fit neatly into key learning areas or traditional school subjects. Rather, our students should learn to draw on whatever knowledge, from whatever sources, that will support a relevant response to the issues they identify. The aim of this book is to portray social sustainability in praxis by providing a number of case studies of teachers who are working with students in lower socio-economic communities and seeking to respond to the challenges faced by those communities.

Each of these case studies is drawn from the findings of an Australian Research Council (ARC) industry linkage research project (LP0454869) that ran between 2005 and 2007 in Adelaide's northern urban fringe. This project, entitled *Redesigning Pedagogies in the North* (RPiN), was the result of collaboration between the Centre for Studies in Literacy, Policy and Learning Cultures (LPLC) at the University of South Australia (UniSA), the Northern Adelaide State Secondary Principals Network (NASSPN), the Australian Education Union (AEU) SA Branch and the South Australian state government's Social Inclusion Unit (SIU). The RPiN project involved over 1,000 participants and relied on a research team that included researchers from UniSA[*] and 31 teacher-researchers from the 10 NASSPN schools.[†]

Using the public title *Connecting Lives and Learning*, the aim of the RPiN project was to develop a university–school professional learning community that collaboratively built knowledge and practice around engaging middle years learners. The fact that each chapter is co-authored by a teacher-researcher and one or more of the university-based researchers, is a tangible demonstration of the strength of the partnership.

As a project set in a region of recognised socio-economic challenge, RPiN also focused on contesting deficit assumptions about students and their communities, as well as contributing to regional capacity building. More specifically, the project aimed to support teacher research around the following questions:

- How do teachers understand, design and talk about their middle years pedagogy in the light of current practice, its history and their location?
- What happens when teachers design curriculum and/or pedagogy by connecting with young people's life-worlds?
- What is sustainable in these new pedagogies?

[*] The editors wish to acknowledge the contribution of the following UniSA researchers to the conceptual development and implementation of the RPiN project: Assoc. Prof. Robert Hattam (project director); Prof. Marie Brennan; Prof. Barbara Comber; Assoc. Prof. Phillip Cormack; Dr David Lloyd; Mr Bill Lucas; Dr Faye McCallum; Assoc. Prof. Helen Nixon; Dr Kathy Paige; Dr Brenton Prosser; Prof. Alan Reid; Dr Sam Sellar; Dr John Walsh; and Dr Lew Zipin.
[†] The contributions to this edited collection are solely the views of the authors.

- How can we educate and resource future generations to face the significant challenges that inequity produces in their lives?

The focus on learning, connectedness, equity and the future in these questions demonstrates a clear emphasis on social sustainability, which is borne out in each of the chapters that follow. As the authors present their ongoing efforts to encourage social sustainability in their schools and classrooms by grappling with these questions, their discoveries converge on three major themes:

What were the effects on students?

Each of the case studies highlights a process and its outcomes aimed at enhancing the capabilities of young people to build communities that are more socially just and sustainable.

What were the effects on teachers?

In each case study there are examples of how teachers changed their orientation to pedagogy, which not only made their projects possible, but also contributed to building more sustainable pedagogical practices for the future.

What were the effects on communities?

To a greater or lesser extent, each of the case studies contributed to making current communities more sustainable (including those communities beyond the geographical boundaries of the communities studied).

As the reader considers the responses to these questions documented in each chapter, it is important not to forget what Thomson (2002) called the 'thisness' of each school, teacher, year level and class. To do so would overlook the specificity of the complex and challenging contexts in which each of the teachers work.

If a reader approaches this book looking for 'gold standard' research and revolutionary pedagogical redesign, then she or he may be disappointed. The book does not pretend to offer a formula for complex teaching situations. Rather it seeks to record and analyse – warts and all – the struggles of a number of teachers at very different points in their careers, researching aspects of their practice as they design and implement approaches to teaching that connect to students' life-worlds. Using an action-research model, the teacher-researchers, supported by their university-based colleagues, devised questions about what they found perplexing in their practice, systematically researched these questions, reflected on what they discovered and then devised a new series of questions. In short, the authors of this book do not purport to present the answers; just honestly share the experiences of their journeys and their questions.

It is our hope that as these authors document their critical reflections on their attempts to foster more socially sustainable schooling practices in their classrooms, it may offer inspiration to other educators as they think about their professional practices.

Acknowledgements

There are a number of people and groups we would like to acknowledge and thank for their part in the RPiN project and in the development of this book. They are:

- the 31 teacher researchers who participated in the RPiN project
- the 10 NASSPN principals and their school communities for their generosity in releasing the teachers so that they could be involved in the project
- the industry linkage partners – NASSPN, the AEU (SA Branch) and the South Australian Social Inclusion Unit – whose funding and commitment made this project possible
- our colleagues in the RPiN research team whose collaborative sharing of ideas contributed to the conceptual development and implementation of the project. Each of the UniSA researchers were involved in supporting all of the teacher-researchers at different points during the three-year project
- Associate Professor Robert Hattam, who as project director, oversaw every stage of the project's development and completion. Without him neither the project nor this book would have been possible
- the project support team of Andrew Bills, Kathy Brady and Pippa Milroy, as well as Sarah Rose and the research support team in the Centre for Literacy, Policy and Learning Cultures
- the editors who contributed to preparing the book for publication (Katie Maher and Paul Wallace)
- the publishers, Wakefield Press and the Hawke Research Institute, whose vision in creating this social sustainability series made the book possible. More specifically, we would like to thank Associate Professor Gerry Bloustien who coordinates the social sustainability series and Stephanie Johnston at Wakefield Press for their patience and support through the publishing process
- the Australian Curriculum Studies Association (ACSA) for its willingness to support the publication and distribution of the book.

Finally, we wish to acknowledge the researchers, based in the schools and in UniSA, who volunteered the time and made the effort to contribute a chapter to this book. With ever increasing workloads in both schools and universities, their willingness to contribute cannot be underestimated.

Brenton Prosser, Bill Lucas and Alan Reid
Mawson Lakes, January 2010

Contributors

Department of Education and Children's Services (SA)	University of South Australia
Debbie Henderson	Marie Brennan
Jennifer Jones	Rob Hattam
David Kinna	David Lloyd
Monica Lee	Bill Lucas
Sandrine Poissonier	Faye McCallum
Brendyn Semmens	Kathryn Paige
Jo Temme	Brenton Prosser
Peter Voudantas	Alan Reid
Jane Wilson	Lew Zipin

Acronyms

ABS	Australian Bureau of Statistics
ACDE	Australian Council of Deans of Education
ACER	Australian Council for Educational Research
ACSA	Australian Curriculum Studies Association
AEU	Australian Education Union
ARC	Australian Research Council
CDROM	compact disc read only memory
CEO	chief executive officer
COAG	Council of Australian Governments
CSIRO	Commonwealth Scientific and Industrial Research Organisation
DECS	South Australian Department of Education and Children's Services
DETE	South Australian Department of Education, Training and Employment
HRI	Hawke Research Institute, UniSA
ICT	information and communication technologies
IT	information technology
LaN test	literacy and numeracy test
LPLC	Centre for Studies in Literacy, Policy and Learning Cultures, UniSA
MCEETYA	Ministerial Council on Education, Employment, Training and Youth Affairs
MI	multiple intelligences
NASSPN	North Adelaide Secondary Schools Principals' Network
NEP	negotiated education plan
OECD	Organisation for Economic Co-operation and Development
PETA	Primary English Teaching Association
PD	professional development
R-12	Reception to Year 12
RPiN	*Redesigning Pedagogies in the North*
SACE	South Australian Certificate of Education
SACSA	South Australian Curriculum Standards and Accountability Framework

SES	socio-economic status
SIU	Social Inclusion Unit, South Australia
SOSE	Studies of Society and Environment
SML	Student Managed Learning
SSABSA	Senior Secondary Assessment Board of South Australia
STS	Science, Technology and Society
TAFE	Training and Further Education
TSoF	Technology School of the Future
UniSA	University of South Australia

Key terms

Category	the index of disadvantage used for South Australian schools. Schools are funded according to seven categories (Category 1 being the most disadvantaged). This formula takes into consideration the ethnic and social diversity of the student population, the socio-economics of the postcode, and the general complexities of a site
middle school	the school structure organised around the middle years
middle schooling	the philosophy and practices that are associated with teaching in the middle years
middle years	the years of schooling between Years 6 and 10, which equates to the ages of 10–15
the North	the geographic region of Adelaide that was the focus of RPiN, located north of Gepps Cross and bounded by Para West, Salisbury East and Gawler North
rustbelt	a term used to describe communities who experience a significant economic downturn usually associated with the decline of manufacturing industry
School Card	School Card is a South Australian government measurement of poverty, where families receive a range of concessions on school costs

Introduction

Connecting lives and learning:

mapping the territory

Brenton Prosser

As educators, we know that there are persistent problems with engaging adolescent students. We recognise the link between the middle years and later school retention. We are concerned by the differential schooling outcomes due to socio-economic status. Yet, how often do the challenges translate into pedagogical innovation and school reform?

More often than not, efforts to address these problems are nullified with 'we tried that before and it didn't work' or 'the problem is too big to change'. Alternatively, we may hear teachers explain that time constraints or the demands of the senior years are reasons for not moving beyond 'chalk and talk' teaching styles to more inclusive and engaging practices. These observations are confirmed when one considers the area that has most recently been the subject of school reform efforts, namely the middle years of schooling.

According to the *Beyond the Middle* (Luke et al. 2003) report, the middle years reform effort is both unfinished and exhausted, with the engagement of students and the pursuit of academic rigour relying on the efforts of individual teachers. Meanwhile, as a profession, we continue to grapple with the changing realities of teaching. With most of the current cohort of Australian teachers trained pre-Internet (and many pre-computer) the challenge of new technologies and digital culture is immense. Where schools were once the major locale for young people to learn about their world and the worlds of others, this is increasingly not the case. As new generations of technologies make the distinction between 'virtual' and 'actual' lives less relevant to our middle years students

(Carrington 2006), teachers are caught trying to find ways to connect the offline world of the school with the online existence of the student. As we plan for jobs that have not yet been imagined, ponder literacies that do not yet exist, and prepare citizens for an increasingly global world, we find ourselves in a situation where there is a 'greater generational cleavage between teachers and students today than ever before' (Hayes, Mills, Christie & Lingard 2006: 11).

There are also persistent economic, environmental and social inequities that present significant challenges to the educational attainment of students, to the viability of communities and to sustaining alternative pedagogies. The socio-economic status of students still remains a major factor in differential achievement at school while deficit stereotypes and the intensification of social need in struggling communities cannot be left at the classroom door. Supporting social sustainability is a key responsibility of all teachers. Yet, with ever-growing demands on teachers' work, the development of more socially sustainable pedagogical practices, so that learning can occur, remains ever elusive.

For those teaching in poor, urban-fringe communities, socially sustainable practice is a daily challenge that has an immediate visible impact on the lives of students and the community. So significant are the demands of these challenges, it is perhaps not surprising to see rapid teacher turnover and an under-representation of experienced teaching professionals in lower socio-economic school communities. In turn, this presents questions of quality and equity in service provision.

In the light of these (at times overwhelming) challenges, perhaps it is understandable that we often hear Australian teachers say that the problem is too big, progress is too slow, and practical responses too hard to sustain.

Yet, both the current generation of (soon-to-retire) teachers and the next generation of teachers to follow are faced with choices. Do we say it is all too hard and continue as we have, or do we respond to the challenges by attempting more sustainable and innovative pedagogical practices? Do we accept the inevitability of inequity, exclusion and failure, or do we seek better opportunities and futures for our students and their communities? Do we locate the challenge in some deficit quality of the student rather than in our pedagogy, and in so doing condemn our best pedagogical efforts (and ultimately our role as teachers) to irrelevance?

It is a response to these questions that this book documents. Acutely aware of the challenges that stifle innovation and social sustainability in the middle years of schooling, the teacher-researchers in this book tried it anyway. With the support of the *Redesigning Pedagogies in the North* (RPiN) project, these teachers worked on the premise that if we are to address the crisis of relevance and inequity in schooling, then teachers need to learn more about students and their communities through research and critical reflection. Hence, their work not only contributes to debate about education and social sustainability, but also to our understanding of the role of teachers as researchers into their own practice, an area that has been largely neglected in previous renditions of middle years reform (Cumming 1993; Luke et al. 2003; Main & Bryer 2007; Pendergast & Bahr 2005).

RPiN & social sustainability

The RPiN project understood 'social sustainability' to be:

> a positive condition within communities, and a process within communities that can achieve that condition. (McKenzie 2004: 23)

This includes:

- equity of access to key services (including health, education, transport, housing and recreation)
- equity between generations, meaning that future generations will not be disadvantaged by the activities of the current generation
- a system of cultural relations in which the positive aspects of disparate cultures are valued and protected, and in which cultural integration is supported and promoted when it is desired by individuals and groups
- the widespread political participation of citizens not only in electoral procedures, but also in other areas of political activity, particularly at a local level
- a system for transmitting awareness of social sustainability from one generation to the next
- a sense of community responsibility for maintaining that system of transmission
- mechanisms for a community to collectively identify its strengths and needs
- mechanisms for a community to fulfil its own needs where possible through community action

- mechanisms for political advocacy to meet needs that cannot be met by community action. (McKenzie 2004: 13–4)

In the chapters that follow, there are examples of the pursuit of each of these aspects of social sustainability within school communities. As such, the case studies position themselves within the wider 'glocal' and interdisciplinary efforts for social sustainability.*

While, by definition, sustainability is an interdisciplinary concept, different disciplines and fields of practice have approached its implications in different ways. Within education, some explain that the damaging assumptions of the modern capitalist west have been embodied in a hidden curriculum in our schooling systems. This view argues that our schools have practices that reproduce unsustainability. For instance, the competitive academic curriculum (Connell 1993) that handles the lifelong distribution of material resources encourages attitudes of competition and consumption. Thus, students in the senior years, rather than learning how to live in harmony and learn collaboratively, are taught only what they need to learn to maximise what they can earn. As this pressure to compete pushes down from the senior years of schooling, it also stifles the potential for engaged and life-connected learning in the earlier years.

Accepting this view, the central premise of the RPiN project was that such practices are neither equitable nor sustainable. The persistent problems with significant numbers of students experiencing disengagement and poor levels of retention in post-compulsory schooling bear this out (Hattam 2005; Smyth, McInerney & Hattam 2003). Further, so rapidly are the affinities, identities and literacies of our young people changing, that even the lives of traditionally successful students increasingly diverge from the traditional practices of schooling in such a way that it presents schooling practices with a crisis of relevance (Knobel & Lankshear 2003). Added to this is the growing complexity of contemporary schooling (Hattam & Prosser 2008; Hattam & Zipin 2009), which needs to be responsive to changing demography, such as:

- increasing levels of social and cultural complexity at a time when governments have shifted concern from the social to community (Rose 1996)

---

* In the development of the following argument around social sustainability, I would like to acknowledge the important contribution of my RPiN colleagues Alan Reid and David Lloyd.

- a significant collapse of the full-time youth labour market and a normalising of precarious employment (Pocock 2003; Pusey 1998)
- a substantial number of families and youth living in difficult financial circumstances and a concentration of the new poor living on the urban periphery of most cities (Bauman 1998)
- the re-emergence and/or unleashing of deficit views of dis-enfranchised communities, refugees, and indigenous people (Luke 1997)
- the influence of media culture on the identity formation of young people (Sefton-Green 1998)
- the recent changes in economics, which have been popularly labelled a global financial crisis.

Unfortunately, the traditional secondary school curriculum has struggled to shift in response to these challenges and is now more than ever unrelated to the lived experiences of the citizens it is supposed to serve.

In response, the RPiN 'methodo-logic' (Hattam et al. 2009: 304) made an argument that students enter schooling with diverse 'cultural capital' (Bourdieu 1984) due largely to their differing cultural backgrounds, and often this difference is defined in deficit ways by those with the power in schools. This view aligns with the concept of social capital in sustainability theory, where social capital is an asset that allows people to maintain coherence in their lives and overcome change, but that some social capital is valued more than others. This perspective need not assume a solely financial or exchange value for accumulating capital, rather, as explored by Zipin (2009), this capital could also take on an asset or use value. To give this theoretical orientation a practical face, the RPiN project drew on a model of pedagogical development that incorporates the 'funds of knowledge' (Gonzalez, Moll & Amanti 2005; Moll, Amanti, Neff & Gonzalez 1992) from students' lives while valuing the diversity of different cultures (Delpit 1993) in a context of the middle years of schooling (Prosser 2008). As such, the RPiN project sought to advance the complex and vexed notion of 'pedagogical justice' (Hattam & Zipin 2009).

In essence, the logic of the RPiN project was that young people from diverse social backgrounds enter schooling with differing degrees of cultural capital, and that increasingly the gap between students' lived experience and the standards of schooling is understood as a deficit in the student and/or their family. With the funds of knowledge concept we have a counterfoil to cultural capital. While cultural capital embodies a series of codes that can be taught to enable access to power, funds of knowledge uses an understanding of how families generate, obtain and distribute knowledge as a resource for making community assets pedagogically viable for student engagement (Gonzalez & Moll 2002: 278). Pat Thomson gave these ideas practical utility in the teaching context through the metaphor of the 'virtual schoolbag'.

Developed through Thomson's (2002) work in schools in Adelaide's northern urban fringe, the 'virtual schoolbag' is a concept built on the premise that all children come to school not only with their conventional schoolbags, but also with virtual schoolbags full of various familial, cultural and linguistic resources. However, because of the preferences in schools for certain sorts of knowledge, only some students have the opportunity to use what is in these schoolbags, leaving the knowledge, experiences and skill of many students invisible and unused in school. The contents of this schoolbag or funds of knowledge (only some of which count as cultural capital in the school setting) can be used as a resource to help teachers to identify stronger connections between students' lives and learning. In adopting this metaphor, the RPiN project seeks to foster examples of young people contributing to sustainable communities in the future and to regional capacity building in the present, and of teachers designing pedagogies that can be used to encourage sustainable pedagogical practices more generally.

The virtual schoolbag metaphor provokes teachers to ask how we can encourage students to unclip these bags, and then how we may be able to use what is hidden inside them to connect their lives with their learning. It was this challenge that was central to the *Turn around pedagogies* project (Comber & Kamler 2005), which demonstrated how teacher research into the lives of students can turn around deficit views of students and their communities. The *Turn around pedagogies* project demonstrated that teachers could experience a *turn around* in how they saw the student, by *turning to* informed research into diversity and *turning away* from deficit thinking, which could result in pedagogies that made notable differences in student literacy achievement. While the *Turn around pedagogies* project focused on literacy in the primary and middle years, its insights formed an important generative source for the RPiN project, which sought to encourage teachers to identify positive metaphors that emphasise the potential of students and to design pedagogies that could reconnect the students to the broader curriculum.

As the RPiN project unfolded, the 'virtual schoolbags' and 'turn around pedagogies' metaphors resonated with the teacher-researchers and, in part, it is their responses to these metaphors that are documented in this book. However, before proceeding to these accounts, it is important to set the broader context of the communities within which these teacher-researchers work.

Adelaide's northern urban fringe

The region of Adelaide north of Gepps Cross, or 'The North', was developed as a manufacturing hub and a pillar of the South Australian economy during the 1950s. However, as the recession of the early 1990s hit the manufacturing sector hardest in South Australia and Victoria (Megalogenis 2006; Peel 1995), it had devastating effects on income and employment in Adelaide's north. This area now includes suburbs that are listed among the most socio-economically disadvantaged in the nation, state and city (City of Playford 2006; Elliott, Sandeman & Winchester 2005), while School Card use (the government school measure of poverty) is around 10% higher than the state average (Centre for Labour Research 2002). The area is also known for its struggle with long-term youth underemployment and intergenerational unemployment (Office of Employment 2003), as well as a reduction in traditional career pathways due in part to the dramatic decline of the manufacturing industry (Thomson 2002). The rate of early school leaving is higher than the state average in this region and the retention rate to the final year of secondary school year is approximately eight percent lower than the state average (ABS 2005; ACER 2000). These urban-fringe communities have not fared well in the face of these dramatic recent economic and technological changes, and one of the main purposes of the RPiN project was to support the regional capacity building and sustainability of these communities. As noted by Hattam and Zipin (2009), schools in these northern suburbs are at the frontline of struggle to meet the challenges of significant and demographic change, often in difficult policy, media and practical contexts.

The research team selected Adelaide's northern urban fringe as the location for this research, not only because of its position as one of the most socio-economically disadvantaged regions in the nation, but also due to the strong links that already existed between schools in this region and the University of South Australia. This relationship made us aware of the challenges faced by these schools, especially in relation to teacher workload, teacher burnout, teacher retention and the greater amount of responsibility these schools take in early career teacher professional development. The relationship also made us aware of the enthusiasm of these schools to embrace innovation aimed at addressing issues of student disengagement, poor academic success and low levels of student retention.

RPiN project design

The RPiN leadership team decided that a research project that allowed time and support for teachers' professional development would be an important contribution to our partner school communities, not least because we believed that teachers are best positioned to develop curriculum, enact pedagogy and make sense of the challenges in their schools, classrooms and communities. However, we were also conscious of research that shows that teachers and teaching are the most important factors in student success (ACDE 2003; Comber & Kamler 2005), and for this reason we decided that collaboration with teachers would be central to unsettling the deficit views that can be a barrier to student success. Thus, we supported teachers to work with the students as ethnographers in their lives. This approach was decided on partly due to the limited time that teachers had to contribute to the project given their other teaching duties, but mostly because we believed that viewing students as experts on their own lives was an important starting point for challenging deficit views. Thus, from the outset, the RPiN project involved university researchers supporting teachers as they explored the life-worlds and local communities of their students with their students. The method that was used by teacher researchers could be best described as an 'action-research' cycle (Cochran-Smith & Lytle 1999; Kemmis & McTaggart 1988; McNiff, Lomax & Whitehead 1996; Webb 2000).

Although some teachers had to withdraw from the project due to redeployment or new parenthood, when the project finished, more teacher-researchers were involved than when it had commenced. Early in the project we held bi-monthly meetings with teachers to explore generative ways of thinking about the resources young people brought to school. Between these meetings, we met with smaller groups of teachers around themes that they had found to be useful in thinking about how to connect students' lives to learning. Many of the teachers were enthusiastic to learn about students' lives and to use new concepts to inform their curriculum. While many teachers found virtual schoolbags to be a useful concept, some teachers understandably found it difficult to know how to begin to unpack the complex schoolbags of their students. To assist them, the university research team designed a survey that would allow young people to tell their teachers more about their lives and learning. This survey contributed to the action-research design, as did the insights that were gained about the students' attitudes to school and learning (Prosser et al. 2008).

Later in the first year our focus shifted to supporting teachers to develop a first cycle of research projects. In small groups, the teacher and university researchers came together to discuss research approaches, analyse data, explore readings and reflect on the problems that emerged through the teacher inquiry process. This process was built around two main tasks: firstly to design a curriculum unit that used student life-worlds as a resource for learning, and secondly to use action research to collect data about the pedagogical changes that had been made and their effect on student learning. Templates for curriculum planning and resources detailing the principles of action research were produced to give structure to these two tasks. Teachers completed their research projects in the third term of school and devoted the last term to writing up their results and preparing a presentation for an end of year conference. Also during the last term, a university research assistant visited each school to interview the teacher-researchers and selected students about the teaching and research experience.

The above process was repeated in the second year, but with two major differences. Firstly, teachers were grouped according to the school sites in which they worked. Schools were then paired with three university co-researchers. This enabled more strategic support and more detailed consideration of the school context, while the relationships from the interest-based groups of the previous year could be continued through the bi-monthly meetings. Secondly, greater emphasis was placed on providing support for a more systematic collection of data and analysis, as well as exploration of the pedagogical changes that were occurring in classrooms. This re-emphasis on pedagogy not only aligned with one of the key objectives of the project, but also emerged out of our analysis of what we had discovered in the first year of the project, as is discussed below.

In the final year, there was a shift in focus as the teacher-researchers did not conduct a third research cycle, instead becoming involved in the production of web-based and other resources derived from their projects. Time was also devoted to teacher-researchers conducting seminars in the participating schools to report back to their colleagues on their inquiry, pedagogy and connecting students' lives and learning.

Learning about pedagogy & connecting lives with learning

A key theme in recent middle years literature (Carrington 2006; Luke et al. 2003; Pendergast & Bahr 2005; Prosser 2008) is the importance of adopting alternative pedagogical resources to engage students, pursue intellectual demand and improve student learning. However, one of the findings in the first year of the project was that most of the teacher-researchers were unaccustomed to (or uncomfortable with) the concept of pedagogy (Comber & Nixon 2009; Sellar 2009). Initially, teacher-researchers were unwilling to use the term to talk about their teaching practice. While resistance to the term decreased as it became more familiar, the initial round of research reports from the teacher-researchers mainly focused on drawing resources from students' virtual schoolbags to uncover new teaching content and whether work completion had increased (as a sign of student engagement). For many teachers, 'connecting lives to learning' was mostly about what the students did, how well they behaved, and whether they attended lessons (Comber & Nixon 2009). Little consideration was given to what the teacher was doing in the classroom beyond the importance of forming strong teacher–student relationships. In our early interviews, pedagogy and good relationships were almost synonymous in the minds of the teacher-researchers (Comber & Nixon 2009; Sellar 2009) who saw them as the precursor to learning and what was required to encourage students to behave and complete work. However, mindful of Lingard's (2007) observation that supportive relationships by committed teachers do not always result in pedagogies that support intellectual demand and value diversity, in the following year the RPiN project took a more explicit approach to exploring pedagogy.

In so doing, what immediately became clear was that there was no shared language for talking about pedagogy between and among the teachers and researchers (Table 1). In response, a heuristic framework was developed to support dialogue between teacher and university researchers. This 'six recursive pedagogical processes' model (Sellar & Cormack 2009) was produced to emphasise the range of practices that teacher-researchers reported using in their classroom, such as researching, designing, communicating, transforming, performing and reflecting.

From the resulting discussion of this model, several teachers found areas that would become the basis for their research projects, and the use of this heuristic resulted in more teacher-researchers developing a focus on their pedagogical practices in the second research cycle of the project. For these teacher-researchers, 'connecting lives and learning' took on different and layered meanings. For some it was a case of the incorporation of new life-world content requiring the adoption of new pedagogical practices to maintain the integrity and authenticity of the learning. Others developed an interest in the ways of learning that students used in their life-worlds and how this could be incorporated in the classroom. The chapters that

Table 1: six recursive pedagogical processes

Researching	Designing	Communicating	Transforming	Performing	Reflecting
students and teachers research community and personal funds of knowledge in order to negotiate rich and connected curriculum tasks	students and teachers negotiate and collaborate to design learning activities, assessment structures and classroom operation	students and teachers communicate through a variety of modes to share understandings and offer explicit instruction	students actively interact with their worlds and transform knowledge gained through this interaction into a variety of media	students perform their learning and act upon their worlds in high-stakes situations for a variety of school and community audiences	students and teachers reflect on their learning, celebrating successes, 'feeling the quality' and identifying future challenges

From Sellar and Cormack (2009)

11

follow offer examples of these different approaches to the pedagogical implications of connecting lives to learning, as well as the inquiries of the teacher-researchers into the success of their efforts.

About this book

At its broadest, this book reports on a series of inquiries into the role of education in building a more sustainable, equitable and inclusive society for urban-fringe communities that have not fared well in the face of recent dramatic economic change. It is the teacher-researchers' accounts of their action-research inquiries that form the backbone of the book. Each of the chapters details a case study of a teacher inquiry that was an attempt to connect student lives with learning, redesign pedagogical processes and demonstrate more socially sustainable pedagogical practices.

In the first chapter, Henderson and Zipin revisit the theory and rationale of the RPiN project through a project that used clay animation in a Year 8/9 visual arts curriculum. They argue that for schools in urban fringe communities, such as the RPiN group of schools, arts courses are often used as a means to sidestep the serious issues of disconnected curriculum and student disengagement. By shunting problem students into hands-on or easy subjects, schools reinforce deficit views of both students and subjects. They argue that in many ways these practical classes can become as much a trap as a haven. In response, Henderson and Zipin consider how the creativity and vitality of the arts may foster opportunities to demonstrate rigorous learning that engages students and counts academically.

The second chapter shares the reflections of a primary school teacher who, after over 20 years of experience, is still pondering how she can 'make a difference' for her Year 6/7 students. In their presentation of the possibilities and limitations for using urban change to reconnect students to the curriculum, Lee and Prosser discover that while we often clearly see the stifling influence of notions of risk and a 'pedagogy of poverty' (Haberman 1991) in the practice of our teaching colleagues, we do not always see it in ourselves. They document what happened when one teacher realised that because she was committed to social justice she had assumed that she was, by default, supporting justice for disadvantaged children but, in practice, was making little difference. Through grappling with this revelation, this teacher found new energy to attempt and sustain more engaging, connected and inclusive pedagogical practices. This story of reawakening is a reminder for other educators who consider their practices as socially just, as well as a story of renewed understanding, renewed direction and renewed hope.

In Chapter 3, Kinna and Paige describe how a mathematics teacher attempted to shift his pedagogy from a decontextualised, textbook-based, chalk-and-talk approach to one which placed students' life-worlds and interests at the heart of the learning process. Using a local issue as the focus, David Kinna engaged Year 9 mathematics students in the mathematical concepts of scale, ratio and measurement as they planned to improve community facilities such as child-minding centres, sound studios and skate parks. He also discovered how using such an approachcan help teach students about social responsibilities and how they can become active citizens.

In the fourth chapter, Wilson and Lloyd present a case study that outlines how the documentary, *Super Size Me*, was used as the basis for a teaching approach that sought to reengage students in science learning by connecting with their life-worlds. The topic focus was an investigation into student and family eating habits and health. The chapter also reflects on the link between transdisciplinary knowledge creation in schools and socially sustainable pedagogical practices. At its core is the argument that canonical science and traditional pedagogy is resulting in the disengagement of students from scientific content. In response, Wilson and Lloyd present an alternative model that can be both rigorous and engaging.

In Chapter 5, Jones describes, explores and reflects on a two-year research project with an English class spanning Years 9 and 10. The motivation for this project was informed by a perceived strong connection between skills development and engagement in the middle years of schooling, and academic achievement in the senior years. Thus, Jones' goal was to increase literary practice and confidence across the ability range and to do so in ways that would draw on students' virtual schoolbags and funds of knowledge in a sustainable way. Like the chapter by Lee and Prosser, this chapter has a strong focus on place-based curriculum involving negotiation and drawing upon student knowledge about their community to guide the pedagogical journey. Alongside reflections about the value of student ownership of the curriculum, the development of metacognitive awareness and the benefits of authentic assessment as vehicles for engagement and rigour in the curriculum, Jones also considers some of the practical obstacles to making such flexible approaches an intrinsic part of the middle years of schooling.

In Chapter 6, McCallum and Temme report on a project that was driven by a teacher's desire to improve academic outcomes for Year 9 students in a Society and Environment/Integrated Studies class. Specifically, Temme sought to increase an understanding of youth culture and an appreciation of diversity with a group of students disengaged by traditional education practices. The project used students as researchers in an effort to increase their participation in schoolwork through greater choice, group work and research into youth cultures. McCallum and Temme explain that the efforts by the teacher to improve academic outcomes soon revealed a need for pedagogical change, which became the focus of an action-research project.

The seventh chapter emphasises how making changes to teaching practices is a lifelong journey. Poissonnier and Paige together present the journey of a teacher as she encounters and inquires into new pedagogical approaches. Poissonnier's story tells about the effect that working on an action-research project for three years has had on her ability to inquire into and think critically about her classroom practice. The chapter addresses the question of how do teachers like Poissonnier come to discover socially just pedagogical practices and how do they sustain a commitment to innovative practice. It is a story that will be familiar to teachers of all levels of experience.

In Chapter 8, Voudantas and Hattam explore the RPiN rationale in the context of a second-chance high school. While not a typical middle schooling setting, the authors find resonance around issues of student disengagement and disconnection. The project explored the problematic nature of working with adult students to develop their literacy skills. It was found that the main barriers to engagement remain the same external factors that stopped students from continuing with their studies in the first place. The authors detail how the project successfully used the students as researchers to bring in a body of knowledge from outside school to make learning relevant and to help them begin to value their immediate community. Voudantas and Hattam conclude by describing and analysing a number of the barriers to, and difficulties with, making the community curricular.

In Chapter 9, Zipin, Brennan and Semmens argue that the position of principal is a critical one for helping to develop conditions for imagining and turning around student engagement and achievement. The condition of schools in communities of poverty and diversity, such as the RPiN group of schools, means that school leaders are constantly faced with unpalatable choices. Many of these decisions are made outside the school and most are not made on educational grounds. This makes it difficult for schools to maintain a constructive, future-oriented, democratic momentum. Thus, the burden of sustaining teachers and their students is disproportionately large. These schools are asked to do more with less, under conditions that are almost designed for failure. The authors consider social sustainability to be creating the conditions for democratic workplaces for both staff and students, with particular emphasis on conditions that make possible a curriculum that connects student lives and learning.

The book concludes with a chapter by Reid and Lucas which reflects on the benefits of developing 'cultures of inquiry' (Reid 2004) to engage with the complexity of teaching in contemporary times. It makes the critical point that developing a culture of inquiry is not the sole responsibility of teachers in schools – it must permeate the philosophy and practices of education systems as a whole. The chapter highlights some of the lessons learned from the case studies described in this book, and proposes some ways by which inquiry-based professional practices might become the norm in educational institutions and systems, rather than items of curiosity. In this way, the chapter revisits and reaffirms the central commitment of this book: that education is at its core a practice of social sustainability that seeks to support this and future generations.

References

Australian Bureau of Statistics, 2005, *Schools Australia 2005 (ABS cat. no. 4221.0)*. Australian Bureau of Statistics, Canberra.

Australian Council of Deans of Education, 2003, 'The Role of the Teacher: Coming of Age', <www.acde.edu.au/publications.html> accessed 27/04/2009.

Marks GN & McKenzie P, 2000, 'Early School Leaving and 'non-completion' in Australia', *LSAY Briefing Paper No. 2*. Australian Council for Educational Research, Canberra.

Bauman Z, 1998, *Work, Consumerism and the New Poor*. Open University Press, Buckingham.

Bourdieu P, 1984, *Distinction: A Social Critique of the Judgement of Taste*. Routledge & Kegan Paul, London.

Carrington V, 2006, *Rethinking the Middle Years: early adolescents, schooling and digital culture*. Allen & Unwin, Crows Nest.

Centre for Labour Research, 2002, *Living and Learning: a profile of young people, employment, education and training in northern Adelaide*. University of Adelaide, Adelaide.

City of Playford, 2006, *City of Playford Wellbeing Plan 2006–2011*. City of Playford, Adelaide.

Cochran-Smith M & Lytle SL, 1999, 'The teacher research movement: a decade later', *Educational Researcher*, 28(7), 15–25.

Comber B & Kamler B (eds), 2005, *Turn-around pedagogies: literacy interventions for at-risk students*. Primary English Teachers Association, Newtown, NSW.

Comber B & Nixon H, 2009, 'Teachers' work and pedagogy in an era of accountability', *Discourse*, 30(3), 333–345.

Connell RW, 1993, *Schools and Social Justice*. Pluto Press, Melbourne.

Cumming J, 1993, *Middle Schooling for the 21st Century*. Incorporated Association of Registered Teachers of Victoria (IARTV), Jolimont, Victoria.

Delpit L, 1993, 'The "silenced dialogue": Power and pedagogy in educating other people's children', in L Weis & M Fine (eds), *Beyond Silenced Voices: Class, Race and Gender in United States Schools*. State University of New York Press, Albany, NY, pp 119–139.

Elliott M, Sandeman P & Winchester H, 2005, 'Embedding Community Engagement: Northern Adelaide and the University of South Australia', in proceedings of *Engaging Communities*, the 4th Australian Universities Quality Forum, Sydney, 6–8 July, pp 55–61.

Gonzalez N & Moll L, 2002, 'Cruzando el Puente: Building bridges to funds of knowledge', *Educational Policy*, 16(4), 623–641.

Gonzalez N, Moll L & Amanti C (eds), 2005, *Funds of knowledge: Theorizing Practices in Households, Communities and Classrooms*. Lawrence Erlbaum, Mahwah, New Jersey.

Haberman M, 1991, 'The Pedagogy of Poverty versus Good Teaching', *Phi Delta Kappan*, 73(4), 290–294.

Hattam R, 2005, 'The (im)possibility of listening to early school leavers: implications for middle schooling', paper presented at the *Australian Guidance & Counselling Association Annual Conference*, Adelaide, 29 September.

Hattam R, Brennan, M, Zipin L & Comber B, 2009, 'Researching for social justice: contextual, conceptual and methodological challenges', *Discourse*, 30(3), 303–316.

Hattam R & Prosser B, 2008, 'Unsettling deficit views of students and their communities', *Australian Educational Researcher*, 35(2), 15–36.

Hattam R & Zipin L, 2009, 'Towards pedagogical justice', *Discourse*, 30(3), 297–301.

Hayes D, Mills M, Christie P & Lingard B, 2006, *Teachers & schooling making a difference: Productive pedagogies, assessment and performance*. Allen and Unwin, Crows Nest, NSW.

Kemmis S & McTaggart R (eds), 1988, *The action research planner* (third edn). Deakin University Press, Victoria.

Knobel M & Lankshear C, 2003, 'Planning Pedagogy for i-mode: from flogging to blogging via wi-fi', *English in Australia – Literacy Learning: the middle years*, 139 (Summer 2003-04), 78–102.

Lingard B, 2007, 'Pedagogies of indifference', *International Journal of Inclusive Education*, 11(3), 245–266.

Luke A, 1997, 'New narratives of human capital: Recent redirections in Australian Educational Policy', *Australian Educational Researcher*, 24(2), 1–22.

Luke A, Elkins J, Weir K, Land R, Carrington V, Dole S, Pendergast D, Kapitzke C, van Kraayenoord C, Moni K, McIntosh A, Mayer D, Bahr M, Hunter L, Chadbourne R, Bean T, Alverman D & Stevens L, 2003, *Beyond the Middle – A report about Literacy and Numeracy Development of Target Group Students in the Middle Years of Schooling*. Department of Education, Science and Training (DEST) and The University of Queensland, Australia.

McKenzie S, 2004, 'Social Sustainability: Towards some definitions', *Hawke Research Institute Working Paper Series No.27*, University of South Australia, Magill.

McNiff J, Lomax P & Whitehead J, 1996, 'Living educational action research, in J McNiff, P Lomax & J Whitehead (eds), *You and your action research project*. Routledge, London, pp 7–28.

Main K & Bryer F, 2007, 'A framework for research into Australian middle school practice', *Australian Educational Researcher*, 34(2), 91–106.

Megalogenis G, 2006, *The Longest Decade*. Scribe Books, Carlton North.

Moll L, Amanti C, Neff D & Gonzalez N, 1992, 'Funds of Knowledge for Teaching: using a qualitative approach to connect homes to classrooms', *Theory into Practice*, 31(2), 132–141.

Office of Employment 2003, *Regional Profile: Northern Adelaide Statistical Subdivision*, Department of Further Education, Employment, Science and Technology, Adelaide.

Peel M, 1995, *Good Times, Hard Times: the past and the future in Elizabeth*. Melbourne University Press, Carlton.

Pendergast D & Bahr N, 2005, *Teaching Middle Years: Rethinking Curriculum, Pedagogy and assessment*. Allen & Unwin, Crows Nest, NSW.

Pocock B, 2003, *Work/Life Collision*. Federation Press, Annandale, NSW.

Prosser B, 2008, 'Unfinished but not exhausted: a review of Australian middle schooling', *Australian Journal of Education*, 52(2), 151–167.

Prosser B, McCallum F, Milroy P, Comber B & Nixon H, 2008, 'I'm smart and I'm not joking: aiming high in the middle years of schooling', *Australian Educational Researcher*, 35(2), 15–36.

Pusey M, 1998, 'Australia: Once the lighthouse social democracy of the world. The impact of recent economic reforms', *Thesis Eleven*, 55 (November), 41–59.

Reid A, 2004, 'Towards a culture of inquiry in DECS' *Occasional Paper Series*, No. 1, South Australian Department of Education and Children's Services, Adelaide, pp 1–19.

Rose N, 1996, 'The death of the social? Re-figuring the territory of government', *Economy & Society*, 25, 327–356.

Sefton-Green J (ed), 1998, *Digital Diversions: Youth Culture in the Age of Multimedia*. University College London Press, London.

Sellar S, 2009, 'The responsible uncertainity of pedagogy', *Discourse*, 30(3), 347–360.

Sellar S & Cormack P, 2009, 'Redesigning pedagogies in middle years classrooms; challenges for teachers working with disadvantaged students', *Pedagogy, Culture & Society*, 17(2), 123–139.

Smyth J, McInerney P & Hattam R, 2003, 'Tackling school leaving at its source:

a case of reform in the middle years of schooling', *British Journal of Sociology of Education*, 24(2), 177–193.

Thomson P, 2002, *Schooling the rustbelt kids: making the difference in changing times*. Allen & Unwin, Crows Nest, NSW.

Webb J, 2000, 'Action research and the classroom teacher', *Practically Primary*, 5(1), 16–24.

Zipin L, 2009, 'Dark funds of knowledge, deep funds of pedagogy; exploring boundaries between lifeworlds and schools', *Discourse*, 30(3), 317–331.

Chapter 1

Bringing clay to life: developing student literacy through clay animation artwork that tells life-based stories

Debbie Henderson and Lew Zipin[*]

Introduction: staking out a double-democratic approach

In school curriculum, the arts are often seen to offer engaging vitalities of 'creative expression', compared to 'more structured' curriculum areas. In students' perceptions, the arts tend to be seen as 'practical' and 'hands-on', relative to 'theoretical' and 'harder' subject areas such as literacy or maths. In both senses – more creative/engaging; and more practical/hands-on – arts courses can seem a haven from the 'competitive grind' of 'academically rigorous' curriculum areas. However, this dichotomy also signifies the lesser status of arts subjects in curriculum power hierarchies: they do not 'count' for much in the high-stakes sorting and selecting game by which learners move up, down or laterally in society through school success. When, as a Visual Arts teacher, I discussed student achievements with students or parents, I was often on the receiving end of statements such as 'Who cares; it's only Art!'

For schools of high-poverty regions, arts courses that accommodate expectations of 'easy' and (merely) 'practical' can present a trap as much as a haven. When working with students who – through no fault of their own or their families' – do not embody culturally inherited capacities that match the cultural capital encoded in mainstream academic 'standards', to

---

[*] This paper draws from the first author's Master of Education thesis, which was supervised by the second author. Although this is a co-authored text, we use the 'I' voice to sustain the feel of a teacher's story about working with her students.

separate 'creative vitality' from 'academic rigour' functions is to reproduce their lesser access to further education and their chances for improved health and wellbeing beyond schooling (Bourdieu & Passeron 1990; Delpit 1993). The question arises: *how might the expressive appeal of art activities be mobilised to engage students in curriculum work that also vitalises their chances to learn and succeed in domains that 'count' academically?*

The *Redesigning Pedagogies in the North* (RPiN) project encouraged efforts to address this challenge. Focused on the middle years of schooling – when 'less advantaged' learners are often alienated by secondary school's intensified degrees of curriculum standardisation, compartmentalisation and competition, RPiN's aim was to design curriculum and pedagogy that engaged students' energies and interests. This was to foster their academic success, thus creating socially just educational experiences and outcomes for learners typically at risk of leaving school early or barely graduating (Ovsienko & Zipin 2007). The strategy was to develop rigorous curriculum units built around 'funds of knowledge' (Moll, Amanti, Neff & Gonzalez 1992) from students' local community life-worlds. The methodology was teacher action research, negotiating with students to inform design of curriculum units that engaged them in topics of life-world relevance, followed by reflection and redesign in a second action-research cycle.

My school was among the 10 schools; and I was one of three participating teachers from the school. Prior to RPiN, my school had been pursuing middle years experiments, including a focus on literacy development across curriculum areas. In my Visual Arts classes, I aimed to scaffold literacy into artwork that retains the 'practical/hands-on' appeal students expect, but at the same time uses and develops literacy capacities. RPiN provoked a further dimension for realising this aim: to build curriculum units around funds of knowledge that carry rich resonance in students' local community lives outside school, so as to involve them more deeply in learning work that is at once richly engaging and rigorously challenging.

As amplified in what follows, my aims hinged on a *double-democratic* approach: (1) *democratic* opening of curriculum to make use of cultural knowledge based in my students' local community lives; facilitated by (2) *democratic* processes of classroom pedagogy, particularly dialogue and group work in which the teacher also learns from students. In what follows, I narrate how I negotiated units of clay animation artwork with my students; how, in the process, a double-democracy approach to curriculum design and classroom pedagogy emerged; and how literacy development was scaffolded into, and enriched, the clay animation work.

Making clay animations

I learned how to devise, shoot and edit clay (plasticine) animations during a mid-year holiday break, in an intensive one-day teacher workshop at the Technology School of the Future.[†] It was a highly enjoyable learning event for me, and I hoped my students would similarly enjoy such work. Across the two RPiN action-research cycles, I pursued units of work that embedded literacy in – as essential to – 'practical' production of short animations. Cycle 1, with a Year 8 class of students in the first year, was followed by reflection and subsequent redesign for Cycle 2 with four integrated Year 8/9 classes in the second year (some Year 9 students had done animations in Cycle 1, creating peer mentoring opportunities). Units in each Cycle took approximately 4–5 weeks, with each class shooting and editing during a whole-day excursion to the Technology School of the Future.

Students undertook the following sequence of learning activities:

- identifying problems of importance in their local community lives, and that they feel can be changed through constructive solutions
- forming groups based on affinity of issues/interests
- choosing a problem/solution, in groups, that can be portrayed in clay animation plots of approximately 45 seconds
- developing story characters: personality, physical appearance
- storyboarding and scripting scenes, including narration, dialogue and character movements
- modelling characters and producing stage props and backdrops
- shooting animations on computers using webcams and animation software
- editing animations, including voices, sounds and music for each scene, using Audacity software and Windows Movie Maker

† The Technology School of the Future (TSoF), based at the Education Development Centre in Adelaide, provided a physical base for school groups to experience programs involving cutting edge technology. It also offered professional development programs for teachers about the use of new technologies in teaching. The TsoF was dismantled by the South Australian government in 2007.

- presenting animations in class, school assemblies and at school open nights.

The democracy of connecting curriculum to community

Engaging students: building life-world funds of knowledge into curriculum

A key RPiN aim was to design curriculum units that connect students' learning to 'funds of knowledge' (Moll et al. 1992) of rich familiarity in their life-worlds beyond school. Local community knowledge thus enters schooling as a core resource for learning. This requires a 'turn-around' in perspective (Comber & Kamler 2004) for teachers trained in the one-way assumption that students are only learners and have nothing to teach their teachers. The 'turn-around' shows respect – as learning *assets*, not deficits – for knowledge grounded in cultures, histories and environments of students, their parents and other local community agents. 'There is much teachers do not know about their students or families that could be immediately helpful in the classroom', say Moll et al. (1992: 136), if teachers find ways to learn about and from their students, with an attitude that 'people are competent and have knowledge, and their life experiences have given them that knowledge' (Gonzalez & Moll 2002: 625). To make effective use of these funds of knowledge in school learning, teachers need to communicate to students, in practice, that they recognise the validity of life-world based knowledge.

An assumption is that, built into curriculum, the familiarity of life-world ways of knowing stimulates learner engagement. Thomson's (2002: 1) metaphor of a 'virtual schoolbag' suggests the resonant force of life-world knowledge for learning: 'each [learner] brings ... to school a virtual schoolbag full of things they have learned at home, with their friends, and in and from the world in which they live'. Oldfather (1995: 136) observes how both teachers and students benefit from curriculum work that researches life-world knowledge and learning processes:

> Students who participate in research about their own learning and
> motivation may inform teachers, researchers, and themselves about the
> contexts and processes in which they are able to become deeply engaged
> in learning. In the end, their 'songs come back most' to them.

The importance of 'the local'

I have long noted that students in the middle years have a very local sense of their world and 'the world' more broadly. I thus sought their identification of issues of *local* community concern for animation stories. In Cycle 1, I began with a set of questions, based on a protocol from Comber et al. (2001: 455), to enable students to link 'personal' to locally extended issues in which they have both concerns and a sense of agency to change conditions. In opening their 'virtual school bags' to identify issues that mattered to them, they drew out tales about a nuisance neighbourhood dog, drug use in their surrounds, the rundown state of the nearest skate park, beach pollution and more.

While such storylines may seem of limited connection to 'the big world', funds of knowledge based in specific social spaces allows learning to scaffold, over time, to a wider community ambit. Such 'place-based' learning, says Chin (2001: 6), 'provides students with opportunities to connect with themselves, their community, and their local environment through hands-on, real-world learning experiences'. Students' community connections are then further strengthened, and their school becomes an integral part of its surrounding communities. 'The metaphor of the community developing school', say Hattam et al. (1999: 2), 'carries the need by schools to be able to develop educational experiences that are sensitive to context'. Teachers are thus challenged to create learning activities 'responsive to the local – an approach that designs curriculum around "generative" themes from everyday life' (Shor 1992, quoted in Hattam et al. 1999: 3). Carrying such generative experiences in their virtual schoolbags from early years on, students can participate in building curriculum that investigates life-resonant themes in age-appropriate ways.

Contexts of poverty: difficult life-world knowledge

If the invitation to draw on life-world knowledge is serious, and trust is established, students from high-poverty regions are apt to show 'expertise' in troubling life aspects. In focus groups with students in a different cohort (prior to RPiN), they conveyed various negative views of their locales – concerns about impoverished infrastructure, and fears about violence – and a sense of being powerless to change these conditions. Yet most saw their future in their suburb. It is thus crucial that invitations to tell life-based stories include ways to work with difficult dimensions of local experience. The first step is to treat such stories not as 'deficit' knowledge to be banished from classrooms, but as dimensions of lived identity to be respected. As Jones (2004: 668) argues: 'Teachers and researchers have choices to make when we hear these stories – either ignore them or we can hear and sanction them'. By accepting, not judging, such stories, teachers foster a learning environment that feels safer for honest, critical and creative storytelling.

A problem-solving approach: re-imagining community life

To establish a safe climate for curricular use of life-based experience – especially tapping into difficult knowledge – I negotiated a story-telling genre with students in which they would identify 'problems' in their lives and, crucially, pose 'solutions'. As Starnes (1999: 2) notes, 'the most powerful learning experiences are those that engage learners in posing and solving problems, making meaning, producing products, and building understandings'. Hayes et al. (2006: 98) suggest a necessarily *creative* quality of such work: 'Problem-based tasks … [have] no specific correct solution, requiring knowledge construction on the part of the students, and requiring sustained attention beyond a single lesson'. In their stories, students imagined themselves working on problems with community groups and agencies: police, town council, the RSPCA. Such *imaginings* of constructive change stirred senses of possibility that they could be agents of actual and sustainable community change: in every class I heard optimism along lines that 'we can find ways to solve problems in our community, or the community can'. As Wood (1992: 211) says, 'opening up the school to the world around it helps students develop the skills and commitment necessary to be involved and make a difference in the world'. Smith (2002: 589) offers a rationale for how such issues-based curriculum design, and the student-centred learning it involves, arouse participatory-democratic energies:

> Called real-world problem solving, this orientation to curriculum devel-
> opment is deeply grounded in particular places and highly democratic
> in its processes. Students play a pivotal role in identifying problems,
> selecting one as a class focus, studying its characteristics and dynamics,
> developing potential solutions, and then organizing and participating
> in efforts to solve the problem.

In my classes, students chose and developed problem–solution storylines in small groups. In exploring different possible solutions for stories, we discussed ethics and legalities of scenarios proposed in groups, which sometimes led to plot changes. For example, one group worked upon an incident related by a group member who had watched her next-door neighbour kick her family cat to death. The group's eventual story involved a dog rescued from neighbourhood cruelty rather than killed. Another group devised a plot in which the Royal Society for the Prevention of Cruelty to Animals (RSPCA) intervened on a group of animal-abusing children, teaching them to understand and reconsider their behaviours; and these children in turn educated another group of animal-abusing children. In an all-girls group that considered a school incident in which a girl was teased and bullied by classmates because she could not afford up-to-date or popular-label clothing, they devised a story in which a girl is given a 'reality TV-style' makeover by her friends to combat the teasing of others. Beyond this clay animation story, these girls had very frank group discussions about cruelties among young people towards those who differ in cultural ways.

As students came to trust the invitation to work from life experiences, some darkly violent features of local context arose in their conversations, including instances of murder, rape, robbery, beatings, hit-and-run accidents and more. Many groups discussed direct and corollary effects of poverty in their lives. At the same time, they showed self-protective impulses to manage pains of difficult knowledge through self-censoring as needed. During problem identification and plot development stages, groups tended to discard issues that felt inappropriate to reveal to people outside their communities. In the process, I felt privileged to be seen by them as a safe person to hear their conversations: as a teacher who made meaningful connection with their lived experiences. Their honesty and depth, in dialogues with me about their stories, increased my knowledge and imagination about their life-worlds and communities, generating stronger teacher–student bonds for mutual learning from each other.

Connectedness & art

Other teachers facilitating RPiN units spoke of student resistances to linking work done for school to their lives beyond school. Some speculated that middle years students lack sufficient extension into social life beyond family and peer groups. More likely, I suggest, is that students' prior school experiences had not built sufficient trust for them to be ready to take vulnerable risks in revealing aspects of out-of-school life that carry deep significance in their identity formations (Zipin & Reid 2008). Yet I did not find my students greatly resistant to linking life-world cultural contents to their clay animation projects. Without much prompting, most students readily breathed life-based vitalities into their animation stories. I do not doubt my colleagues' accounts. My interpretation is that students feel less threatened in narrating life experiences – especially 'difficult knowledges' – through 'practical' storytelling arts (Jones 2004), as compared with high-stakes 'standard literacy' work in English classes, in which they experience greater struggles and humiliations.

Creating animations is similar to puppetry – a medium known to allow young people to engage life dimensions they might otherwise not express. Storytelling through surrogate characters, rather than as firsthand accounts, removes some of the emotional distress surrounding violent and fearful aspects of life. Constructions of 'solutions' to 'problems' in their local communities are not so much a watering down of 'realities' as acts of incorporating realities within emotionally manageable boundaries. Storytelling of this nature is akin to the mythological world of violent fairytales that envelope 'real-life horrors' within the creative genre of a problem-solving story, enabling re-imaginative use of the darker 'funds of knowledge' within students' lived experiences.

The ethnographic teacher: 'hooking' into life-world vitalities

In learning to listen to students in dialogue about clay animation tasks and goals, I became an *ethnographic* teacher: a researcher of their cultural lives. I began to listen for 'hooks' into 'funds of knowledge' that, if built into curriculum projects, I could be confident would engage students. Maney (2005) uses the 'hook' metaphor to signify attentive listening that 'fishes' for domains and ways of knowing that resonate deeply among students. To listen with such ethnographic ears requires teachers to become open learners about students' lives, rather than project our own assumptions about their lives. Such openness enables teachers to recognise life-world based themes that are not peripheral or casual but touch on vital registers of lived cultural meaning and identity. Says Maney (2005: 105): 'this is what "turn-around" pedagogies are all about – being willing to turn around our own assumptions and practices as teachers and be open to change in order to turn around our students'.

My best discovery of a 'hook', early in Cycle 2, was serendipitous. In my classroom, when students are working on technical aspects of artwork, I let them watch videos as they work (they are very capable of such multi-task attention). Across the four classes of Cycle 2, I observed that the most frequently favoured video was an animated cartoon, *Ice Age*, in which students actively identified with animal characters: 'You're like the mammoth; you're like the tiger; you're the little squirrel'. I finally asked 'What is it about this movie?', and students said 'They fight a lot; they have these huge issues with each other'. It struck me that they identified with relationships featuring violence. I carefully probed: 'Let's look at relationships, let's look at their problems'. They engaged readily, dissecting how characters in the film, and in life, interacted with each other. From this, a broad theme – problems suffered through bullying/harassment relations – emerged as an agreed-upon common focus.

Across the two action-reflection cycles, my ethnographic ear developed from idle listening to hearing with intent to appreciate hooks of authentic engagement. My discovery of a hook in querying the popularity of the *Ice Age* narrative was a major breakthrough in my development as an ethnographic listener to, and negotiator with, students in designing curriculum units that would sustain their engagement through the unfolding duration of clay animation stages and tasks. Ongoing listening to their group discussions about local community issues was ear, and eye, opening. After many years teaching, I thought I 'knew' the dimensions and complexities of their home and community lives; but I gained far greater ethnographic grasp of the tunings of their lives through the pedagogical 'turn-around' in which I learned to listen for hooks into deeper identity resonances.

The democracy of classroom pedagogy

Establishing safety & trust

As discussed above, students' considerations of life-world stories evoke some dark dimensions of their lives. In establishing trustworthy classroom environments for broaching and working through such issues, teachers play pivotal pedagogic roles. Every teacher needs to self-assess the ways and degrees in which they are positioned to create comfort zones. In my case, having been at the same school for eight years and having taught older siblings of students in my classes, they were predisposed to my 'belonging' in their lives, giving me a head start towards credibility that safe spaces for dialogue and collaboration were possible. Still, I had to work hard to appreciate their young identities, and to enable their creative courage to translate 'private' community stories into animations for 'public' audiences.

Collaborative & dialogic classrooms

For this unit of work, collaborative processes were essential in many ways. At a basic level, students needed each other's help to complete the many complex tasks of clay animation production within the time line. In Cycle 1, an initial protocol of analytical questions about life-world issues was the only task students did individually. In Cycle 2, initial question analysis was based on the film *Ice Age*, and students worked in small groups to complete analysis sheets. The latter proved more manageable and lessened resistance to what, at this early stage, students tended to see as an undue 'literacy' activity. (I will later discuss how literacy activities required careful scaffolding into the animation work.) Groups of 4–6 students became the 'critical mass' that sparked reciprocal energies yet kept tasks achievable. I was explicit at the outset about groups needing to work together to complete animation tasks, with each individual making responsible contributions to group tasks. In both Cycles, after preliminary whole-class conversation/analysis about life-world events, groups formed almost 'of themselves'.

Beyond 'technical' reasons for group collaboration, more important learning gains were realised. Democratic communication and decision-sharing in groups fuelled learners' energies, working with and off each other to sustain rigorous effort. Groups thus embedded a practical learning of democratic civics within their artwork. Collective vetting of potential storylines also reinforced a sense of 'safe place', since students shared stories with peers who had reasonable familiarity with their lived conditions, relating incidents that in some cases had been experienced mutually.

After initial whole-class brainstorming of different ways to work together to achieve common goals, I let groups determine just how to tackle tasks. In both Cycles, diverse decision-making methods emerged.

Most common were following a leader, voting democratically, selecting randomly and assigning different jobs to those seen as good at them. For the most crucial decision – what story to build a clay animation around – the most frequent method was adoption by consensus of one member's idea after democratically inclusive discussion. Interdependence within groups noticeably increased over time, with improved individual engagements, both through the security of company, and a sense of responsibility to contribute to common goals and not let the group down. Often one person would start a task, then others would join and help finish or take over if that person was away or busy with other tasks. As peer trust developed, greater collective responsibility and less conflict followed.

Peer trust also enabled those with low confidence about certain skills – written and oral literacy, and drawing – to work on skills with less sense of risking failure and humiliation, and so to gain a safer sense that they can develop skills through practice. As groups formed, I created some informal mentoring situations, steering class members who had been viewed as 'disruptive' or 'unpopular' into association with classmates who showed strong work and leadership capacities. Left to individual work, they would likely have fulfilled negative prophecies. However, working in group environments on stories that held shared meaning, with a shared sense of need to accomplish tasks on schedule, such members gained acceptance and experienced their contributions as valued by others, reinforcing self-belief, communicative skills and attention to tasks. For some, this was a turning point in social relations not just in the group but the whole class.

Group activities, a stock in trade of primary school teaching-and-learning, abruptly decline with middle year entry into secondary school settings, where high-stakes competition intensifies, furthered by pedagogies of individualism. This favours students from relatively powerful social positions, who – in family interactions of early childhood – inherit prowess in the 'cultural capital' encoded in mainstream academic 'standards' (Bourdieu & Passeron 1990), which they carry in their virtual schoolbags, priming them to succeed 'individually' in school contests. However, those from less powerful positions need schools to reveal and explain the power codes, and to provide *socially interactive* contexts for gaining prowess in them through practice (Delpit 1993).

They thus fare better under cooperative pedagogies than in competitive, individualist regimes.

Along with student–student collaboration, teacher–student collaboration developed dynamically, particularly in negotiating assessments. At first I was worried about how to know that all contributed within groups. I found, however, that this type of project thrives on different individuals contributing diverse strengths to the overall project, and I became comfortable with this, so long as all were developing in written literacy work such as script writing. Rather than individual evaluations at the end of the unit, I used evaluative assessment at various stages as a means to further group discussion and direction. Explicit assessment criteria for each part of the project stimulated group discussions of how to achieve tasks at each learning stage, helping students to gain clarity about what they were aiming for in each task.

Evaluation criteria were not simply determined by me, but forged in whole-class discussions. Evaluations thus became an embedded part of the learning processes. 'Research demonstrates', say Hayes et al. (2006: 117), 'that when … assessment tasks … are connected to [student] experiences, are intellectually challenging and mediated by supportive classroom practices, [students] are far more likely to remain engaged in learning'. Importantly, evaluation criteria included how well group members worked both individually and together. Groups became skilled in evaluating their progress collectively, often contributing as cohesive units to class discussions, with various members joining in to tell their group story and rate their group and each other's progress. As they became adept in this process, I came to trust their self- and group-evaluative reflections. As well, my own pedagogic self-reflection grew as I circulated among groups, giving feedback on how I saw their progress.

Shared power in the collaborative classroom

The pedagogy of student–student and student–teacher negotiations challenged me – in my 'teacher' position – to share power in the classroom. I had to learn to let go of the reins and not fear issues students raised when they had real autonomy, but to listen with a balanced sense of when to intervene to help develop safer approaches to problematic issues. Reciprocal student-teacher trust develops through practical success, but begins when teachers and students both make courageous moves to unlearn deep habits of accustomed power in roles and relations. In the 'move to collaborative power sharing', outlines Hyde (1992: 67), key domains include 'assessment, valuing students' knowledge and experience, developing negotiation skills (rather than directing skills), developing collaborative skills (sharing, discussing, group work) and establishing less rigid roles for students and teachers'.

Foremost, for teachers, is democratic appreciation that the learning environment belongs to all classroom participants, and student empowerment is not a loss for teachers but builds multi-layered agency in teaching-and-learning. A pedagogy of 'less control, not more, is the key to real learning', suggests Wood (1992: 206), in enabling a more engaging and challenging curriculum in which 'teachers and students are free to explore the world as it comes to them, not after it's pre-packaged', and so 'to understand the world in its complexity'.

It is wholly reasonable for students to share power in decisions that shape their curriculum work, and the classroom pedagogy that supports it. After all, their learning is the central purpose of schooling, including learning of capacities for democratic participation. Moreover, to realise democratic curriculum that includes their life-world funds of knowledge, power sharing is essential for eliciting and developing capacities to negotiate contents and themes. As Delpit (1993: 288) argues, 'The teacher cannot be the only expert in the classroom. To deny students their own expert knowledge is to disempower them'. Teachers can facilitate dialogic evocation of such life-based expertise. For example, in negotiating problem-solution stories for animations, I raised leading questions such as 'What are some problem-solving stories in your lives?' After they responded, we analysed examples they provided. In such dialogue, I often struggle with balance between facilitating real freedoms of student voice while taking sensitive care for their vulnerabilities and boundaries. I remind myself not to impose my idea of 'valuable' knowledge, but to listen for life motifs and themes that they identify (Smith 2002), and which, sensitively 'handled', can be put to curricular use as learning *assets*.

Scaffolding literacy & other higher-order rigours into artwork

Literacy & life-world connection

Literacy is not primarily learned in schools, but inheres in everyday social life. Whilst students from less powerful social positions do not inherit the 'literacy capital' for ready success in academic modes that schools privilege, they do embody vernacular literacies, which – taught, learned and used in families, peer groups and other lived sites – constitute valuable funds of knowledge. '[C]hildren's language and literacy development', say Vacca et al. (1997: 447), 'are influenced by … social and cultural interactions … [in] home and community language learning environments … often rich in ways not fully explored'. Curriculum connection to vernacular literacies is thus vital for enabling 'less advantaged' learners to engage with school literacy work. As Luke et al (2003: 40) state:

> There is considerable documentation that literacy instruction can be tailored to better 'fit' and build upon the cultural background knowledge and identity issues both of minority students, Indigenous students, and the increasing body of at-risk readers from lower socio-economic groups.

Jones (2004: 463) suggests that, when embedding literacy work in creative and practical story-telling tasks, 'teachers invite students' worlds into the classroom as young writers transform their lives into narratives … [and] make explicit connections between literature, their experiences and the wider society'. When curriculum thus recognises forms of communication at the heart of community-based identities, this ameliorates fears of judgement as 'illiterate' that often induce student resistances to mainstream school literacy work. When given opportunities to use their 'funds of knowledge' in explicit tasks, they are able to engage in rigorous learning challenges that develop both familiar and new literacy capacities.

Engaging multi-literacies in clay animation projects

As part of our middle years plan, I sought to embed student literacy development within art projects. I reckoned that students would be more open to literacy tasks encountered as integrally necessary to 'practical' art productions (as against 'add-on theory work'). Producing clay animations fits the bill in requiring multiple dimensions of literacy application: oral, written, visual and computer.

Oral literacy – generally less alienating to students whose past school experiences have bred resistances to written literacy work – is thus a good starting point within a strategy of progressively scaffolding literacy development. Oral literacy featured in group and class dialogues and negotiations at all production stages, in more formal analytical work using systematic question-and-answer approaches, and in construction of dialogue for the animation figures in the sound-recording stage. In group interactions, many showed outstanding visual and verbal plot construction capacities, revealing familiarity with the beginning, middle, end story genre that works from 'problem' towards 'solution', inherent in much popular media such as the *Ice Age* video. In Cycle 2, students initially analysed the *Ice Age* story together, pausing the DVD to discuss interactions among characters. Although groups were not yet set, class members actively communicated to help each other complete the sheets I used to structure their analyses. They were responsive to my questions while brainstorming possible animation plots and identifying local community incidents, including 'difficult knowledge', which they discussed meaningfully and honestly.

From oral work on plot development, groups moved on to draw characters and storyboard scenes in more formal steps. Light writing work came into play in initial discussion questions, *Ice Age* analysis, plot development, storyboarding and scripting during planning stages of the animation process. In Cycle 1, I learned a lesson about starting with too strong an emphasis on written literacy. I sought at first to generate plot ideas in written form, but this stymied the momentum of plot development. Only five in the class of 22 had reasonably developed written literacy skills to start with; others needed much assistance from me to complete the task. In my action-research journal I reflected on the need to take pressure off this stage, seeking only minimal written responses to discussion questions and making these a collaborative group task rather than individual work.

I expected students to greet 'hands-on' tasks more eagerly than 'academic' tasks; and indeed, the highest engagement levels were during the intensely 'hands-on' modelling of plasticine characters (other popular activities included construction/drawing of animation props and back-drops). Done mostly in a double lesson of 90 minutes, this modelling is a very intricate activity, as the plasticine characters are no taller than 10 centimetres. Models produced by all groups were of incredible complexity, with fine details of all manner of hairstyles, facial features and decorative clothing. An all-boys group, with members not known for their patience, carefully crafted characters with tiny-letter brand names on clothing items, hoods on sweatshirts with wisps of hair poking out, miniature shoes and contrasting coloured shoelaces. An all-girls group produced an array of ant-like creatures, six centimetres long with body segments and finely rolled legs, and three rats – central characters for their animation – that wore shirts, trousers and dresses with polka dots, and had precise cartoon-style faces. Another group's skate-park characters were dressed in designer clothing with tiny labels and rode little plasticine skateboards. In both cycles I noted virtually 100% on-task engagement.

I too was terrifically busy during these lessons, acting as gofer and distributing plasticine to students too occupied with modelling characters to access supplies from a central table. Some groups still worked on characters and backdrops on the train to the Technology School of the Future, showing no signs of public embarrassment (an unprecedented sight), so engrossed were they in their tasks.

It was important neither to let literacy components of the overall project disrupt student engrossment in 'practical' work, nor to weaken the literacy work, but to scaffold literacy work as integral to the artistic holism. Within this strategy, students appreciated that their clay characters were meaningless in isolation from story development and all its literacy tasks. After Cycle 1, I reflected that plot development, storyboarding and scripting stages were better junctures to scaffold more rigorous literacy work. I stipulated that all individuals needed to demonstrate contributions to the literacy dimension of group projects, but left to each group how they tackled literacy tasks. Two variants emerged. In some groups, members took turns writing as the group discussed and decided on stories. In other groups, dominant scribes helped less confident students when they took writing turns. In both approaches, all students contributed in some way to writing, and motivation grew to write well. Indeed, some groups, not satisfied with first drafts, chose to rewrite their scripts.

For shooting and editing, animation productions required use of computer software with which students and I were unfamiliar. An instructor at the Technology School of the Future taught the skills and processes, which students picked up with remarkable quickness, some (primarily male) with such proficiency that they could mentor others. In shooting the animations, some groups designated different roles among members: for example, one person directing, one working the mouse, others moving plasticine characters or working on sound. In other groups, individuals rotated through specialisations, often teaching each other the different functions as they swapped positions. My roles were to facilitate and help troubleshoot. Under strict time frames, students worked with speed and skill, successfully finishing their animations in all but one instance (of computer malfunction). Eight students from my Cycle 1 class, who were spread across my classes in Cycle 2, mentored new learners in storyboarding, shooting, editing and computer processes, showing high levels of retained knowledge and understanding.

Such student facility in gaining computer literacies suggests that, in their life-worlds, they were already familiar with multiple literacies through engaging varied media. Buckingham & Sefton-Green (1994) note that '"at-risk" adolescents can be artistic, creative, innovative, and daring at using a variety of popular media ... texts, including video, images, and print, to represent themselves and their world intelligently' (cited in O'Brien 2001). Visual arts are well-suited for use of 'new literacies', and highly compatible with students' everyday explorations of technologies. While prowess in 'traditional' *written* literacies is a learning challenge for them, creating a multi-literate learning environment in which 'academic' literacies can be scaffolded, is the challenge for many teachers. As McDougall (2002) puts it:

> literacies are always evolving; as technologies change, so too do the ways we practise literacy and perceive its social role. Thus, we are alerted to the need for a range of new kinds of literacies: 'information literacy', 'digital literacy', 'critical literacy', 'media literacy', 'visual literacy' and so on.

Integrating multi-literacies within a holism of group creativity

Complex clay-animation productions constituted the most rigorous teaching-and-learning I have ever set for students and myself. It required synergising diverse multi-literate efforts within group projects, integrating literacy work in 'authentically' life-resonant story creation. Such holistic creativity both demands, and generates, far more learning energy than simply applying art skills and techniques to create objects. Moreover, core English literacy genres – oral and written – are more readily practised by 'less advantaged' students when embedded within a holism of artistic production than when taught in isolation.

Developmental literacy practice was also furthered through *co*-labouring. Reciprocal reliance generates motivation 'not to let the group down'; and within collective effort, member contributions gain *social* value, ameliorating isolations of 'individual failure' for those with initially weak literacy skills. Peer mentoring and skill sharing reinforce belief in one's learning-*and-teaching* abilities to contribute to group success and satisfaction. As Starnes (1999: 1) states a core principle of the Foxfire education movement: 'A constant feature of [democratic education] is its emphasis on peer teaching, small group work, and teamwork'.

Rigorous learning through authentically creative engagement

My focus on literacy development was within a broader aim to provoke so-called 'less advantaged' students to rise to rigorous learning challenges. I was convinced they were as capable as any other learners, but understood that they shied away from risk of failure that schooling had already *taught* them to fear. I sought a unit of work in which their *creative intelligence* was engaged, there were incentives to work hard, and they could anticipate *success*. By this logic, they needed to feel themselves working towards an *'authentic'* product in two senses. First, they needed belief that their work would result in effectively realised creations; to encourage this, I showed them clay animations done by students elsewhere (and, in Cycle 2), as tangible artefacts that students like them had produced. Second, they needed a sense of the authentic relevance of their animated stories to *their* lived concerns and identities.

The animation work was staged to build both senses of authenticity. Once groups had formed and identified issues, engagement grew considerably as students moved into plot development. Collaborations picked up in pace and time-on-task, often without any prodding from me. In Cycle 2, two boys who at the outset had refused to join the end-point visit to the Technology School of the Future notably changed their minds during the storyboard/scripting stage, stating – as I recorded in my journal notes – that 'They would return their excursion consent forms because they wanted to make the animation from their story'. In ringing 'true' to their experience, their story (about a robbery) animated a vital sense of investment to complete the work for showing to others. This heartened their whole group of four students, as fruition could not have been achieved without them. I later noted that these two students became dedicated driving forces within their group. Home group teachers who accompanied my classes on excursions to the Technology School of the Future remarked on the 'unusual' intensity, concentration and persistence of students in shooting/editing activities of complexity and length for young people of this age level.

Student sense of authenticity began, in my view, with trust in my invitation to bring funds of knowledge from their lives into curricular use. Actualisation of this sense came with genuine opportunity to *construct* – not simply to 'replicate' but to *interpret and create* – social-cultural knowledge about their local community environments. As Smith (2002: 593) observes 'learning experiences that allow students to become the creators of knowledge rather than the consumers of knowledge created by others can only serve to heighten students' engagement in their schooling'.

To grasp such authenticity is, for both students and teachers, to head collaboratively into the *unknown*. Indeed, any knowledge *about* lived experience is, to some degree, *interpretation*, or *re-creation*, of 'experience'. As such, neither teacher nor students can know definitively in advance how life-world *re*-presentations might take form. 'Enquiry means asking questions for which you do not know the answers', say McNiff et al. (1996: 13). This *constructive* nature of re-presented knowledge is fundamental to the problem-identifying/solving narrative genre. 'It is the job of the teacher', says Smith (2002: 589), 'to facilitate this process, linking the problem to the required curriculum, finding resources, and acting as a general troubleshooter'. The teacher thus becomes an authentic *learner of how to follow* students' creative leads. As Hayes et al. (2006: 90) state:

> When students engage in the construction of knowledge, an element of uncertainty is introduced into the instructional process and makes instructional outcomes not always predictable: that is, the teacher is not certain what students will produce. In helping students become producers of knowledge, the teacher's main instructional task is to create activities or environments that allow them opportunities to engage in higher-order thinking.

In such interaction, however, the teacher becomes more than mere 'facilitator'. At a point in my action-research journal, I started noting how I was integrating into the production of their stories, as much involved in their activities as they, and not just a teaching 'stranger' looking into their life-worlds. Through our interactive dialogues I had become so familiar with, and to, their stories that they were including me in them:

my likeness modelled as a school principal in one animation; my voice used for characters in others.

Conclusion: realising a double-democratic approach

Principles of uncertain knowledge creation, and of teacher as learner, underlie teachers and students becoming power-sharing 'colleagues' in forging directions that teaching-and-learning take. To embrace them requires a *pedagogical democracy* of collective and participatory dialogue in which students gain real voice in their learning. Authentically dialogic classrooms generate energies vital to sustaining rigorous work effort, and to engaging *curricular democracy* that invites genuinely meaningful funds of knowledge – deep contents from students' virtual schoolbags – into an inclusive and living knowledge interplay.

Ultimately, this double-democracy, curricular and pedagogical, came to fruition in clay animations created not just *from* student life-worlds, but *for* their life-worlds. That is, they gave critical and constructive knowledge back to their life-worlds in exhibiting their animations to school audiences that included local community members. As Delpit (1993: 288) says, 'merely adopting direct instruction is not the answer. Actual writing for real audiences and real purposes is a vital element in helping students to understand that they have an important voice in their own learning processes'. In this two-way exchange – taking from, and giving back to, local community (Zipin & Reid 2008) – the students became democratic agents in a profound sense: the 'problem-*solving*' creativity of their stories about community life offered new possibilities for local communities to re-create and vitally sustain themselves. They also became more adept and confident in their multi-literate capacities for engaging critically, creatively and proactively in such community-building work.

References

Bourdieu P & Passeron JC, 1990, *Reproduction in Education, Society and Culture* (2nd edn). Sage Publications, CA.

Chin J, 2001, *All of a place: Connecting community schools, youth, and community*. Bay Area Reform Collaborative, San Francisco, CA.

Comber B & Kamler B, 2004, 'Getting out of deficit: Pedagogies of reconnection', *Teaching Education*, 15(3), 293–310.

Comber B, Thomson P & Wells M, 2001, 'Critical literacy finds a 'place': Writing and social action in a low-income Australian Grade 2/3 classroom', *The Elementary School Journal*, 101(4), 451–464.

Delpit L, 1993, 'The 'silenced dialogue': Power and pedagogy in educating other people's children', in L Weis & M Fine (eds), *Beyond Silenced Voices: Class, Race and Gender in United States Schools*. State University of New York Press, Albany, NY, pp 119–139.

Gonzalez N & Moll L, 2002, 'Cruzando el Puente: Building bridges to funds of knowledge', *Educational Policy*, 16(4), 623–641.

Hattam R, McInerney P, Smyth J & Lawson M, 1999, *Enhancing School-Community Dialogue*. Teachers' Learning Project Investigation Series, Flinders Institute for the Study of Teaching, Adelaide.

Hayes D, Mills M, Christie P & Lingard B, 2006, *Teachers & schooling making a difference: Productive pedagogies, assessment and performance*. Allen and Unwin, Crows Nest, NSW.

Hyde S, 1992, 'Sharing power in the Classroom', in G Boomer, N Lester, C Onore & J Cook (eds), *Negotiating the Curriculum: educating for the 21st Century*. Falmer, London.

Jones S, 2004, 'Living poverty and literacy learning: Sanctioning topics of students' lives', *Language Arts*, 8(16), 461–9.

Luke A, Elkins J, Weir K, Land R, Carrington V, Dole S, Pendergast D, Kapitzke C, van Kraayenoord C, Moni K, McIntosh A, Mayer D, Bahr M, Hunter L, Chadbourne R, Bean T, Alverman D & Stevens L, 2003, *Beyond the Middle – A report about Literacy and Numeracy Development of Target Group Students in the Middle Years of Schooling*. Department of Education, Science and Training (DEST) and The University of Queensland, Australia.

McDougall J, 2002, 'Teaching the visual generation: Teachers' responses to art, media and the visual literacy challenge', paper presented at *AARE Annual Conference 2002*, University of Queensland, Brisbane, viewed 18 March 2007, <www.aare.edu.au/02pap/mcd02235.htm>.

McNiff J, Lomax P, &Whitehead J, 1996, 'Living educational action research', in J McNiff, P Lomax & J Whitehead (eds), *You and your action research project*. Routledge, London, pp 7–28.

Maney B, 2005, 'Re-positioning the reluctant high-school reader', in B Comber & B Kamler (eds), *Turn-around pedagogies: Literacy interventions for at-risk students*. Primary English Teaching Association (PETA), Sydney.

Moll L, Amanti C, Neff D & Gonzalez N, 1992, 'Funds of Knowledge for Teaching: using a qualitative approach to connect homes to classrooms', *Theory into Practice*, 31(2), 132–41.

O'Brien D, 2001, 'At-Risk' adolescents: Redefining competence through the multiliteracies of intermediality, visual arts, and representation, International Reading Association, Inc, Australia, viewed 18 March 2007, <www.readingonline.org/newliteracies/obrien/index.html>.

Oldfather P, 1995, 'Songs "come back to most of them": Students' experience as researchers', *Theory into Practice*, 43(2), 131–7.

Ovsienko H & Zipin L, 2007, 'Making social justice curricular: Exploring ambivalences within teacher professional identity', in P Jeffrey (ed.), *Proceedings of the Australian Association for Research in Education Annual Conference*. Adelaide, 2006.

Smith G, 2002, 'Place-based education: Learning to be where we are', *Phi Delta Kappan*, 83(8), 584–594.

Starnes B, 1999, *The Foxfire approach to teaching and learning: John Dewey, experiential learning and the core practices*. ERIC Clearinghouse on Rural Education and Small Schools, Charleston.

Thomson P, 2002, *Schooling the rustbelt kids: making the difference in changing times*. Allen & Unwin, Crows Nest, NSW.

Vacca R, Vacca J & Bruneau B, 1997, 'Teachers Reflecting on Practice', in J Flood, S Brice-Heath & D Lapp (eds), *Handbook of research on teaching literacy through the communicative and visual arts*. Macmillan Library Reference USA, New York.

Wood G, 1992, 'The school and the community'. In G Wood (ed.), *Schools That Work: America's Most Innovative Public Education Programs*. Plume, New York.

Zipin L & Reid A, 2008, 'A justice-oriented citizenship education: Making community curricular', in J Arthur, I Davies & C Hahn (eds), *SAGE Handbook of Education for Citizenship and Democracy*. SAGE, Los Angeles, 533–544.

Chapter 2

Making a difference: community change as a resource for connected primary curriculum

Monica Lee and Brenton Prosser

How teachers make a difference to the learning and lives of their students is not always immediately apparent. As teachers in the middle years of schooling, the year or two that we have with our students is but a small part of their overall education. It is often not until years later (when we have the good fortune to meet them as adults) that we come to understand how we may have influenced them. But what is immediately apparent on a daily basis, at least in our experience, is when we are not making a difference.

Our students tell us quite blatantly how they feel about the curriculum and tests that we are required to deliver, as well as how we deliver them. In our work with students, it is not uncommon to hear 'this is boring' or 'this is shit', followed by the slam of the door or furniture being upended. For these students, official learning is over before it has begun, while the remaining students also suffer as time is taken away due to subsequent classroom management responsibilities.

It is with such challenges in mind that we developed a unit of work and an action-research project that took into account (and provided for) these students who regularly tell us that we are not 'making a difference'. For us, this notion of 'making a difference' remains constantly perplexing. As teachers, we often feel at odds with the official expectations of schooling, which we believe to have evolved around a competitive academic curriculum (Connell 1993) that promotes 'learning to earn' (Gruenewald 2003; Hattam & Howard 2003), rather than learning how to live and learn. Further, as the priorities of schooling are increasingly welded onto the economy (Smyth et al. 2000), even in the primary-school context, we see a growing culture in which schools are expected to merely prepare children for the job markets of a globalised economy. While we do not deny that this is important, we do not believe that it should be almost to the exclusion of everything else. Thus, we are constantly caught in the tension between teaching the curriculum content that is handed down to teachers (in the context of an already crowded primary-school curriculum) and finding the space to foster authentic and community connected learning with our students.

In our experience, traditional transmission or 'banking' (Freire 1972) approaches to teaching do not encourage engaged learning amongst students, nor are they good for teachers and their school communities. We believe that education should be about social sustainability, which seeks a better future for our students, their communities and their environment. But if our classroom context of tears, verbal outbursts and flying chairs shows us anything, it is that traditional, competitive and learn-to-earn approaches are mismatched, disengaging, alienating and unsustainable. Thus, we set ourselves the challenge to educate our students in social sustainability by better understanding their social conditions, recognising the politics of power around them and acting as effective agents of change. We see this goal as being all the more important as urban fringe students find themselves in a context that often acts strategically to pacify them, to marginalise them, or to tell them that they are powerless or unimportant.

In this chapter, we tell the story of our attempt to take up this challenge. More specifically, we document how Monica (with the support of Brenton as her Masters' supervisor) tried to make a difference for her students by using recent urban renewal in the Salisbury region of Adelaide's northern suburbs as a resource for exploring students' 'funds of knowledge' (Gonzalez, Moll & Amanti 2005; Moll, Amanti, Neff & Gonzalez 1992) and developing community connected curriculum (Zipin & Reid 2008).

'Thisness' at school
Monica reflects:

> I have taught in Adelaide's northern suburbs for the past nine years, and have spent most of my 20-year teaching career in other 'rustbelt' schools (not that I am comfortable with the term). In that time I have

become increasingly frustrated with government policy and ideology, along with community and media expectations, that have become increasingly unrealistic in my view. I have witnessed an almost deliberate erosion of public schools, curriculum and social justice. The reduction in funding for public schools and my school in particular, has made teaching extremely difficult, as we are continually asked to do more with less. Meanwhile, the curriculum increasingly has become based around a series of outcomes that do not reflect how our students learn, nor is it necessarily relevant to the knowledge that is important to our students, or even to the increasingly diverse and complex identities of our students. These things have become increasingly apparent over the decade that I have been at this school.

Monica currently teaches Year 6 and 7 students at a Reception to Year 7 school on the northern urban fringe of Adelaide. It can be a difficult place to work. A large proportion of students struggle to achieve the literacy levels specified by the national and state benchmarks in Literacy and Numeracy (LaN) tests. Due to a high level of disengagement, it is often a battle for teachers to get students to complete the tasks that enable measurement against set outcomes. Staff are constantly under pressure to obtain results with students, and students in return resist these efforts in a number of ways, including chronic lateness, absenteeism, work refusal, apathy, verbal outbursts and/or physical disruption during classes.

However, these challenges must be viewed in the context that there is much from students' lives outside school that interferes with their learning. A number of difficult issues impact on the daily lives of students. These include poverty, complex family relationships, unemployment, underemployment, substance abuse, crime and changing government policy. Many families live in Housing Trust homes* that offer cramped living conditions, little privacy from neighbours and limited access to information technology.

Our conversations with students have revealed difficult and troubling lives, and there is a darker side to many of their daily experiences (Zipin 2009). We frequently find that the students who cause the most harm to their peers and learning environments have themselves been subject

---

* Public housing in South Australia is referred to as Housing Trust. These homes were built across the state in the 1940s and '50s. By the 1980s, in Salisbury North 37% of houses were Housing Trust homes and nearly 80% of these were concentrated around the school.

to the most harm. In this context, teachers cannot expect students to drop all their troubles at the door so that they can be willing and carefree learners when they enter the classroom. Many students are sleep deprived, hungry and poorly clothed, while some also see themselves as carers for their parents and siblings. All these things can distract them from their learning and disrupt the learning of others.

The school context

There are also contextual barriers to learning on a school-wide level. For instance, schools in South Australia are funded on an index of disadvantage that has seven categories. The school consists of two schools combined (with the junior primary listed as a Category 1 school and the primary school listed as a Category 2 school). Further, school data show that over 50% of the families qualify for a School Card and the suburb has one of the lowest socio-economic statuses in the nation (City of Playford 2006; Elliott, Sandeman & Winchester 2005). Clearly, the school operates in a context of significant complexity and need.

Adding to this, enrolments have been declining due to an urban renewal initiative which sees many families being moved to other suburbs as their Housing Trust homes are bulldozed to make way for more modern housing, or renovated for sale in the private housing market. While this is not necessarily a negative policy, it has had significant implications for the school, as public schools in South Australia are funded according to enrolments. So, not only has this policy resulted in greater instability in the school, but the student population has halved in three years, dramatically affecting funding for social justice and equity programs.

The classroom context

Monica's classroom is situated in the north-west corridor of a 1965 U-shaped building. It is located between the counsellor's room and the other Year 6/7 classroom. The room measures approximately 40 square metres and is typical of most classrooms in the school, with a whiteboard at the front and pin-up boards at the back. The room is painted a lilac colour (supposedly due to its calming influence) and the carpeted floor shows the scars of many years of art activities. Two computers (loaded with Windows 98) at the back of the classroom allow for Internet access. Seating arrangements are negotiated with students, but there are space restrictions which inhibit classroom activities and students often complain about the lack of room. It is not exactly a space that is conducive to modern teaching, nor suitable for a class of 25 to 30 middle years students. At the time of this project, the class was made up of nine girls and 17 boys. Thirteen of these students were considered to be 'at risk' by the school for reasons due to learning, family or social issues.

Such information is important to an appreciation of what Thomson (2002) called the 'thisness' of schools and classrooms. A major factor that is often overlooked in the current political climate, which emphasises standardised curriculum and assessment, is the importance of contextual influences and the learning needs of any one child. We believe that a one size fits all approach to learning is a major impediment to student engagement and learning, irrespective of the school that a child is attending.

For us, the concept of 'thisness' is helpful, namely because we believe it assists the teacher to consider the particularities of any school site, classroom or student cohort when planning learning experiences. It was the notion of the 'thisness' of a particular class, in a particular school, in a particular place, at a particular time, that was central to the planning of this teaching unit and the resultant action-research project, which is the focus of this chapter.

Planning the action-research project

As part of the RPiN project (Prosser 2008), this inquiry drew on conceptual resources such as 'funds of knowledge' (Moll et al. 1992), 'virtual schoolbags' (Thomson 2002) and 'turn-around pedagogies' (Comber & Kamler 2005). From these, the notion of using resources from the students' lives and community as curriculum, as well as strategic efforts to challenge deficit views of students, was a powerful one for us. However, there were two further conceptual resources that influenced this project, namely 'democratic schooling' and 'place-based education'.

Democratic schooling

Relinquishing teacher power in a classroom and instigating a more democratic or collaborative approach is not easy for most teachers. However, it can provide a rich learning experience not only for students, but for teachers themselves (Apple & Beane 1995). Trust in students and in yourself is needed to negotiate learning. This can be a threatening, yet gratifying, experience. Importantly, negotiation does not mean giving in to the low expectations of, or deficit views of, students. Teachers still set rigorous standards and use their expertise to guide learning, but democratic schooling acknowledges that the teacher is not the source of all knowledge.

Consequently, pedagogical approaches are developed that are different to the traditional method whereby knowledge is merely disseminated by the teacher. Instead, pedagogy is focused on the mutual interrelationships between teacher, learner and knowledge (Lusted 1986). In democratic schooling, knowledge is created, explored, discussed and theorised by teacher and student alike, with the lives and interests of the student as the basis of learning, rather than traditional school subjects (Beane 1991, 1995). Such approaches can result in greater student engagement, participation and active citizenship, each of which was an aim of this project.

Place-based education

A second conceptual resource, often called placed-based education (Smith 2002), allows us to explore when students are participating and engaging with their contexts and environments in meaningful ways. This approach acknowledges that despite teachers' best efforts, the types of learning that occur in schools will always be qualitatively different to those which occur in the real world. By getting out of the classroom, students are encouraged to become involved in environmental activities, community service and actively solve community problems.

> Place-based education can take a wide range of forms. One of its primary strengths is that it can adapt to the unique characteristics of particular places, and in this way can overcome the disjuncture between school and children's lives. (Smith 2002: 593)

Gruenewald (2003) suggested that learning needs to be based on home, school and community experiences. Doing so can create a society in which citizens are better connected to their communities and in turn are better able to identify with, care for, and work towards sustaining that community. By reconnecting, rather than disconnecting, students from their worlds, place-based education works to foster social sustainability and seemed an exciting way to engage marginalised students in a 'Society and Environment' curriculum unit.

Action-research question and method

With these concepts in mind, a research question was developed that took into account both student learning and pedagogical change. This question was: '*How can local community changes and experiences be used to motivate my students in their learning and assist in redesigning my pedagogy by defining deficit views about the ways students produce and apply knowledge?*'

To support an investigation of this question, we decided on a multi-pronged approach to collecting data. In addition to official school records, information was collected in the following forms:

- observations of classroom events recorded in a teacher's journal
- video recordings of classroom activities
- final work products from students
- structured interviews of students and the Deputy Principal by RPiN researchers
- structured interviews between the teacher and RPiN researchers.

The rationale for collecting these data was to record both student engagement and teaching practices.

The student interviews were intended to discover not only how focus students experienced the unit of work and their learning about the community, but also how they interpreted the meanings of 'successful at school' and 'a good teacher'. The teacher and Deputy Principal interviews were intended to supply additional information about good pedagogy at the school and the pedagogical strategies commonly used by Monica. Video observations were expected to offer an independent perspective to help compare the intended curriculum with the enacted curriculum (Manning 1996).

A chronology of a unit of work

Monica's initial question was 'If urban renewal was causing so much instability and concern for the school itself, then what sort of effect was it having on school families?' Monica set out to determine how the urban renewal policy was affecting the day-to-day attitude to school of the students, as well as the implications for their learning. All the students were aware of what was happening in their community, but unlike Monica, did not see it as a problem. In fact, most of the students reported that they were looking forward to the opportunity of being moved to a new home (which would possibly be in a different area). They were not worried about being moved out of Salisbury as they believed that they could stay in contact with friends via mobile phone and the Internet.

Monica had not taken into consideration the 'glocal' opportunities that modern technology had given to students so that they could 'transcend the physical neighbourhood' (Carrington 2006) through virtual communities and networks. Neither had she considered that an issue based on her own immediate concerns may not be such a concern for her students. She was then faced with the need to change the initial research aims of the project. Such change is not inconsistent with action-research methods and, in response, Monica decided to refocus the research aims by maintaining an interest in the changes in the local community, but not restricting it to the urban renewal project.

Specifically, Monica chose to address 'Time, Continuity and Change', a strand in the Studies of Society and Environment (SOSE) learning area of the South Australian Curriculum Standards and Accountability (SACSA). She had a particular learning outcome in mind, namely; the student explains why local and international communities have changed and are likely to change in the future. She felt that this would give her the opportunity to link a local issue to place-based learning and focus on a group of students who often disengaged from their learning across most curriculum areas.

Getting started

Monica started by devoting time to teaching research skills and giving students time to decide on their area of research. She provided the opportunity for this during Student Managed Learning (SML) time, which was held in the last session of the day.

There were three planned aspects to this project:

1. *Investigating the Past*: involving students in researching the past of Salisbury, looking into how and when the suburb started and what changes had occurred

2. *Investigating the Present*: involving students in interviewing staff and councillors from the Salisbury City Council about how change is determined, who makes decisions, and in whose interests these decisions are made

3. *Contemplating the Future*: where students would be given the

opportunity to plan how Salisbury could be designed, taking into consideration the issues and resources they consider important. Due to numerous interruptions to the project and time constraints, the class focused mainly on the *Investigating the Past* component, which involved interviewing staff and councillors from the Salisbury City Council. Timing difficulties due to the calling of local government elections meant that Monica covered *Instigating the Present* aspect in a lesson. Likewise, the *Contemplating the Future* component was conducted through a survey rather than interviews and presentations to a council representative. The survey Monica developed asked students what they liked about the area and called for them to suggest other possibilities for it.

While all students participated in the *Investigating the Past* component, Monica identified nine focus students. They were students who the school had recorded as lacking motivation, as under-achieving, or as at risk of school failure. The majority of them were boys; only one was a girl. These students fell into two categories:

1. students who lacked motivation and/or students who under-achieved due to complex domestic and/or social issues
2. students who lacked motivation and/or students who under-achieved due to learning difficulties.

When Monica first presented to the students the idea of researching the history of the area, she was met with silence. One student offered an explanation. Many of the students had completed a similar project when they were in Year 3. They indicated that the project had been fun, but they were underwhelmed because they had done it before. Monica then asked them to consider ways they could run the project without repeating what they had already done. To frame their collaborative efforts, Monica adapted and explained the model of 'head work, field work and text work' (McWilliam, Lather & Morgan 1997).

Head work

During the next session, the class looked at what they already knew 'in their heads'. Some students drew on their previous research experiences and could remember who the founding father of Salisbury was. Other students were surprised that the area was not always like it is now. Monica then communicated to the students the research work that she had already completed and told them what options were available to them during this project. She indicated that she was happy to support any options, as long as they were reasonable and the students could articulate what resources and skills they needed.

An extensive brainstorming session followed – more headwork. Students were particularly interested in visiting the Salisbury Library and the Salisbury and District Historical Society. It was possible for a history walk of the city centre to be organised through the Salisbury and District Historical Society, an idea that was very well received by students. They then looked at the different ways they could present information. Initially students suggested charts and written reports, but Monica presented a mini-documentary that a previous class had made. Suddenly, the ideas were flying and suggestions included models, maps, interviews and even a television program.

The class then discussed the skills they would need to complete their projects, which skills would benefit the whole class and which would benefit individuals. Once they had established the skills required, Monica set about explicitly teaching writing genres that would benefit specific projects. While the head work involved topic selection, working out what information needed to be gathered, where it could be found and what skills would be needed; the projects also required fieldwork to gather, filter and organise information.

Fieldwork

The fieldwork component included students visiting the Salisbury City Centre. After they had decided on their projects, they walked to the places they were researching to look for historic sites and to compare them with historical photos. A local historian agreed to visit the school and be interviewed by the students. During this time, Monica worked with students to interpret text and discuss their proposed content. Results from Internet searches were very limited, which surprised many students as they thought their community would be as important as Salisbury in the United Kingdom, about which they found plenty of information. During these activities students developed basic skills in identifying information sources, using information retrieval strategies, assessing the utility and reliability of evidence and comparative analysis of information. As students were gathering information in the fieldwork stage, Monica had frequent conversations with students about how they wanted to present the information that they had uncovered.

Text work

The text work that followed centred on the best form for presentation. Some students had very clear ideas about how they would present their work, while others took more time as they frequently changed their topic. Monica felt it important not to dictate how a project was presented and to allow students to find a way to present their projects so that they developed confidence in completing tasks. However, she did need to frequently present ideas to them to keep them motivated and engaged. When students kept changing their minds about what information they would present, she sat with them and brainstormed a number of ideas until they were satisfied with an idea that would work for them. She also regularly reminded them of the assessment criteria for the SOSE component so that they could negotiate to meet those criteria. As they explored the SOSE outcomes and she showed students the ones she needed to assess; and students understood what was expected of Monica in her role as teacher in relation to assessment. That they were still able to maintain control by choosing their area of research and how they presented their work, was satisfying and motivating for them. However, this transition from fieldwork (researching) to text work (assessment) still presented the greatest challenge to maintaining engagement.

Learning outcomes for students

During the project a number of practical issues emerged in relation to the learning of both Monica and the students. For instance, students were starting projects and realising that their initial concept was not working. Following this, they discussed what did not work in their initial attempt and then brainstormed other options. In these discussions, students focused on ways they had felt had worked in the past, but also talked about new things they would like to try. They were re-establishing their projects and not just giving up. Students took little interest in researching the history of the establishment of the district, yet negotiated their own areas of interest in the history of Salisbury. They discussed their projects with their parents and, when Monica spoke to the parents, they related how their children were enjoying the work and that they had never had so many discussions about school.

There were plenty of excuses why they should give up on their project when faced with difficulties; it required hard work on Monica's part to anticipate problems and look for ways for students to reconnect with their projects. Students were only given one hour on four days a week for their project, but they often enthusiastically asked if they were doing RPiN that day. The term RPiN became part of classroom language.

Throughout their projects, students also demonstrated a range of SACSA learning outcomes, including:

- understanding and valuing people's past
- understanding concepts of time, continuity, change, causation and heritage
- gathering and analysing primary and secondary sources of information
- presenting arguments based on historical evidence
- investigating the roles, intentions and motives of people and groups in relation to past and current events and issues
- a commitment to positively influencing present and future events and issues
- using electronic forms of technology and gathering and analysing statistical data
- understanding identity, both individual and group
- applying creative problem solving and conflict resolution skills
- valuing diversity, cohesion and justice
- recognising the roles and relationships of people and groups in political, legal and economic settings and systems.

While these were not as extensive as Monica had initially hoped for (she had hoped for more success in the areas of critical questioning, active citizenship and commitment to redressing oppression), these were still important outcomes for her students. However, the students were not the only ones learning, Monica was also learning about her contribution to socially sustainable schooling practices.

Reflecting on socially sustainable practices

As long-time readers of teacher research reports, and having attended many teacher conferences, we think that we can be forgiven for thinking that we are the only teachers who feel like we are not making a difference. Often, as we hear others report their success and the dramatic change in their students, we struggle to see classrooms that we recognise. Everyone else's classroom appears free of behaviour problems, chaos and constraints, with learning outcomes achieved and clear research results delivered. It can seem so detached from our daily experience that we wonder how it could possibly work in our classroom.

This, however, is not what action research is about. Action research is based on the struggle with the nagging concerns and unsolvable challenges in our practice as we embark on cycles of questioning and re-questioning. And so it has been with this project. Due to the complexity of contexts, unexpected interruptions, competing curriculum demands and time constraints, this project did not achieve all we had hoped it would to foster social sustainability. However, we believe that these challenges will be familiar to teachers and make this research report all the more real and believable.

However, just because this project did not reach its high ideals does not mean we should overlook the positive steps it made. We do not know what changes it made in the lives of the students involved in it. In fact, we may not know unless we have the good fortune to meet them as adults. The influences on curricular and pedagogical approaches that emanate from the underpinning philosophy should not be discounted, and neither should the subtle influences that this can make on students in the long term. While negotiation or democratic decision-making may seem like small things to the teacher, their contribution to a student and their future contribution to social sustainability should not be discounted. However, research reports require tangible outcomes. So, what did this project contribute to our understanding of socially sustainable pedagogy?

Monica used thematic coding to analyse the data that were collected. More specifically, she looked for keywords and phrases related to her main themes of good pedagogy, community as curriculum and democratic classrooms. She did this not only in her journal, but also in the student interviews and in her interview with the Deputy Principal. She then looked at the video footage to see if she was demonstrating any of these themes in her practice. Monica wanted to see how her understanding of these things related to her enacted pedagogy. This analysis resulted in three main discoveries, which we will frame according to the main themes of this book: the effect on students, the effect on teachers and the effect on communities.

Firstly, there was an effect on students. Through this project students were more engaged – indicated both by the way they expressed their enthusiasm 'to do RPiN', as well as by the rate of work completion. Students who had not previously submitted work did so for this project and there was not the normal struggle to get all the work completed and submitted, which is far from usual at this school. Further, each student had some success at school, which for many spilled over into having the confidence to try new things in other lessons. This is the core of the funds of knowledge and cultural capital approaches. If we can engage students and build their identities as learners, we can then start resisting deficit views and teaching the codes that can allow greater success in schooling.

When asked about what it was that worked for them in this unit of work, the focus students replied that they liked getting out of the classroom, exploring the community, working in groups, choosing what they were learning about and the challenge that this provided. There were also improved performances in rigour, both through focus students applying knowledge in new contexts and through performance against SOSE assessment criteria. These students also had success in enjoying, completing and being assessed for their work through negotiation and democratic decision-making.

The focus students were asked what they thought were the qualities of a 'good' teacher. They said that a good teacher:

- explains things clearly
- is a good listener
- is patient and has a sense of humour
- is organised
- is positive
- assists all students equally.

As these interviews were completed towards the end of the project, Monica was curious if the students made these comments because they believed it was her teaching practice or they felt these were qualities she was lacking and they wanted to communicate this to her. To check this, she reviewed the video footage and watched the way she interacted with students. This process leads to a consideration of the second of the key themes, namely the effect on teachers.

In watching the video, Monica found that for most students it was easy to consistently demonstrate the above 'good' pedagogies. However, it was with the focus students that she found that she was less successful. By looking closely at the video, Monica found that while she had assumed she was negotiating and being democratic, often she was merely giving focus students a list of options, rather than allowing them to explore possibilities for themselves.

As the qualities of a 'good teacher', as described by interviewed students, were becoming more evident and as Monica was more receptive to their ideas, she realised afresh something that she thought she already knew: instead of dictating narrow parameters for these students, she needed to listen more to their ideas and facilitate their own project design. For many teachers, this may not seem a very significant insight. However, this was confronting for a teacher with over 20 years experience in schools who believed that she is a good teacher who negotiates successfully with all students and who has created a democratic classroom. It reminded Monica again of the difference between the intended and enacted curriculum.

The third theme was the effect on the community. Clearly, if external constraints had not limited the linkage with the local council, it would have been more possible to foster active citizenship, advocacy for the community and an orientation to the future. That said, the project still provided a new understanding of the role of local government, as well as new links with community members, including community historians. Students developed a heightened sense of their community (as well as its namesake overseas) and participated in advocacy on the part of their community. Monica hopes to build these small steps in future renditions of this action-research program.

Reflecting on the 'redesign' in RPiN
Monica reflects:

> If someone asked me if using local community change can motivate student learning, I could confidently say 'yes'. However, it is answering the question about what I have learned from redesigning my pedagogy that shocks me most.
>
> I believe myself to be a socially just teacher, always seeking what is best for my students – this belief is why I became part of the RPiN project in the first place. However, through RPiN, I realised that I had become complacent in my practice for some students, namely those identified as being at risk.
>
> In essence, this project was a wake up call for me. I realised that

the only risk associated with these students was the risk I gave them. Whether I realised it or not, I was acting as though they were in deficit and I blamed them for their inability to learn and/or complete tasks. 'They lack motivation', 'they are frustrating', 'they continue to unreasonably resist', 'they refuse to take responsibility for their learning', all these things I found myself thinking. I do not know how these views snuck up on me, given my commitment to being a socially just teacher. Maybe I was not prepared to relinquish control, to really listen to them, to motivate rather than dictate. Maybe students were not necessarily resisting, they were just waiting to be heard.

There were many things I learnt from RPiN, and they have challenged the way I think about making a difference for my students. Most importantly, I learned that place-based learning and virtual schoolbags can generate a democratic learning environment where teachers and students create knowledge together. Not just in curriculum content, but also in providing students with the words, ideas and space to articulate why teachers have not made a difference in the past, and what they need for that difference to be made in the future.

But, despite my best intentions, I have found that previously I have been no better than teachers who practise the 'pedagogy of poverty'. However, through revisiting and renewing 'good pedagogy', I have had an opportunity to practise what I preach. I hope this reawakening can be a reminder for other educators who also call themselves socially just.

Conclusion

We began this chapter by reflecting on the fact that the ways that teachers make a difference to the learning of their students are not always immediately apparent. However, as this study has detailed, the barriers to doing this are not always clear. As experienced educators, we can assume that our commitment to social justice makes us immune, but we must not underestimate the subtlety, influence or invisibility of deficit views of our students and communities.

Through systematic examination, Monica discovered that what she thought she was doing well, she was doing superficially. And while it would be easy for Monica to give reasons for this, perhaps based on deficit views or unrealistic work demands, ultimately this would bring her no closer to her goal of being a socially just educator.

So what does this mean for Monica and sustainable pedagogy? In realising that she was thinking more than she was doing for her students that struggle most, Monica has found new energy to attempt and sustain more engaging, connected and inclusive pedagogical practices. She now has renewed understanding, renewed direction and renewed hope.

So while the steps taken in this study may not have been revolutionary in terms of pedagogical redesign, the study was an important step that we must all take. We hope that by realistically documenting its successes and limitations, other professionals will be encouraged to either think afresh about their long-term pursuit of social sustainability, or perhaps to look again at how they can make a difference in their practice.

References

Apple MW & Beane JA, 1995, 'Lesson from democratic schools', in MW Apple & JA Beane (eds), *Democratic Schools*. ASCD, Alexandra, 101–105.

Beane J, 1991, 'The Middle School: natural home of integrated curriculum', *Educational Leadership*, 49(2), 9–13.

Beane J, 1995, 'Curriculum Integrations and the disciplines of knowledge', *Phi Delta Kappan*, 76(April), 616–622.

Carrington V, 2006, *Rethinking Middle Years: early adolescents, schooling and digital culture.* Allen & Unwin, Crows Nest, Australia.

City of Playford, 2006, *City of Playford Wellbeing Plan 2006–2011.* City of Playford, Adelaide.

Comber B & Kamler B (eds), 2005, *Turn-around pedagogies: literacy interventions for at-risk students.* Primary English Teaching Association (PETA), Newtown, NSW.

Connell RW, 1993, *Schools and Social Justice.* Pluto Press, Melbourne.

Elliott M, Sandeman P & Winchester H, 2005, 'Embedding Community Engagement: Northern Adelaide and the University of South Australia', in proceedings of *Engaging Communities*, the 4th Australian Universities Quality Forum, Sydney, 6–8 July, 55–61.

Freire P, 1972, *Pedagogy of the Oppressed.* Penguin, London.

Gonzalez N, Moll L & Amanti C (eds), 2005, *Funds of knowledge: Theorizing Practices in Households, Communities and Classrooms.* Lawrence Erlbaum, Mahwah, New Jersey.

Gruenewald DA, 2003, 'The Best of Both Worlds: A Critical Pedagogy of Place', *Educational Researcher*, 32(4), 3–12.

Hattam R & Howard N, 2003, 'Engaging Lifeworlds: public curriculum and community building', in A Reid & P Thomson (eds), *Rethinking Public Education*. Post Pressed, Flaxton, Qld.

Lusted D, 1986, 'Why Pedagogy?' *Screen*, 27(5), 2–14.

McWilliam E, Lather P & Morgan W, 1997, *Headwork, field work, textwork: A text shop in new feminist research*. The Centre for Policy and Leadership Studies, Brisbane.

Manning A, 1996, 'Look before you Leap' (Plenary Address), *Literacy: getting insights from classroom research conference*, Balyana, South Australia.

Moll L, Amanti C, Neff D & Gonzalez N, 1992, 'Funds of Knowledge for Teaching: using a qualitative approach to connect homes to classrooms', *Theory into Practice*, 31(2), 132–141.

Prosser B, 2008, 'Unfinished but not exhausted: a review of Australian middle schooling', *Australian Journal of Education*, 52(2), 151–167.

Smith G, 2002, 'Place-based education: Learning to be where we are', *Phi Delta Kappan*, 83(8), 584–594.

Smyth J, Dow A, Hattam R, Reid A & Shacklock G, 2000, *Teachers' work in a globalizing economy*. Falmer, London.

Thomson P, 2002, *Schooling the rustbelt kids: making the difference in changing times*. Allen & Unwin, Crows Nest, NSW.

Zipin L, 2009, 'Dark funds of knowledge, deep funds of pedagogy; exploring boundaries between lifeworlds and schools', *Discourse*, 30(3), 317–331.

Zipin L & Reid A, 2008, 'A justice-oriented citizenship education: Making community curricular', in J Arthur, I Davies & C Hahn (eds), *SAGE Handbook of Education for Citizenship and Democracy*, SAGE, Los Angeles, 533–544.

Chapter 3

Connecting Year 9 mathematics to the community: an action-research project

✂✐✂✐✂

David Kinna and Kathryn Paige

Introduction

In this chapter David describes how mathematics can be taught in the classroom using community issues as a focus. His project explores the way in which an issue in the local community can engage middle years students in meaningful and rigorous mathematics, as well as teach students about their social responsibilities to the community. The study demonstrates that connecting to student life-worlds – drawing from the backgrounds and experiences of individuals and their families as well as from the local community – negotiating boundaries and incorporating explicit mathematical concepts and skills in a rich task, can motivate students in mathematics. Using an action-research model, he completed several cycles in two different middle school settings as he attempted to offer a rigorous curriculum to students through an approach to teaching mathematics and science that was influenced by connecting students to community.

The challenges David had in designing and delivering relevant curriculum, and in the process questioning entrenched institutional structures and personal practices, have important implications for sustaining pedagogical change over the long term. Working in groups, using a range of modelling materials, relying on broader strategies than textbooks, and encouraging students to negotiate boundaries are quite common in humanities classrooms, but very uncommon in secondary mathematics classrooms. David used these strategies to build a more democratic classroom by engaging students in meaningful mathematics. The longer-term aim was to build this notion of a democratic classroom into the middle years of schooling in his school.

The research context: school & teacher background

David has been a secondary schoolteacher of science and mathematics for over a decade, and is currently a coordinator of mathematics and numeracy. He has worked primarily in disadvantaged northern suburbs schools and has a strong commitment to social justice and equity. For this study David was situated in two schools. In both locations there is a disproportionately high level of complex and aggregate disadvantage in the school population. Many problems arise from poverty, generational unemployment, high youth unemployment and individual and family transience. The area immediately surrounding the schools comprises semi-detached public housing and there is a large number of single parent families. The schools have a long history of commitment to working with and supporting students at risk of not completing a full secondary education. While the project ran in two schools, the emphasis in this report is on the community-based nature of the classroom practice, rather than on the similarities and differences between the two schools.

The student profile and middle school structures were drawn from the second site, where David spent the last two years, and where the cycle of the research project reported here was located. The students came from a wide range of cultural backgrounds representing at least 22 different nationalities. Consequently there was a significant enrolment of students from non-English speaking backgrounds. In the last four to five years the region has been undergoing an urban renewal project to improve safety in the area and make it more attractive for families to move to. This urban renewal was occurring at the same time as the RPiN project (Hattam, Brennan, Zipin & Comber 2009). The latter aimed to help teachers understand their students' lives more clearly, and their school communities more deeply, by supporting teachers to redesign their pedagogy to provide a relevant and more equitable curriculum. It aimed to build curriculum and pedagogical practices that engage young people's 'funds of knowledge' (Gonzalez & Moll 2002; Moll, Amanti, Nett & Gonzalez 1992) that arise from the life-worlds of their communities, as a way to encourage academic success in the mainstream curriculum.

For the 13 years that David has been teaching, a question that he has often asked himself is: how do I make the curriculum interesting and relevant to students and engage them in rigorous schoolwork? He has been working on this question in his two main teaching areas, mathematics and science. When he started his action-research projects on these aspects of pedagogy, his teaching and research focus was centred on re-invigorating middle school science. The first cycle of the research, based in the first school, focused on a special needs Years 8 and 9 science class in which the students tested water at the local wetlands; and in the second cycle, David trialled a model-making project in a mainstream science class. This coincided with the first year of the *Redesigning Pedagogies in the North* project, which gave added impetus and resources to David's interest in curriculum redesign.

After the first two cycles of action research, David won a leadership position as Mathematics Coordinator in another northern suburbs high school, and the focus changed to re-invigorating middle school mathematics. The research, although important at the classroom level and for David as a teacher, became even more important from a faculty point of view, given David's leadership position. It was important to model contemporary practice in mathematics so as to influence teachers in the middle school team. The focus of this chapter is on describing and analysing the third iteration of the project, conducted in his second school, this time using a Year 9 mathematics class to explore the local community and what students think would improve it.

The unit of work

David wanted to use a community issue that students were passionate about and could relate to, something that was tangible to them and would spark their curiosity. After reading an article by Moll et al. (1992) about teachers using students' funds of knowledge in a middle primary classroom, he decided to use a similar methodology with a Year 9 mixed ability Mathematics class. The community issue that was identified by the class was the lack of recreational areas in the local district, places where students felt they could go after school and on weekends with friends and family. After designing a survey and interviewing at least one family member about what they knew about the street on which they lived and what they felt was needed around the area, they collated the results and presented their findings to the class. From this, the students' brief was to work out what they thought was needed in the community and then, in small groups, to choose a concept and design and construct a model of such things as a playground, zoo, crèche, skate park and sport playing fields. Mathematics was central to the model building, focusing on three key strands in the mathematics curriculum – measurement, data and statistics, and number – and emphasising the mathematical concepts of budgeting, scale and ratio.

How was this mathematics unit of work different and what did it look like? Model building and blueprint drawing are skills not often used in a Year 9 mathematics class. Yet students' mathematical skills and concepts were developed when they drew blueprints and built scale models of their recreational areas. Estimation and accurate measurement of linear distance and surface area saw numbers being manipulated mentally and with pen and paper. By constructing surveys and analysing data, the students also developed a critical numeracy perspective. This was achieved by comparing recreational areas (surface area and facilities available) in different Adelaide suburbs of different socio-economic status. This information was incorporated when they designed their own solutions.

Tables were moved to the edge of the classroom to allow for group planning on the floor, students were solving problems in small groups, and people were moving around the room to collect material and seek help. A store was set up in one corner where students could use their allocated budget to purchase consumable materials such as balsawood, cardboard, paint and pipe cleaners at a cost per unit. They could also hire equipment such as glue guns, paint brushes, Stanley knives and cutting boards on a per 15 minute basis. David's role was one of facilitation, helping students solve problems as they emerged. While the noise level was up, it was a constructive noise and quite different from a traditional mathematics classroom in a secondary setting.

The unit was run over most of one term with all lessons focused on this task. Planning for these lessons consumed lots of David's thinking, as it was the first time he had used this approach in mathematics. He used his imagination and support from colleagues to scaffold students' learning. With this flexible approach there was less emphasis on the traditional method of using texts to cover a certain amount of mathematics in each lesson.

During the eight-week block of lessons, there were a number of key changes to David's pedagogy. Except for two double lessons on biased and unbiased questions and budgeting, the textbook was not used and there was little explicit whole-class teaching. Students were helped with any questions they had on a need-to-know basis. There was ongoing negotiation with students and class discussion time was planned for the final session each week to identify successes and problems and negotiate ways forward.

Group work was also encouraged with students choosing the size and membership of their group. While this might not seem revolutionary to teachers in other subject areas, this is not common practice in many mathematics classes.

Assessment was by peers. Students negotiated criteria, and rubrics were constructed to cover learning outcomes evident in the models, PowerPoint presentations and surveys. After each presentation they received oral and written feedback from their peers.

The orientation to numeracy was a mix of the traditional, constructivist and socially critical (McInerney, Hattam & Smyth 2002). The traditional orientation was used to teach the students about the surveys and budgeting, and a constructivist orientation to numeracy encouraged students to build on their knowledge of scale and ratio. Students also had the chance to compare the quality of recreational areas in different suburbs of Adelaide, which allowed for a socially critical orientation to numeracy. From this they could study why those differences might occur and suggest what could be done about them.

In summary, in the unit of work – entitled *Your community: What is missing?* – secondary students in a mathematics classroom in a middle school setting developed their functional numeracy through model construction. The three main changes made to the teaching of mathematics involved connecting to students' life-worlds through place-based projects, providing opportunities for students to negotiate, and engaging students by using mathematics in the real world.

Action research in David's classroom

The processes and outcomes of the project were explored using an action-research methodology, a definition of which was provided by Kemmis and McTaggart:

The linking of the terms action and research highlights the essential feature of the method: trying out ideas in practice as a means of improvement and as a means of increasing knowledge. (in McNiff, Lomax and Whitehead 1996: 4)

David's action research investigated the impact of his changed pedagogy on students' engagement in mathematics. A key issue David and other teachers experienced with this class was a lack of interest in schoolwork and a consequent lack of engagement in learning. This was most evident in the first two terms of the year in the lack of work completed, and questions such as 'why are we doing this?' and 'how long until the bell?' Students' work also lacked the level of rigour expected from a Year 9 class. In short, they were not connected to their learning in mathematics.

Thus the pedagogical questions underpinning David's action-research project were:

1. *Is there a way to teach mathematics concepts so as to engage students and teach them how to use real mathematics skills in a wide variety of contexts?*
2. *Can we create a rigorous and engaging mathematics program around these community issues?*
3. *Can a more democratic classroom in mathematics that focuses on group work and negotiating within real life contexts contribute to socially sustainable practices?*

Four methods were used to collect data to answer these questions:

- At the start of the project, students filled out a survey in which they said what they liked and disliked about maths, what they felt their maths skills were and what they would like to see more of in classrooms. At the end of the project students took the same survey again and David compared those results to track changes in attitude over the eight weeks of the project. In the initial survey there were few positive comments about mathematics; students did know that it was important but could not see why. In the post-project survey, students said that they found mathematics more interesting and relevant. Most significantly, they could see how it related to life outside school.
- David kept a journal of his observations from each lesson as well as student issues that arose.

- Two colleagues observed some of the lessons and their feedback was used to improve teaching.
- Student work samples – the completed models and rubrics for peer assessment – complemented the written test at the end of each unit of work. Students shared their models and PowerPoint presentations with students transitioning from Year 7 to 8.

This mix of methods gave us a number of insights into the impact of the approach. The next section on project findings is based on the data gathered.

Project findings

Our examination of the data during the project led to incremental teaching changes over the eight-week teaching period. We found that reflecting on journal entries and using feedback were particularly useful, and critical incidents helped David to focus and alter his teaching.

The summative findings from the project highlighted a number of achievements. First, the students were very engaged with their work, as evidenced by a number of indicators. The questions of 'why are we doing this?' and 'how long until the bell?' were rarely asked. Students wanted to come to the class during lunchtime and, even on Friday afternoon, students were concentrating and did not know when the lesson had finished. Students wanting to show the model that they had made to others was further evidence of their engagement. Another indicator of engagement was that students took the models home on the weekend so that they could spend time working on them. In their spare time, students would also measure things such as car parks and air conditioner systems and use these measurements to scale their models.

During this project, David's Year 9 students' attendance and participation improved. Managing behaviour in mathematics lessons became less of a focus, as students were engaged in learning and were thinking and working mathematically during the problem-based learning task. Another aspect of student engagement was ensuring that students could see how the mathematics they were learning linked with their daily life. Working with their parents in the shed, contacting the council by letter and using the expertise of graffiti artists all connected aspects of the students' life-worlds with their community. And, most importantly, the students were developing a connection to place and a sense of belonging.

The challenge is for this project to be repeated on a broader school basis in an effort to improve students' engagement in mathematics and increase enrolment in senior years.

Importantly, student engagement was achieved without any loss of rigour – indeed we believe that the approach increased the depth of student learning. By studying a community issue that affected them personally, the students developed knowledge and skills in budgeting, estimating and measuring, calculating scale, surveying others and analysing data. Explicit teaching of mathematics also involved measurement, angles, cost of construction and budgeting. Students' learning in spatial sense and geometric reasoning was documented, and they were engaged to think and work mathematically through the construction and use of rotograms to estimate and replicate angles. This is part of using a constructivist approach to developing conceptual understanding (Van de Walle 2007).

We also learned a lot about the challenges involved in achieving a balance in implementing a more democratic classroom. Some of the negotiations with the students worked well, but a number of students wanted wider scope for negotiation and found it difficult when the brakes were put on by the teacher, such as being required to set a budget based on a negotiated ceiling on prices for materials. While six groups worked well to complete their projects, some did not. By allocating lesson time to develop students' ability to successfully work in groups, and having some non-negotiables about who could work together, may have helped more groups to be successful. Democratic classrooms do not equate with lack of structure: by specifying what could and could not be negotiated, David was able to support the evolution of a democratic classroom. Small steps were taken in this project, but it is an important area worthy of future teacher and student development.

Another challenge was the time involved in planning. It takes a lot of time to plan a unit of work such as this and to organise the materials needed for model building. These were not big factors for David, as the RPiN project gave time support to his project, but if a teacher was to try this project while teaching a full class load, the preparation time could be prohibitive. A solution to this could be working with other mathematics teachers or integrating the topic across two subject areas.

A further challenge was the traditional timetable structure at the school. Since lessons have a set length, it was difficult for students to spend extra time working on the project. In addition, if David's approach was to become mainstream, then time for teachers to meet would need to be made. In order to attempt a project like this with more than one teacher and to allow the students a chance to study the issues seriously, schools would need to be more flexible with timetables.

Implications for teaching mathematics

After three years' research on this project, David's pedagogy has shifted from one which uses traditional exercise-based mathematics lessons to one which places greater value on students' life-worlds and uses this as a context for learning. When asked at the end of the project about what his current focus in teaching involved, David replied:

> Mine is community issues and place-based education, and that's what I'm looking at, so I suppose I'm a lot more interested in what's happening in the local community for the school now, and how I can link that into the kids' learning.

This revitalised view of teaching and learning, based on the connection between students' lives and learning, has changed David's classroom practice in three key ways. First, he is moving away from a textbook focus to more hands-on learning in the mathematics classroom. Second, he is trying to learn more about students' lives and to incorporate this knowledge into the classroom. Third, he is developing the capacity and skills to offer students more voice in the classroom, allowing for a more democratic classroom. Two of the innovative practices, keeping a democratic classroom and learning more about students' lives will be explored in the next section.

Keeping a democratic classroom

An area of significance for teaching and research was the change made to classroom pedagogy to implement classroom democracy. A democratic classroom allows all the people involved in the classroom, the students and teacher, to participate in decision-making processes (Pendergast & Bahr 2005). Allowing the opportunity for negotiation needs work and practice from both the teacher and student, as the traditional roles of teacher and student no longer work. The students felt that they had more ownership of their work, as they were involved in discussions about planning in the classroom, ways to present their work, the materials they could use and what recreational area they could build. The use of a community issue was important, as the students could become a part of their community, and it taught them how they could influence the community that they live in. Developing negotiation skills helped increase students' respect for their community and become responsible citizens. This leads to the notion of a socially sustainable curriculum. Students see the importance of their own place in the world and develop an understanding about what they can do to improve it and work positively with the community. Students who do develop these ideas can contribute to the school community while they are at school, as well as to the wider community when they leave school.

David's negotiation in the classroom and efforts to make it a more democratic place was effective but far from easy. The students were engaged and this helped them become more effective contributors in the classroom and have a greater say in the work done. However, due to the nature of schools and the 'powerful discourse which seeks to affirm far more utilitarian values and purposes of schooling' (McInerney, Hattam & Smyth 2002: 19), there can still be conflict over which aspects of the work remain non-negotiable. For instance, students need to learn mathematical concepts, and these cannot be negotiated away in the democratic classroom or this will damage students' chances in future years. So the ongoing dilemma for the teacher is how to achieve a balance between the tasks which involved students applying the knowledge they have gained, and the need to build for rigour and course content, in order to ensure viable options for career pathways in the senior years of schooling. However, it was David's experience that, after students have learned the non-negotiable mathematical concepts, they are better placed to negotiate other matters such as community issues to be investigated. One example of how this might be done is to have students ask questions which can be the focus for further rich tasks (Hyde1992). Hence, mathematical questions that arise in the contexts of students' part-time jobs, future careers and contemporary music can all become possibilities for connecting with students' interests. It is our belief that a combined understanding between teacher and students of what can be decided collectively and what must be learned is the foundation for any democratic classroom to succeed.

Learning about students

The idea of finding out about students and using their funds of knowledge in the classroom has been influential in David's pursuit of pedagogical change. Through connecting to, and having discussions with, students throughout the course of the project David developed a knowledge of their interests and what they enjoy doing outside the school. He learnt about students' love of sport. He also learnt that the students recognised the importance of family relationships and responsibilities, especially with and for younger brothers and sisters, whom they often have to baby sit. As a result some of the students built playgrounds or a child-care centre for their younger siblings, as they saw these as important resources for their communities.

This is but one example, and of course it is not easy to use all the students' interests at one time. A possible solution is to use a particular student interest in one piece of work and then use another in a second. Another possible solution is to allow greater student choice in their work. Whatever a teacher's approach, it is most important to always employ the students' funds of knowledge in maths to help increase their connectedness to their learning.

The significance of the project

From a teaching and research perspective, David felt that his project was significant for a number of reasons. These included:

- the capacity to develop numerate citizens by using and choosing mathematics in context
- using a community issue to connect students to place
- exploring the use of student voice in a democratic mathematics classroom.

The project demonstrated that there need not be a gap between students' lives, learning and the curriculum as there are many aspects of the physical and biological environments that can provide authentic contexts for teaching and learning mathematics and science. Admittedly connecting community issues to the classroom cannot occur all the time, but it can happen often enough for students to see connections between science and mathematics and their life-worlds. Hodson (2003) made the point that school science needs to change, as it no longer meets the needs, interests and aspirations of young citizens, and suggested that the science curriculum be orientated more towards socio-political action. Mathematics, through a numeracy lens (Zevenbergen 2004), can also connect mathematics to students' life-worlds, as this project demonstrates.

David found that this project opened his eyes to the different strategies that can be used in science and mathematics classrooms, as well as to the different resources that are available to the teacher. Encouraging middle school students to work in groups and to negotiate aspects of curriculum by using community issues, can invigorate their interest and lead to students working harder in mathematics classes. David found that using models is an excellent way to get to know students and incorporate work that interests them. Mathematics can be taught through real-life tasks and students can develop their functional numeracy by using real-life issues that challenge them to use problem-solving skills. Sharing these insights with mathematics colleagues and those in other learning areas in the school has ensured that the innovative pedagogical practices developed by the project have spread to other classes in the middle school. These are important outcomes from a three-year project.

David's professional growth shows that changes can be made to classroom pedagogy if long-term support is available. Being part of the RPiN project over a three-year period, with ongoing access to teacher peers and university colleagues, has contributed to the change. For this to continue in the long term, support must come from school structures to enable team teaching and time to co-plan. What has become clear in this project is that a link between being informed through literature and educational theory is vital to teachers developing more innovative classroom practice.

References

Gonzalez N & Moll L, 2002, 'Cruzando el Puente: Building bridges to funds of knowledge', *Educational Policy*, 16(4), 623–641.

Hattam R, Brennan M, Zipin L & Comber B, 2009, 'Researching for social justice: contextual, conceptual and methodological challenges', *Discourse: Studies in the Cultural Politics of Education*, 30(3), 303–316.

Hodson D, 2003, 'Time for action: Science education for an alternative future', *International Journal of Science Education*, 25(6), 645–670.

Hyde S, 1992, 'Sharing power in the Classroom', in G Boomer, N Lester, C Onore & J Cook (eds), *Negotiating the Curriculum: educating for the 21st Century.* Falmer, London.

McInerney P, Hattam R & Smyth J, 2002, *Improving Numeracy Outcomes: A review of the Literature.* Flinders Institute for the Study of Teaching, Adelaide.

McNiff J, Lomax P &Whitehead J, 1996, 'Living educational action research, in J McNiff, P Lomax & J Whitehead (eds), *You and your action research project.* Routledge, London, pp 7–28.

Moll L, Amanti C, Neff D & Gonzalez N, 1992, 'Funds of Knowledge for Teaching: using a qualitative approach to connect homes to classrooms', *Theory into Practice*, 31(2), 132–141.

Pendergast D & Bahr N, 2005, *Teaching Middle Years: Rethinking Curriculum, Pedagogy and assessment.* Allen & Unwin, Crows Nest, NSW.

Van de Walle J, 2007, *Elementary and Middle School Mathematics: Teaching Developmentally*, 6th edn. Pearson Education, Boston USA.

Zevenbergen R, 2004, 'Reconceptualising numeracy for new times', *Curriculum Perspectives*, 24(3), 1–7.

Chapter 4

Connecting lives and learning:

Super Size Me with science

❤❤❤❤

Jane Wilson and David Lloyd

In this case study we discuss the way in which a documentary, *Super Size Me,*[*] was used as a basis for a number of learning activities that connected with students' life-worlds by using an inquiry approach based on a transdisciplinary methodology. The aim of this action-research project was to increase student engagement in science learning and contribute to social sustainability through encouraging healthier eating.

Motivation for the project

The motivation for this research project was a concern about the limited degree to which students engaged in science learning. This observation challenged us to examine pedagogical strategies in order to improve student engagement and the quality of their learning. School data and the broader research literature indicate that the uptake of science in the senior years of secondary school and tertiary institutions is declining, and that junior school science is not connected to students' life-worlds. This project takes on the idea that science education, to be relevant and empowering for students, must be an exercise in socio-political action and directed towards sustainable living – economic, social and cultural, as well as environmental. Science learning that takes such an approach contributes to social sustainability and shifts towards a more transdisciplinary methodology. In our case study, the social issue that was tackled

---

[*] *Super Size Me* (Ronin Films 2004) is a documentary that serves as a springboard for discussion on fast food, nutrition, food advertising and obesity in children. It also encourages students to examine their own eating habits and societal changes taking place in food production and consumption.

is the quality of students' nutrition and its associations with personal health, obesity and family and community life. Media reports indicate that the diets of our students are not always healthy. Noakes and Clifton (2005: vii) reported that 'Obesity rates have doubled in Australia in the past twenty years. It's a fact that today more than 60% of Australians are overweight or obese – men, women and children'. This project aligns with efforts by education authorities to implement pro-active strategies in schools to tackle the problem of overweight youth.

Significance of this project for teachers & research

If an inquiry approach to learning and a socio-political orientation to curriculum can be shown to engage reluctant students in science learning, then other teachers can, with some confidence, embrace this approach. As we briefly report later, science education research literature and government reports indicate a worrying decline in the uptake of science in senior years and a general disenchantment with science as an area of learning. This literature also indicates the need for our community to be scientifically literate, as science 'is a tool we use to make sense of and guide us in our decisions about the world' (Lee & Roth 2002: 43). Scientific literacy is more than a matter of interest to scientists and science educators. When one considers social sustainability, scientific knowledge and literacy is vital to its development. However, current science curriculum is primarily canonical, textbook-based and directed towards preparing a few for work as scientists. It therefore lacks relevance for all but a few enthusiasts. However, a number of authors 'advocate a politicised, issues-based curriculum focused on seven areas of concern' (Hodson 2003: 645), one of which is human health, an idea that is central to the topic investigated by the students in this study.

Key question

The aim of the research was to see if, by using a student inquiry approach and connecting learning to life-world interests and concerns, student learning could be improved, and the learning experience could be seen by students to be a positive one likely to sustain their interest in science.

> [An] inquiry-based approach to science stresses the active engagement
> of students in their own learning, the development of appropriate
> strategies to solve personally relevant problems and the undertaking of

these strategies with the aim of producing data that can be analysed and presented to a variety of audiences. (Jones, Melville & Bartley 2000: 18)

The research task was to evaluate a science topic structured on a number of learning experiences in which a documentary, *Super Size Me*, was used to connect science learning to students' lives, both at school and at home. The action-research intervention was a transdisciplinary study of health and nutrition in the community that used an inquiry-based approach. Transdisciplinary studies are problem, or issue-based, studies that use as many ways of knowing as are needed for their resolution. The *Super Size Me* topic replaced a programmed chemistry topic covering the Periodic Table. Jane argued that learning about food chemistry and dietary requirements would introduce students to many of the ideas (e.g., elements, atoms, compounds, molecules, mixtures and chemical change) that would have been normally addressed, but in a context to which students could relate. Although a transdisciplinary approach should ideally have be followed in collaboration with other teaching areas (i.e., been truly trans-), the rigid school structure and curriculum requirements made this too disruptive or novel for other subjects. Innovation rarely takes place in ideal environments.

The research question that drove this project was: *How is student learning, about their disposition towards their diet and their engagement with their learning, enhanced by using an inquiry approach that connects students' learning to their life-worlds?*

The research context

The school

The school we worked in is a Category Two Disadvantaged school of 1,100 students in the northern suburbs of Adelaide. It is a single campus school, Reception to Year 12, and consists of three sub-schools, Junior (R–6), Middle (7–9) and Senior (10–12). The retention rates are below the state average and attendance rates decrease progressively as students move from the Middle to the Senior School. Completion rate of the Senior Secondary Certificate (SACE) is also below the state average.

The school is socio-culturally diverse and complex and a large percentage of its community experiences economic hardship. This is demonstrated by the high proportion of School Card holders (approximately

60%), high rates of unemployment (Office of Employment 2003) and transience in the region. There were a significant number of students from cultural backgrounds other than English (approximately 20% Cambodian and Vietnamese) and it had one of the largest enrolments of Aboriginal students in the Adelaide metropolitan area.

The class

Middle School class sizes in the school were less than 24 students; smaller than the South Australian average. Most of the home group teachers taught Mathematics, Science, English, or Society and the Environment and took their home group for at least one subject.

The group of students that participated in this study, a Year 9 class, was taught science by Jane and was the only class to take part. This was the only contact Jane had with these students as a subject teacher. All the students came from English speaking backgrounds. Two students had special learning needs that affected their comprehension of text, and one student was on a Negotiated Education Plan.

The class was typical of the wider school population in their lukewarm enthusiasm for traditional subject-based learning and textbook driven pedagogy, and were not confident in taking risks to move away from what they knew. It was our challenge to offer something different that students could be successful with and enjoy.

The science lessons were usually held in the science laboratory and sometimes in the Resource Centre and computing rooms. Unfortunately, booking problems often meant these rooms could not be used. Apart from accessibility, the configuration of specialist rooms, although ideal for the purposes for which they were designed and the needs of subject-based curriculum, did not lend themselves to learning approaches that required multiple ways of engaging with the subject matter. Being in an inappropriate space can inhibit students' progress. Ideally, a room with wet areas, access to computers and spaces for individuals and small groups to work collaboratively would have been more suitable for the *Super Size Me* topic.

The teacher

For five years Jane was Assistant Principal and Head of the Middle School as well as a science teacher. She has taught in a variety of locations. Her main goal for teaching was to encourage all students to work independently to the best of their ability, think scientifically and to take risks with their learning. As a teacher (and administrator), it was important to understand students' lives and the school community, so that pedagogies could be redesigned to be better connected to students' 'funds of knowledge' (Gonzalez & Moll 2002). The challenge was to develop pedagogical practices that engaged students in learning they valued. A related challenge was to move from planning and learning that relied primarily on a textbook, to an approach that valued learners' ability to collect and interrogate primary data. It was also seen by Jane as being important to recognise the role of the teacher as a learner and to renew and review the curriculum to ensure students engaged in their learning.

Influential ideas

To inform our work, we have primarily drawn on the middle schooling and science-education literatures, although we have also taken note of transdisciplinary research connected to community problem solving. The middle schooling literature notes the nature of students in the middle years and how society constructs them as a cohort (Barratt 1998; Beane 1997; Carrington 2006; Eyres, Cormack & Barratt 1993; Groundwater-Smith, Mitchell & Mockler 2007; Pendergast & Bahr 2005). The science-education literature is a rich source of ideas on how science can be taught in ways that relate to students' lives and interests (Aikenhead 2006; Fensham 2003, 2004; Goodrum, Hackling & Rennie 2001; Hodson 2003; Jenkins & Pell 2006; Lee & Roth 2002; Lemke 2001; Osborne, Simon & Collins 2003; Skamp & Logan 2005; Tytler 2007; Tytler & Symington 2006a; Venville, Wallace, Rennie & Malone 2002). Transdisciplinary research has helped us to understand and value pluralistic methodologies when working towards community sustainability (Balsiger 2004; Costanza 2003; Després, Brais & Avellan 2004; Esbjörn-Hargens & Zimmerman 2009; Horlick-Jones & Sime 2004; Lawrence & Despres 2004).

Two aspects of the middle schooling literature are particularly relevant. The first is the need to connect curriculum to students' interests and needs. It is a strong theme in the middle school literature to see curriculum as primarily addressing the needs of young adolescents (Beane 1997; Eyres, Cormack & Barratt 1993). Carrington (2006), Groundwater-Smith,

Mitchell and Mockler (2007) and Pendergast and Bahr (2005) also saw the need for curriculum to primarily and explicitly address the needs of young adolescents and to connect students' learning to the world outside the school, rather than focus on discrete subject areas.

The second, and related, aspect is the need to integrate curriculum across learning areas so that students can make connections between various subjects and the wider community (Pendergast & Bahr 2005). Such a curriculum encourages students to participate in a curriculum that they believe is worth doing (Eyres, Cormack & Barratt 1993).

Our observations that students are not engaging with science learning are supported by the science-education literature. A number of studies have highlighted a reduction in the number of students selecting post-secondary careers that involve science, particularly the physical sciences (Fensham 2004; Jenkins & Pell 2006; Osborne & Collins 2001; Osborne, Simon & Collins 2003). Skamp and Logan (2005) reported that Australian and international studies have shown that students in the middle years lose interest in science, with girls losing interest more than boys (Osborne, Simon & Collins 2003).

The last 30 years of research on science learning also indicates that 'most students tend not to learn science content meaningfully (that is do not integrate it into their everyday thinking)' (Aikenhead 2006: 27). Many students are disenchanted with the school science curriculum due to its emphasis on 'canonical science concepts' (Aikenhead 2006: 31) and consequently science becomes 'unimportant, unengaging and irrelevant to their life interests and priorities'. For them, 'science has little personal or cultural value' (Rennie 2006: 6). Too often, current practice in science 'ignores the realities of students' own lives, interests and feelings' (Tytler 2007: 38). There is also a need to show science as 'a way of understanding the world and engaging with issues that are meaningful to them' (Tytler 2007: 13).

The science education literature indicates that at present, with the knowledge dominated curriculum, teachers largely adopt a transmissive style of pedagogy and the majority of students 'learn to fail' and do not understand science. Students increasingly describe it as boring – an outcome of a combination of low interest and high cognitive demand (Fensham 2003: 18). Goodrum (2006), Goodrum et al. (2001), Rennie (2006) and Tytler (2007) have all pointed out that this is not due to the nature of science, but to the failure of many teachers of science to offer relevant and engaging science experiences to their students. Science courses that connect to students' life-worlds, on the other hand, are 'located in the multiple societal contexts within which citizens are involved – at home, in their neighbourhood, in their work, at leisure, and as members of local, regional and national communities' (Fensham 2003: 8). Such approaches are situated, engaging and relevant. They are also vital for the future. Understanding the physical and biological world, the realm of science, is essential for engaging meaningfully in practices that lead to environmental and social sustainability (Berry 1999; Cross & Price 2002; Lowe 2009; Suzuki & McConnell 1997).

Ways forward

From a science, technology and society (STS) perspective, Ziman (1994) suggested a number of ways forward, four of which informed this study. They are:

- making science relevant to everyday life
- using a transdisciplinary approach
- using a sociological approach (citizen science) in which science becomes embedded in social action
- using a problem-solving approach where students look at current issues.

These ways forward clearly correlate with the emphasis on relevance, interdisciplinarity, social justice and integration in the latest wave of middle schooling literature (Prosser 2008). Further, they share an aspiration similar to that at the core of the RPiN project to engage students by connecting curriculum to their life-worlds and community.

Relevance

Osborne and Collins (2001) found that students are most interested in the aspect of science that they perceive as relevant to their lives, and least interested in topics that they see as having little personal relevance – in the main, science learning needs to be authentic to be engaging. Students need science to be interesting and exciting, and also intellectually challenging, if it is to engage their interest and commitment (Tytler & Symington 2006b: 11–12). Sousa (2006) maintained that the more information relates to, and can be packaged in, a real-world context, the easier it is to learn. This notion of relevance found in the science education literature is consistent with the studies of middle schooling mentioned earlier.

Problem solving & transdisciplinarity – a pedagogy for sustainability
While much has been written about integrated curriculum (Venville, Wallace, Rennie & Malone 2002) and multidisciplinary and interdisciplinary studies, there is less about a transdisciplinary approach to learning (Costanza 2003; Gidley 2002). The initial three approaches may be termed 'multidisciplinarity' where the 'implication is a division of labour in which different disciplinary frames survey separate aspects of the same whole' (Horlick-Jones & Sime 2004: 444). For transdisciplinarity, understandings are 'exchanged across disciplinary boundaries, in an evolved methodology which transcends "pure" disciplines' (Horlick-Jones & Sime 2004: 444). The key feature of a transdisciplinary approach is that transdisciplinarity is issues-based, where the issue does not stem from 'its own disciplinary context but is driven by a concrete problem' (Balsiger 2004: 416). The issue being investigated is seen as not bounded by any one discipline and values disciplinary as well as local knowledge (Klein 2004). This approach is 'strongly sensible to social needs and aspirations' (Balsiger 2004: 407) and contributes to the solution of the issue (Balsiger 2004; Després, Brais & Avellan 2004; Lawrence & Despres 2004).

While learning within subject boundaries leads to disciplinary understanding, it also leads to segmentation and methodological reduction of reality (Després, Brais & Avellan 2004: 475). It is unlikely to address in any meaningful way issues arising in day-to-day living, and that may threaten social sustainability. In epistemological terms, transdisciplinarity involves an integration of knowledges (Horlick-Jones & Sime 2004: 410).

The call for a transdisciplinary approach to knowledge production goes back at least to the early 1970s (Horlick-Jones & Sime 2004) when debate on the appropriateness of reductionist science for a comprehensive understanding of reality was challenged. For example, Balsiger (2004: 407) argued that the concept of transdisciplinarity is closely related to Feyerabend's criticisms of the philosophy of science, which concluded that 'the only principle that does not inhibit progress is: anything goes' (Feyerabend 1988: 14), by which he meant the refutation of any dogmatic, scientific approach. Després, Brais and Avellan (2004) drew on Habermas' (1984) idea of 'communicative action', arguing that cognitive rationality or scientific knowledge alone cannot explain everything. For these thinkers, transdisciplinarity was a post-rationalist approach to knowledge building, in which 'aesthetic, instrumental and ethical knowledge are considered as valuable as scientific knowledge to inform a problem', and where

> [i]nstrumental is about the approach to, or procedure for, the resolution of a problem; ethical knowledge is about customs, beliefs, values and past experiences which bring people to determine what is wrong and what is right on a specific issue; and aesthetic knowledge refers to tastes, preferences and feelings that help define what is beautiful and what is ugly. (Després, Brais & Avellan 2004: 476–477)

In our study we wanted students to look for pragmatic solutions to the problems of food preparation, eating habits, diet and personal and community health, rather than only develop a scientifically based understanding. This requires an approach that crosses the boundaries between disciplines and defines a mediation space. Such a space includes, among other things, personal and family eating habits, means of sourcing food, and the complex issue of food preparation, health and diet. The topic required a combination of research methods and collaboration between the researchers (Després, Brais & Avellan 2004).

While we applied the principles of transdisciplinarity pedagogically, we did not try to theorise the approach with students. We, in the main, relied on students' intuitive understanding of the differences between the true (science), the good (ethics) and the beautiful (aesthetics) and the insight of Nobel prize-winning physicist, Murray Gell-Mann that:

> Ben [Murray's brother] and I wanted to understand the world and enjoy it, but not to slice it up in some arbitrary way. We didn't differentiate sharply among such categories as the natural sciences, the social and behavioural sciences, the humanities, and the arts. In fact, I had never believed in the primacy of such distinctions. What has always impressed me is the unity of human culture, with science being an important part. (Gell-Mann 1994: 14)

Science education as social action

The idea that science education should be for citizens living in a sustainable world and in which they take responsibility for personal and collective action has been informative for our work. Much of science that is taught today in schools is the antithesis of a transdisciplinary approach and more in line with the narrow topic-centred approach of some disciplines (Paige, Lloyd & Chartres 2008). Transdisciplinary learning, when applied to education, encourages students to inquire into an issue that has implications for both today and the future. When students are engaged in transdisciplinary studies (such as obesity in our society) and are actors in their resolution, they become socio-political players (Lemke 2001) and agents of social sustainability. Hodson (2003) maintained that:

> [It is] … time for science curriculum to be oriented toward socio-political action. If current social and environmental problems are to be solved, we need a generation of scientifically and politically literate citizens who are not content with the role of the 'armchair'. (Hodson 2003: 645)

Rather than being told how to eat by distant people in authority, or being subliminally influenced by the corporate sector through advertising and clever marketing, students can come to their own construction of what is appropriate for their good health and the health of their family. They can, through their own research and deliberations, come to understand personal needs and addictions, ethical food production and distribution, socially empowering eating practices and nutritional balance.

The Australian Science Education Action Plan (Goodrum & Rennie 2007: 3) suggests that science education should develop scientific literacy so that students can 'contribute to debate about significant science-related issues'. We have taken the stronger stance suggested by Hodson that involves participation of society in science-related matters to foster social and ecological sustainability. That is, practical scientific knowledge in action that Irwin & Wynne (1996) called 'citizen science' rather than scientific literacy.

We believe that science education should not only inform, but also 'shape the personal and public worlds of adolescents' (Goodrum 2006). This quite different approach to exploring scientific literacy began to be discussed during the 1990s. It involves identifying the need of adults for scientific knowledge as they function in the variety of societal contexts that make up life in increasingly technological societies (Fensham 2003: 7). Tytler and Symington (2006b: 13–14) also argued that schools 'need to offer a science program that will prepare students to be citizens able to engage with community discussion and action around science-based issues' and that school science should be 'part of the life long process of the education of citizens'. Citizen science, as discussed by Fensham (2003), is practical science knowledge in action and aims to develop the ability of citizens to participate fully in the political and social choices that face members of a technological society. This approach to science learning focuses on learning that is about everyday situations that have an enduring relevance (Fensham & Harlen 1999: 761). Citizen science, as constructed by Fensham (2003), has four perspectives: personal well-being (science for me); socio-economic wellbeing (science for society); democratic wellbeing (science for all of us); and scientific wellbeing (science for scientists).

These themes resonate with our aspiration to connect with students' life-worlds and the community to develop socially sustainable practices. We have focused primarily on the first two of these in this study. The *Super Size Me* topic sought to develop an understanding of the science of nutrition and personal dietary habits that promote family and personal wellbeing. Critiques of food availability, both locally and globally, assist students to act responsibly and ethically when purchasing food.

What we did – the intervention

The topic selected was students' diet and built on the documentary *Super Size Me*. The enquiry topic was scaffolded using a set of open-ended research activities that, to be successfully completed, needed students to develop positive relationships, group skills and mutual trust. This approach was a shift in teaching practices from a textbook centred approach to one requiring students to collect primary data and research their own secondary information. The important focus of this approach was to ensure that students' life experience and the science curriculum were connected.

In practice, this inquiry approach was transdisciplinary in that students drew on local knowledge (personal and family) as well as on the traditional learning areas of science, studies of society and environment, English and literacy, information communication technology (ICT) studies, mathematics and numeracy, health and personal development, and careers education.

The *Super Size Me* topic was, for the students, a new type of task. They were required to generate new data through surveys and practical investigations, offer personal opinions and produce reflective writing, gather and comprehend information from textbooks and Internet sites, read food labels and newspapers, and re-present data in different formats.

The topic was built around six tasks containing a range of semi-structured learning activities that structured student inquiry. The tasks included exploring eating habits, energy in food, quality of food in fast food outlets and an audit of food in the school canteen. As part of these of activities, students were required to collect information from family members and friends, which connected their learning to their lives outside school (life-worlds) and used 'a lot wider range of learning activities than they would have done normally' (extract from interview with Jane (author)). This approach was seen as authentic, student-centred learning that encouraged students to reflect on their life-worlds, enabled them to connect their life-worlds to school and empowered them to make decisions that affect their daily lives.

What we documented

Records of student work and observations of what they did were collected before and during the intervention. We wanted to monitor what students learnt and how they engaged in the learning to evaluate the effectiveness of the curriculum content and the pedagogical approach. Interviews with students and researchers, including teacher focus group discussions and interviews associated with the RPiN project, supplied valuable data.

Student learning & engagement

To gauge the effectiveness of the teaching approach and curriculum planning, data were collected on student attendance (by lesson roll), student achievement (via assessment tasks and practical reports which were given on a regular basis), the quantity and quality of written work (including media reviews, journals and reflective reports) and teacher observations on collaborative learning (including photographic records).

For example, the students' inquiries into their diet included a weekly diet sheet that they completed before starting the topic and one they completed at the conclusion of the topic. A before and after survey was used to see if what the students learnt about their diets had an impact on their diet (Table 1). As an extension of this questionnaire, they also kept records of meals for each week and comments on how balanced they were.

Observations and reflections on pedagogy and curriculum

Throughout the topic a reflective journal or planner was kept on the development of the topic in which were recorded lesson plans, observations during the lessons on student behaviour and engagement in the tasks, and evaluations of the learning objectives. Photographs were used to support observations on student engagement. A survey (Table 2) was also given to students. It was aimed at revealing students' degree of acceptance of the new practice of inquiry and its presentation.

Interviews & focus group discussions associated with the RPiN Project

Interviews with students and researcher, including teacher focus group discussions and interviews associated with the RPiN project were also valuable data. Data were collected during the introductory and case study years and included documentation associated with the study school and class, (school profile, teaching topic), taped focus group discussions (four occasions), interviews with the researcher and students (five occasions), and

Table 1: diet survey

Questions
What do you consider is a healthy diet? (asked as a prior knowledge question)
What have you learnt?
Have you or your family changed your diet?
Will what you have learnt make you change anything in the future?
What do you now consider a healthy diet?
What else have you achieved during this topic?

Table 2: student survey of pedagogy and curriculum

Questions
How difficult/easy have you found the work?
How interesting (or not) have you found the work?
What is your opinion of the range of activities?
In what ways were the activities different from before?
Do you feel that you have learnt more in this topic than in previous topics?
What suggestions would you make to the teacher when planning the next topic of work?

taped conference presentations by the first author, including PowerPoint presentations (two occasions).

Inquiry findings

What the students did & learned

We have used a review of student artefacts, test results, teacher observations and student interviews to identify learning. We have categorised this into three areas: new understandings (the knowing); learning skills (process learning) and behaviours (dispositions to life and learning). Although the students, in the main, rejected a 'bookish' approach to learning, they did embrace an inquiry approach that was evidenced by the quantity of work they completed. Ten of the 18 students showed a significant improvement in their final grade when compared with previous topics. Improved achievement measured by work completion and test scores correlated with positive comments students made about the topic content and the inquiry approach.

New understandings

Test results and student presentations revealed significant learning about diet. Students were able to describe the chemical composition and function in the body of different food types and learnt how to identify these food types on labels. They were able to read the energy content of foods from labels and charts and calculate the total energy content of a meal. By measuring their own body mass, they were able to understand the idea of energy intake for an active life. Through researching the functions of nutrients needed for healthy living, students were able to explain why different foods are important in their diet and draw links between diet and wellbeing. They were able to make critical comments about lifestyle and eating habits, and various trendy diets, such as the Atkins and CSIRO diets.

Learning skills

The literacy focus in this topic was scientific report writing. Students were able to demonstrate this via practical reports and presentations. As part of the report preparation process, they were able to show that they could design surveys, collect, collate and interpret data, use laboratory techniques to test for food substances such as sugars, starches, proteins and fats, calculate dietary intake and analyse food labels. Students effectively used ICT as part of their learning and became proficient at using the Internet and applications such as PowerPoint. For example, each student group used PowerPoint presentations to report their findings and conclusions to the class and invited teachers.

Behaviours & engagement

The most pleasing aspect of this project was students' enhanced ability to engage with their studies and work collaboratively in small groups and with the teacher. Students found the work interesting and enjoyable, and there were fewer days of absence. Students on a Negotiated Education Plan improved their attendance the most. Student engagement also seems to have been improved by extensively using structured group work that enabled each student to use their skills and knowledge to contribute to the group product. The students engaged in a wider range of learning activities than they would have done normally. One student commented that 'First of all we were like "Oh, this is going to be boring", and then once you got into it, it was like, it was pretty good' (extract of an interview with students).

Students willingly took their school learning home and brought their home activities to school. They readily talked about home behaviour in class and were able to discuss it openly with colleagues and in presentations. They considered decisions they needed to make about their diet and there was evidence that suggested that they had made changes to their eating habits at home. Their homework was based on their home: what they watch on TV, what they eat; what kind of foods are brought into the home; whether they eat at the dining room table or on the couch watching TV. Students' comments supported their increased engagement as a result of connections to their life-worlds. All of this learning was done in the context of their home lives and community. There were fewer canonical science concepts and better links with students' personal interests and social concerns.

Student wellbeing

Interviews with students revealed that they felt successful and more engaged with learning and were prepared to take risks. In their reflective journals, they described how they had assumed responsibility, made decisions and had become more critically aware. For example, they were able to audit what was sold in the school canteen and come up with healthier alternatives.

Interestingly students were prepared to share their feelings, which for such a sensitive topic as diet and obesity, indicates their comfort in the learning environment and their 'at easeness' with colleagues and teacher. Students were not reluctant to offer constructive suggestions to improve activities, an indication that they felt comfortable in their learning environment and had a sense of belonging with their peers and teacher. For example, one student, Chantel, reported that:

> We enjoyed doing this unit of work because it was exciting and also interesting to know what we're eating. It was a change from our usual science work – it required our own thoughts and opinions on things.
> (student survey of pedagogy and curriculum)

A pleasing outcome was students' explicit statements about their motivation to achieve. For example, there was a group of girls who all wanted to get top marks, they didn't mind if one of the others beat them by one or two, but they all believed they should be up there getting full marks. A couple of the boys said 'I'm doing really well, I'm going to keep [it up]'. Students developed a quite competitive disposition, not in an aggressively competitive way, but 'they were all really striving to be up there' (extract of an interview with students).

What we learnt

Pedagogy

Action research allowed the researchers to develop a deeper understanding of classroom dynamics and adapt and change pedagogy to meet students' needs. It contributed to the deconstruction of the deficit view of students by demonstrating that students can work independently and with enthusiasm to achieve outcomes that they value. The change made to pedagogical practice was by connecting students' lives and learning through inquiry, and it seemed to work by increasing engagement that led to positive learning outcomes for students. This shift from teacher directed learning only, to allowing students to take control of well-structured tasks, seems to have increased student engagement and learning.

Interestingly the data suggest that the inquiry approach to diet better supported girls' learning than did didactic approaches of telling and textbook research. Girls were observed to manage their time and multiple tasks and were much better at meeting deadlines than boys. They were also able to work independently with less supervision and were observed to work collaboratively in groups and teams, collecting information and sharing. Observational and photographic records show that boys were off-task more often than girls. The better engagement of the girls may be because they were more interested in healthy diets and obesity.

Student achievement and improved engagement in learning in the *Super Size Me* topic suggest that an enquiry or transdisciplinary approach encourages students to reflect on their life-worlds and empowers them to make informed decisions about their eating habits and diet. Our findings suggest that the inquiry approach used in this topic offered life experiences that enhanced the development of personal capabilities such as independent learning, being a team player and asking questions.

The use of scaffolded activities, as well as being very explicit about what outcomes were required, enhanced students' learning. What was also observed was that a transdisciplinary approach encouraged students to become critical thinkers and actors in their school and at home. Student engagement was increased by using local knowledge and involving community members. This project also reminded us that coming to an understanding of, and implementing, new pedagogical practices is hard work. It is not only the new planning for learning and the added time needed to research that takes effort, but also the selling of the approach to workplace colleagues.

Curriculum

The shifts from generic, textbook science learning, which makes at best weak connections to student interests and concerns and therefore has limited relevance, to an inquiry approach that used students' collected data as the primary resource, increased student engagement and achievement. By linking students' life-world experiences to global issues such as personal health and wellbeing also seemed to enhance engagement in learning and improve learning outcomes. Information on world food issues (famine for example) and world health issues related to diet seems to have had more meaning for students in the context of this topic – transdisciplinary means richer and more meaningful connections.

At a broader level, it is important to note that not all teacher inquiry needs to be into the practices of the individual teacher. The pedagogical practices of subject areas and disciplines are also worthy of consideration. A significant aspect of our learning has been the opportunities for science teachers to embrace transdisciplinarity and engage students in community and life-world connected science learning. By exploring how to redesign the conventions of science pedagogy, we are not only offering a lens through which others might look at individual practice, but we are also reaffirming the centrality of education and scientific education in the development of a socially sustainable future.

Concluding reflections

This project has been an opportunity to deepen our understanding of teaching and learning using inquiry and transdisciplinary approaches. The evidence suggests that the shift from formal classroom-based teaching to one that connects learning to students' interests, and values students' experiences outside school, improves student engagement and learning. Our hope is that such an approach can, in the longer term, lead to more empowered communities and sustainable societies in the future. While the RPiN project focuses on connecting students' funds of knowledge to the curriculum, there are clear resonances in both science and middle schooling literature. This project sought to draw on the resources these provide. Of course, the outcomes of one case study cannot do more than suggest a better way forward, but we are confident enough to document and suggest this approach for others.

References

Aikenhead G, 2006, *Science education for everyday life*. Teachers' College Press, New York.

Balsiger PW, 2004, 'Supradisciplinary research practices: History, objectives and rationale', *Futures*, 36(4), 407–421.

Barratt R, 1998, 'Shaping Middle Schooling in Australia: A report of the National Middle Schooling Project', Australian Curriculum Studies Association, Deakin West.

Beane JA, 1997, *Curriculum integration: Designing the core of democratic education.* Teachers College Press, New York.

Berry T, 1999, *The great work: Our way into the future.* Bell Tower, New York.

Carrington V, 2006, *Rethinking Middle Years: early adolescents, schooling and digital culture.* Allen & Unwin, Crows Nest, Australia.

Costanza R, 2003, 'A vision of the future of science: Reintegrating the study of humans and the rest of nature', *Futures,* 35(6), 651–671.

Cross R & Price R, 2002, 'Teaching controversial science for social responsibility: The case of food production', in W-M Roth & JD Desautels (eds), *Science education as/for sociopolitical action.* Peter Lang, New York, pp 99–123.

Després C, Brais N & Avellan S, 2004, 'Collaborative planning for retrofitting suburbs: Transdisciplinarity and intersubjectivity in action', *Futures,* 36(4), 471–486.

Esbjörn-Hargens S & Zimmerman M, 2009, *Integral ecology: Uniting multiple perspectives on the natural world.* Integral Books, Boston, MA.

Eyres V, Cormack P & Barratt R, 1993, '*The education of young adolescents in South Australian government schools: Report of the Junior Secondary Review*', Education Department of South Australia, Adelaide.

Fensham PJ, 2003, 'What do the "All" need in science education?' in D Fisher & T Marsh (eds), *Proceedings of the Third Conference on Science, Mathematics and Technology Education.* Key Centre for School Science and Mathematics, Curtin University of Technology, Perth, Western Australia, pp 1–20.

Fensham PJ, 2004, 'Engagement with science: An international issue that goes beyond knowledge', paper presented at the *Science and Mathematics Education Conference (SMEC)*, Dublin City University, Ireland, 23–24 September.

Fensham PJ & Harlen W, 1999, 'School science and public understanding of science', *International Journal of Science Education,* 21(7), 755–763.

Feyerabend P, 1988, *Against method.* Verso, London.

Gell-Mann M, 1994, *The quark and the jaguar: Adventures in the simple and the complex.* Freeman, New York.

Gidley J, 2002, 'Global youth culture: A transdisciplinary perspective', in J Gidley & S Inayatulla (eds), *Youth futures: Comparative research and transformative visions.* Praeger, Westport, CA, pp 3–18.

Gonzalez N & Moll L, 2002, 'Cruzando el Puente: Building bridges to funds of knowledge', *Educational Policy,* 16(4), 623–641.

Goodrum D, 2006, *Inquiry in science classrooms: Rhetoric or reality?* <www.acer. edu.au/research_conferences/2006.html> accessed 27 November 2007.

Goodrum D & Rennie L, 2007, *Australian School Science Education National Action Plan*, 2008–2012, <www.dest.gov.au/sectors/school_education/publications_resources/profiles/Australian_School_Education_Plan_2008_2012.htm> accessed 17 September 2007.

Goodrum D, Hackling M & Rennie L, 2001, *The status and quality of teaching and learning of science in Australian Schools.* Department of Education, Training and Youth Affairs, Canberra.

Groundwater-Smith S, Mitchell J & Mockler N, 2007, *Learning in the middle years: More than a transition.* Thompson, South Melbourne, Victoria.

Habermas J, 1984, *The theory of communicative action: Reason and the rationalization of society* (T McCarthy trans.). Polity Press, Oxford, UK.

Hodson D, 2003, 'Time for action: Science education for an alternative future', *International Journal of Science Education*, 25(6), 645–670.

Horlick-Jones T & Sime J, 2004, 'Living on the border: Knowledge, risk and transdisciplinarity', *Futures*, 36(4), 407–421.

Irwin A & Wynne B (eds), 1996, *Misunderstanding science? The public reconstruction of science and technology.* Cambridge University Press, Cambridge.

Jenkins EW & Pell RG, 2006, *The relevance of science education project (ROSE) in England: A summary of findings.* Centre for Studies in Science and Mathematics Education, University of Leeds, Leeds.

Jones D, Melville W & Bartley A, 2007, 'Science, inquiry and professional learning', *Professional Educator*, 6(2), 18–21.

Klein JT, 2004, 'Prospects for transdisciplinarity', *Futures*, 36(4), 515–526.

Lawrence RJ & Despres C, 2004, 'Futures of transdisciplinarity', *Futures*, 36(4), 397–405.

Lee S & Roth W-M, 2002, 'Learning Science in the community', in W-M. Roth & J Désautels (eds), *Science education as/for sociopolitical action*. Peter Lang, New York, pp 37–66.

Lemke JL, 2001, 'Articulating communities: Sociocultural perspectives on science education', *Journal of Research in Science Teaching*, 38(3), 296–316.

Lowe I, 2009, *A big fix: Radical solutions for Australia's environmental crisis* (2nd edn). Black Inc, Melbourne, Australia.

Noakes M & Clifton P, 2005, *The CSIRO total wellbeing diet.* Penguin, Victoria.

Osborne J & Collins S, 2001, 'Pupils' views of the role and value of the science curriculum: A focus group study', *International Journal of Science Education*, 23(5), 441–467.

Osborne J, Simon S & Collins S, 2003, 'Attitudes towards science: A review of the literature and its implications', *International Journal of Science Education*, 25(9), 1049–1079.

Paige K, Lloyd D & Chartres M, 2008, 'Moving towards transdisciplinarity: An ecological sustainable focus for science and mathematics pre-service education in the primary/middle years', *Asia-Pacific Journal of Teacher Education*, 36(1), 19–33.

Pendergast D & Bahr N, 2005, *Teaching Middle Years: Rethinking Curriculum, Pedagogy and assessment*. Allen & Unwin, Crows Nest, NSW.

Prosser B, 2008, 'Unfinished but not exhausted: a review of Australian middle schooling', *Australian Journal of Education*, 52(2), 151–167.

Rennie L, 2006, 'The community's contribution to science learning: Making it count', presentation to ACER Research Conference, *Boosting Science Learning: What Will It Take?* August 14, 2006, ACER Press, Camberwell, Victoria.

Skamp K & Logan M, 2005, 'Students' interest in science across the middle school years', *Teaching Science*, 52(4), 8–15.

Sousa D, 2006, *How the brain learns* (3rd edn). Hawker Brownlow Education, Heatherton, Victoria.

Suzuki D & McConnell A, 1997, *The sacred balance: rediscovering our place in nature*. Allen & Unwin, St Leonards, NSW.

Tytler R, 2007, *Re-imagining Science Education: Engaging students in science for Australia's future*. ACER Press, Camberwell, Victoria.

Tytler R & Symington D, 2006a, 'Boosting science learning and engagement: what will it take?' proceedings of the ACER Research Conference, *Boosting science learning – what will it take?* 13–15 August, Canberra, www<research.acer.edu.au/research_conference_2006/1> Accessed 22 July 2009.

Tytler R & Symington D, 2006b, 'Science in school and society', *Teaching Science*, 52(3), 10–15.

Venville G, Wallace J, Rennie L & Malone J, 2002, 'Curriculum integration: Eroding the high ground of science as a school subject?' *Studies in Science Education*, 37, 43–84.

Ziman J, 1994, 'The rationale of STS education is in the approach', in J Solomon & G Aikenhead (eds), *STS Education International Perspectives on Reform*. Teachers College Press, New York, pp 21–31.

Chapter 5

Place-based and community learning:

engaging and sustaining student interest

*Jennifer Jones**

Introduction

Decades of research show that there is a pedagogy of poverty (Haberman 1991) that makes assumptions about the capabilities and aspirations of students of schools in low socio-economic areas. Students are considered not to have the aptitude to engage in intellectually demanding work. Focusing on crisis management and embracing a deficit view, schools tend to become trapped in a mode that perpetuates these perceptions, reinforcing the notion that these students need to go back to basics, that they have little to offer and that our job as educators is merely to prepare them for relatively unskilled employment (Johnston & Hayes 2008).

More recent research presents alternatives in the form of productive pedagogies, suggesting that it is both possible and worthwhile to design and negotiate curricula that increase the engagement and achievement of a broader range of students. Although the productive pedagogies focus on intellectual quality, connectedness, a supportive classroom environment and working with and valuing difference, studies of what actually happens in classrooms suggest there is often a lack of intellectual richness (e.g., Hayes, Mills, Christie & Lingard 2006). *The challenge for me was, in the context of the challenges posed by the school setting and by these research dilemmas, first, whether and how I could engage my students in rich intellectual activity, and second, how I might sustain that kind of learning both for the students and for myself.*

* I would like to thank (my co-researchers from UniSA) Helen Nixon and Phil Cormack for their valuable comments and support with this chapter.

In thinking about how the kind of pedagogical adventures described here might be made sustainable, and the potential extent of their impact on student learning, it is pertinent to consider the limitations on such activities, and conversely, what facilitates them. David Berliner (2006) pointed out how poverty and social dysfunction present compelling limitations to innovation in pedagogy. Obstacles to sustainability include teacher turnover, costs that accompany work beyond the classroom, time and energy involved in organising community-based expeditions and approaches and, not least, the complexity of school organisation and timetabling.

I was a teacher-researcher for two years in the action-research project, *Redesigning Pedagogies in the North* (RPiN). In the first year I worked with a Year 8 class in both English and Homegroup, in keeping with middle schooling principles. The following year, wanting to continue to build relationships and skills, I worked with these same students in Homegroup, English and Studies of Society and Environment. Such continuity, still relatively rare in secondary school contexts, offered me opportunities to pursue paths embarked upon in the first year, and to actively incorporate reflection in planning, leading me to adjust the curriculum accordingly.

Intrinsic to action research is the continuous loop of reflection that leads me to make observations about how the work we did has influenced our students in the longer term. At the time of writing I am teaching several of these students in a Year 11 class; conversations about questioning and higher-order thinking flow easily, and student Kate – once at risk of leaving early – has developed the capacity to produce perceptive discussion about poetry and to craft coherent arguments. She is actively constructing a pathway to university. Clearly, continuing and positive working relationships between teachers and students can benefit both. Students share their views and experiences with teachers and vice versa, making the pathway to learning more open. When teachers make learning the topic of conversation, they create opportunities for at least some of their students to go further and deeper in their learning and to embrace rigour.

Context of the school

The school, situated north of Adelaide, has an enrolment of over 900 students, 60 teaching staff and a dozen non-teaching staff whose tasks include supporting students on Negotiated Education Plans (NEPs) that are designed to enable students with behavioural or learning difficulties, or high intellectual potential, to access the curriculum. The school, built in 1970, is currently being significantly upgraded. Recent training and development for staff has focused on issues such as authentic assessment, engagement through community connection, career pathways and curriculum relevant to our students. Change, and recognition of the need for it, is a key element in the school environment. Enrolments at Year 8 level, coming from over 20 primary schools, are at around 220 (almost the maximum number that can be accommodated), while the number completing Year 12 stands at approximately 90. Many students gain employment or follow alternative pathways as they progress through the school.

The student body is varied, comprising around 30% eligible for a School Card (which offers financial assistance for educational costs to full-time students from low income families), with a significant number living in extended, combined or sole parent settings. Several students are under the guardianship of the Minister for Families and Communities. The Year 8 intake in the second year of the project included 40 (of 220) students with social, emotional, behavioural and or learning difficulties that necessitated intervention and guidance from external agencies. Weak literacy and numeracy skills, as evidenced by the results of state and national basic skills tests, pose problems for a significant proportion of the student body, with approximately 12% of 850 students on NEPs. Results in the final year of secondary school are below the state average, and the school seeks to address poor academic achievement in a number of ways.

Curriculum changes aimed at increasing relevance and engagement with the purpose of improving retention and achievement include the introduction and extension of vocational education courses and school-based apprenticeships, and basing a regional apprenticeship broker at the school. Many senior students attend TAFE (Training and Further Education) courses and a growing number of students engage in Community Studies subjects. These do not attract a tertiary entrance score, but do allow students to work towards completion of their secondary school certificate while actively pursuing their own interests. A small but increasing number of students gain entrance to university through an alternative entry program, and students are supported in finding work through active work experience and a range of over 30 mentoring and support programs.

Fostering & sustaining deep learning in the context of community

The fundamental motivations driving the action-research projects described here were frustration and a desire for change. As a teacher of both middle school and senior students, I was acutely aware of increasing levels of disengagement among senior students, and of how weak literacy skills make successful study in the challenging final years of school difficult. I reasoned that if we could strengthen student interest and engagement in the middle years, maybe we could influence outcomes in the senior years. I wanted to help middle years students expand their skills base, giving them confidence to develop aspirations and achieve their goals. I hoped that I might develop new insights into the dynamics and practical dimensions of transformative learning, deepening my understanding of how to engage students and sustain their interest in a curriculum that incorporates intellectually rich activity.

In both research cycles I took as a particular focus the use of existing student interest and knowledge to enable inclusion of rigour in the curriculum, with a view to extending and expanding students' repertoires of literate practice, their thinking skills and their confidence in organising and presenting work. This approach acknowledges the potential value of student cultural and everyday knowledge – the often-overlooked students' virtual schoolbags – in the school setting (Thomson 2002), and the possibilities of using a number of strategies to achieve transformative learning (Haberman 1991; Pearson & Somekh 2006). Pat Thomson's (2006) suggestion that my aim as a teacher should be not to make *the* difference in the way my students approach their work, but to make *a* difference, encouraged me to take risks in my teaching practice.

The first year – Our Place

My focus on place was sparked by David Homer's (2004) use of the power of place to stimulate adult learners to write creatively, drawing on expedition and immersion in place as a trigger for developing short stories and poems. I saw for myself the ways in which place-based learning could unleash creative responses in English. Further, the example of Murray-Darling primary students' rich exploration and representations of their local areas through poetry, short stories and artwork (Comber, Nixon & Reid 2007; Cormack, Green & Reid 2008) also encouraged me to use place-based curriculum as a base for broadening literate practice in my Year 8 class. Class discussions on students' life-worlds reinforced my decision, as students revealed their strong interest in, and knowledge of, some local landmarks, most students having lived in the local area for most of their lives.

Having made the decision, I now faced the challenges that come with engaging in place-based learning, a process that involves dissolving some of the usually rigid boundaries between classroom and community. Long inculcated patterns of schooling tend to keep teachers and students separated from the community, making school and classroom synonymous (Gruenewald 2003: 10). When classes venture into the community, school administration has to accommodate more flexible delivery of curriculum and resolve many practical obstacles, including the effect of teacher absence on other classes and the costs associated with out-of-school activities. Issues confronting teachers when initiating place-based coursework include increased complexity and time involved in planning, the development of authentic assessment tasks, the management of diverse activities during and following expeditions, and the unpredictable nature of student responses to their experiences.

To undertake this work I, and the school, needed to be prepared to take risks, just as I was asking the students to venture beyond their usual experience. By acknowledging student knowledge and interests in the context of place, and by bringing them into contact with people and places in the community, I wanted to 'allow space for students to learn autonomy and selfhood ... help students take risks' (Comber 2001) and stimulate their interest and competence in literate practice along the way. As Comber and Nixon (2005: 117) observed, 'If as literacy educators we want children to learn that texts matter ... a key goal of literacy ... then children need to be involved in producing texts that matter to them'. This became a clear goal of my action-research project. Importantly, to achieve my goals I needed to be prepared to take risks myself, and I needed the school's support.

We began by reading, in class, several place-based texts: *Belonging*

(Jeannie Baker 2004), *Window* (Jeannie Baker 2002) and *My Place* (Nadia Wheatley & Donna Rawlins 1987). Each of these texts presents a child's view of place and introduces the notion of change over time, providing powerful stimuli for students to create their own *My Place* page, including detail about change in their environment, favourite and interesting places and experiences, and descriptions of family, pets and neighbourhood.

From this point we negotiated a series of excursions to explore places of interest to the students. Negotiation was integral to the planning process, including negotiating the places to be visited and what we would do there. The process involved group brainstorming and discussion, scribing and voting, all of which encouraged development of group skills, as students needed to listen, interact, reflect, compromise and collaborate.[†] These skills, developed in a whole-class context, helped students make the shift to individual negotiation in the following year.

Our first excursion, an all-day trip to Port Adelaide, involved taking students beyond the familiar. We walked, visited the Museum of Childhood and the Maritime Museum, heard ghost stories in the basement of a local hotel, went on a small cruise boat on the river, with dolphins hugging the hull, climbed the lighthouse and met locals. Students took photos, spoke to camera and used workbooks they had helped design. Later excursions focused on the local area and included visits to a primary school, the Adelaide–Mannum water pipeline and the Olive Grove (local landmarks), fire and police stations, the local Australian Rules football club, a cemetery and Uleybury School Museum. In the latter, students experienced a nineteenth century lesson in which they used slates and learnt handwriting.

The series of excursions was intensive and involved the collection of still and moving images later used as prompts for written responses by using information and communications technologies (ICTs). The project involved collaboration with the ICT Coordinator who created a short film based on each excursion, and with the students' science teacher, who accompanied us and followed up with activities aimed at increasing students' ecological literacy (e.g., compiling a field report on bird and plant life). She observed that the students' competence and interest increased during the study.

---

† These elements of the research design are consistent with those outlined by Farrell and McCarthy (2002) and by Gruenewald (2003).

Flexibility characterised the curriculum, taking account of student interest and requests to develop some tasks in greater depth or in different ways. This brought a new intensity into the classroom at times as students became animated in discussion. Use of ICTs allowed students to develop varied responses, but created frustration due to difficulties with the availability and functionality of equipment. The research design included publication of student work in a number of forms. Possible tasks for a student folio of writing included creative writing, letter writing, production of a brochure for incoming Year 8s about going on excursions, research about a selected place, and interviews with local community members. The inclusion of real-world tasks encouraged students to produce quality work, as they knew that their letters would be sent to those we had visited and worked with, and that several of their other products would be displayed, either in the classroom or library, or would be published on the school's intranet and on the annually produced CDROM.

Students responded positively to our pedagogical adventures. When I surveyed the class about their views on English part way through the unit, students remarked that they enjoyed our excursions and 'going out, seeing things and learning stuff'. Most considered that they had improved their writing skills and most thought that they had learnt more about place, understood more about how they learn and had learnt more about teamwork and listening skills.

For the purposes of the study, I followed four students closely throughout the unit: Jon, a boy on NEP; Sam, a boy of average achievement with anger management problems; Pam, a girl who had learning difficulties and a complex home life but who did not qualify for NEP support; and Meg, a girl of average achievement. I also noted the reactions, behaviours and work output of high achievers. High achieving students generally responded well to the tasks available; several swiftly completed basic tasks and moved on to experiment with creative writing pieces or to create PowerPoint presentations. Towards the end of the unit, a few students, having completed their own work, assisted others. Peer tutoring emerged naturally within this unit due to the nature of the activities. Of the students we tracked closely, all reaped some benefit from our activities. Jon gained confidence in creative writing, working well with another boy and showing enthusiasm and willingness to proofread his work, where previously he had tended to be satisfied with a rushed effort. Sam engaged strongly with the excursions to the football club and the police and fire stations, and took pride in the resulting letters and imaginative writing. Pam also connected strongly with the excursion work, developing greater confidence in speaking and in her written work, where previously she had been tentative. Meg surged ahead, showing high motivation, strong organisational skills, thoughtful responses and greater confidence in written work. Three of the four considered that these activities had taught them something about themselves.

Implementing this curriculum confirmed the view for me that a key outcome of place-based education is that it 'strengthen[s] children's [and adults'] connections to others and to the regions in which they live' (Smith, in Gruenewald 2003: 11). My students did gain a deeper understanding of their local area, its history and ecology, and showed interest in the community organisations we visited. A logical next step would be to explore the experience of others in that environment, strengthening understanding of the significance of, and connections to, place. Student involvement in an oral history unit would allow them to gather information about older residents' experience of the local area and would enrich connections between school and community.

Projects like Our Place can lead to a more sustainable curriculum. The rich differentiation it involves encourages students of all abilities and backgrounds to engage, and the unit incorporates flexibility in planning and assessment, resulting in a high level of student negotiation and ownership of the curriculum. These characteristics make the learning process one that sustains both students and educators by enlivening the curriculum, acknowledging student knowledge and building real connections with the community. Ongoing benefits that come from student work of this kind include a broader skills base and increased confidence. These qualities can enrich student experience in other subjects and in following years. However, to deliver such programs to more than one class in the course of a year, as would be desirable, would require enormous effort at individual, faculty and cross-curricular levels, and the wholehearted support of the school involved.

The second year – questioning & journalism in a community context

Once begun, the kind of work described above is sustaining for teachers and worth sustaining for both teachers and students. In the second year of the research I wanted to challenge the students, and myself, to go further down the path of negotiation, collaboration and community exploration, all the while using community-based curricula as a vehicle for rigour and as a means to expand students' literacies.

Inevitably, the composition of the class changed a little, with new students joining and a few leaving. The 26 students of mixed ability included four students who formally qualified for NEPs, others with learning difficulties and behavioural and emotional problems, and several students with complex and challenging family circumstances. I taught the group in Homegroup, which includes a personal development component, and in English and Studies of Society and Environment, giving me the opportunity to continue to build sound relationships with the students, to recognise and accommodate their interests and strengths, and to identify and address weaknesses.

The experiences of the previous year, together with readings, workshops, discussions with colleagues and academics involved in the RPiN project, and my own reflections, all influenced the design of, and inquiry into, the new unit of work, as well as modifications along the way. I wanted to minimise my use of those 'teacher acts' that define the 'pedagogy of poverty', including giving information and directions, settling disputes and punishing non-compliance (Haberman 1991). While some of these acts remain an inevitable feature of teaching in a large urban school, I worked to integrate approaches that Haberman nominated as characteristic of good teaching. Of 12 approaches described, the following six particularly influenced and feature in this unit of work.

- Whenever students are being helped to see major concepts, big ideas and general principles and are not merely engaged in the pursuit of isolated facts, good teaching is going on.
- Whenever students are involved in planning what they will be doing, it is likely that good teaching is going on.
- Whenever students are actively involved, it is likely that good teaching is going on.

- Whenever students are directly involved in a real-life experience, it is likely that good teaching is going on.
- Whenever students are involved in redoing, polishing, or perfecting their work, it is likely that good teaching is going on.
- Whenever teachers involve students with the technology of information access, good teaching is going on. (Haberman 1991: 293, 294)

The place-based unit and my new unit incorporated several of Haberman's approaches, along with features of Pearson and Somekh's (2006) provisional model of transformative learning, which involved students:

- Learning creatively: contributing, experimenting, solving problems;
- Learning as active citizens: acting autonomously, taking responsibility for their own learning;
- Engaging intellectually with powerful ideas: using thinking skills, grappling with ideas/concepts;
- Reflecting on their own learning: evaluating their own learning through metacognition. (Pearson & Somekh 2006: 520)

The problem: background to the second unit

Once again, my frustration about student engagement, retention, achievement, skill levels and confidence, and my desire to effect change, shaped the development of the second unit that focused on questioning and journalism in the context of our local community. Early in the year, I had asked the class to write a snapshot biography, based on three important moments in someone's life, and a report on a chosen topic. These tasks called for clear, creative presentation of information, but most students completed them poorly, basing their research on closed questions and producing brief, superficial responses. Lack of confidence and competence in such tasks manifests in senior years too, with students struggling to organise ideas and present them in essay form. This in turn affects student retention and achievement. Research points to the phenomenon of 'alienat[ion] from learning' and of regression rather than progress in skill levels of middle school students, and indications that performance in Year 9 is indicative of achievement in the final year of schooling (Cormack 2005). This motivated me to develop curriculum and use pedagogies that might improve student outcomes.

I wanted to further test my belief that engagement may increase and skills be strengthened if students are supported in investigating a topic of great interest in a way that incorporates rigour. Through negotiating topics of relevance to students, I aimed to honour a key element of the 'active school', which 'reach[es] out to the lives of young people ... not merely responding to them', and seeks to 'construct rigorous curriculum and pedagogy around the lives and experiences students bring with them' (Smyth & Hattam 2002, in Smyth, McInerney & Hattam 2003: 179). Incorporating ongoing negotiation in the unit is an acknowledgment of the evidence that students who have input in the planning of their learning become and remain more engaged (Pearson & Somekh 2006: 524). I also wished to observe the possible effects of the goal of producing an authentic product (e.g., webpage) to be viewed by others in and beyond the school environment.

So, while a focus on acquisition, consolidation and extension of literacy skills informed my planning, I was cognisant of the 'transformative perspective, [which] views the acquisition of functional skills as inseparable from transformative skills of critical thinking that link to broader social problems and concerns' (Brown 2005: 6). In particular, I highlighted the power of questions, introducing students to the quotation, 'Once you have learned how to ask relevant and appropriate questions, you have learned how to learn and no one can keep you from learning whatever you want or need to know' (Postman & Weingartner 1969: 34). By intervening through negotiation and by supporting question development, for example, I intended to initiate enduring shifts in competence and confidence that would lead students to achieve more consistently and understand how to ask and use questions. They would therefore be equipped to make choices in everyday, academic or workplace contexts.

The questioning journey

In the planning phase of the unit I discussed earlier work on snapshot biography and reporting on a topic with students, and worked with them to identify learning goals, including development of skills in questioning, conducting research and presenting information. The class considered possible topics and ways of conducting research, some expressing a particular interest in interviewing. When I explained that they would need to create questions to guide their investigation, one student remarked dismissively, 'Questions? They're easy!' a view that changed as the journey continued.

We began the unit with two sessions with a practising journalist who workshopped question development, interviewing, evidence and article writing. As 'cub reporters' fleshing out a story through interviews with eyewitnesses, students composed and asked questions, identifying which lines of inquiry would lead to particular types of stories. Through these activities, some began shifting from uncritical acceptance of news stories to recognition of the influence of question construction. Students showed heightened awareness of difficulties associated with asking good questions and the responsibility of journalists to report the truth. This hands-on experience was a useful point of reference, as students began to see how their questions could influence the responses of interviewees and the construction of resulting news articles. From this point, journalism, in the form of interpretation and creation of news reports, served as a backdrop, an anchor of traditional curriculum and a counterpoint to our other work. This practical strategy gave students flexibility. Some found the thinking work of question development too challenging at times, and sought more contained tasks.

To support students to develop well-structured questions and to present related findings and creative writing, I used knowledge of their learning styles, developed over 18 months of teaching many of them, and derived from a multiple intelligences questionnaire. Diversity in learning styles, needs and abilities in the class, meant that scaffolding ranged from using a 'Question tool-box' and matrices to explicit modelling of questioning techniques, peer tutoring and extensive one-to-one discussion. Students themselves actively guided my pedagogical approaches and shaped the learning environment by giving direct feedback about their enjoyment and understanding of class activities, a process I facilitated by including written and oral reflection routines in lesson time.

To further model question development and analysis I used the example of 'Ned Kelly – Hero or Villain?' a topic in which several students had previously indicated interest. By devising questions myself and asking students to classify them, I generated discussion of different types of questioning. Able thinkers and speakers responded well. NEP students and those lacking confidence in classification and reasoning tasks did not, prompting me to offer more accessible ways of analysing questioning. Meanwhile, students began the process of topic selection, research and question development.

The whole-class negotiation that underpinned the Our Place unit laid foundations for students to engage in individual negotiation in this unit. Skill development evolved over the two years, highlighting the value of sustaining long-term relationships with students. Throughout the unit I continued to negotiate on significant points, including:

- topic selection
- approach to working processes (including paired study, collaboration and peer tutoring)
- nature and extent of work required
- format of presentation.

To raise student awareness of the processes they were engaging in, and to see if they or I could comment on connections between their work and what we were doing in the classroom, I asked them to give themselves a mark out of 10 for work rate each lesson, and to graph the results. I observed a clear correlation between work output and clarity of understanding of tasks and, not surprisingly, enjoyment of tasks. One student commented that her 'work rate went to a flying 6 instead of a 2 … because I enjoy ice skating so much and Im enjoying reasearching it to [sic]'. Some students had not been aware of how they used time in class and began to take responsibility for this.

Students appreciated having input into the form and pace of their work. I developed a flow chart to guide them through the stages of work to be completed, and negotiated the number and type of task with each student. Some students completed one article, others wrote three, some conducted an interview off-campus, and others created detailed web pages based on their research. A pattern of alternation between brief sessions of whole-class discussion and sharing, and individual, paired or small-group work emerged. I was no longer positioned in the class as the sole teacher, instead becoming an active collaborator. Several students showed that they were aware of the informality of my assistance, noting that I would 'just come and talk' with them individually rather than instructing the class.

Some students took time to settle on a subject of relevance to them and others gravitated to a topic immediately. My own understandings of their 'virtual schoolbags' (Thomson 2002) helped. I knew, for example, that Kate was into black, Mary was in an ice hockey program, James was a prolific reader and writer, David played electric guitar and Adam loved nothing but cricket. David's comment, that 'My connection with my topic … is I have played the electric guitar for one and a half years. It means creation. I chose it because it is one of my favourite things' reflects the importance of acknowledging student interests in the curriculum. The topic range was diverse, including local football, radio, dirt-bike riding, architecture, zoo keeping, local bands and frogs. I was intrigued by the range of interests. Some students who demonstrated little knowledge in conventional academic areas displayed a detailed understanding of their topic of interest.

Whatever the topic and whatever the product, all students were engaged in question development, research and presentation. Interviewing involved trips into the city and the local community, and hosting visitors on-campus. Samples of students' questions and reflections about their learning indicate the potential of this kind of work to help students engage in deep and enduring learning. Early closed questions included 'How many meals do … meerkats eat a day?' and 'How long have you been breeding frogs?' The shift is evident in later open questions like 'Why do zoos exist?' or 'Has the [Ice Hockey] program helped you in any part of your life?' or 'Why do you believe the colour black is … appealing to sub-cultures like the Goths?' or 'What impact do frogs have on our environment?' Through reflection, students responded to processes unfolding in the classroom and developed metacognitive language. One student commented:

> At first … I thought I did a good job … the teacher told us about open and closed questions, then I saw that all the questions I thought of were … closed questions and that there would not be much detail in the answers. Then with some help of the teacher I developed my questions … They are called open questions and seven ninths of my questions were open. At the start I didn't recognize any of this and now I understand it a bit better. (Jo)

As in the first year, I closely followed several students with contrasting achievements, attendance patterns and motivation. The focus students were Adam, a disengaged low achiever with poor attendance; Lisa, a capable student who attended consistently but did not engage well with the regular curriculum; and Kate, an able student whose level of engagement and achievement had weakened across all areas bar music over two years, and whose increasingly poor attendance led her to be identified as being at risk. Most classes include those who share some of these characteristics in terms of attendance, behaviour, engagement and achievement, so strategies that proved successful with my students may well be applicable to similar settings.

Several students showed improved engagement as we worked. Kate liked the freedom to negotiate, and the quality of her written work confirms that a high interest topic can be a vehicle for rigour. She developed skills of collaboration, questioning, research and organisation in writing. Like Kate, Lisa did not engage in traditional units based on films and novels. She too collaborated effectively in this unit. She participated actively in discussion, developed thoughtful questions, conducted an effective interview, developed well-structured articles and creative pieces, and constructed a web page. She assisted others with web page construction, advised me on technological matters and maintained a high level of engagement throughout the unit, responding to the freedom and challenges involved. Kate missed 27 lessons in the period prior to this unit and only eight during it. Adam, by contrast, maintained a high rate of absenteeism, but responded to my calls to attend lessons to work on his interview with South Australian cricketer Graham Manou.

Improvement in grades is evidence of skill development in a context of greater student ownership of the curriculum (Table 1). Several students produced work more consistently and at a higher level during and following our unit. However, achievement in English did not necessarily correlate with improvement in other subjects. For several students, an A, B or C in English was the highest grade on their report. Student views reinforced teacher observations made through marking; of 20 students surveyed near the end of the unit, 11 considered they had improved in confidence in writing, 10 in speaking, eight in listening and six in

Table 1: Achievement by grade before and after the Questioning unit.

Grade	A	B	C	D	Unclassified	Total
Term 1	3	3 (1)	10 (6)			23
Term 4	8 (1)	6	6 (2)	1	3	27

Note: the number in parentheses indicates a modified grade, reflecting accommodations made according to NEP. 'Unclassified' indicates extended absence or alternative programs. Totals reflect the fluidity of enrolments in the class.

reading. Most thought they had improved their understanding of how to ask and use effective questions.

Making place-based, negotiated & community learning sustainable

The notion of sustainability has multiple dimensions. Effective education sustains a community by producing independent, capable and critical thinkers. The research cycles discussed here reflect my efforts to develop and implement curricula that would sustain the interest of students, provide rich intellectual engagement and allow long-term skills development, while being sustainable for the teacher and the school in terms of the time, effort and organisation required. In these units, topics that connected with students' funds of knowledge improved their motivation. Ongoing negotiation led to ownership of the curriculum, and authentic assessment tasks sustained commitment to quality. Throughout, I sought to build confidence and willingness to take risks, and to cultivate students' capacity to sustain the effects of their learning in other contexts.

Concomitant challenges include rigidity of the secondary school timetable, difficulties in bringing staff together across faculties, availability of suitable equipment, and technological problems. In the first year, coordinating whole-class excursions followed by completion of negotiated tasks was an intense effort. In the second year, managing 25 students of mixed ability, each investigating something different, was demanding and complex, even with a traditional print media study. Such programs need to be sustainable for students *and* teachers, and a simpler structure may be more manageable.

Creative and synergistic approaches can overcome the obstacles outlined above – and others – to 'disrupt ... the default modes of schooling' (Johnston & Hayes 2007: 371) and implement productive pedagogies that offer opportunities for student engagement, ownership of curriculum and skill development. Poverty, however, limits the reach of such change. David Berliner pointed out the correlation between 'poverty and educational attainment', and the widespread societal and government tendency to overlook the potency of the connection (Berliner 2006: 961). Students described here did experience poverty and this doubtless affected their educational experience and outcomes. In that context, I can only remind myself that I act to make *a* difference rather than *the* difference.

To make the kind of work described sustainable and sustaining, effort needs to be shared by the school community and be continued over time. An individual teacher can initiate programs involving place-based learning, negotiation, authentic text production and intellectual challenge, and students may engage in the experiences and reap an educational benefit. For benefits to be more than transient, skills need to be reinforced in other subjects and in following years. A whole-school approach could result in deep transformational learning on an ongoing basis, giving educators the potential to make even more of a difference.

References

Baker J, 2002, *Window*. Walker Books, NSW.

Baker J, 2004, *Belonging*. Walker Books, NSW.

Brown ER, 2005, 'Introduction', in ER Brown & KJ Saltman (eds), *The Critical Middle School Reader*. Routledge, New York, pp 1–13.

Berliner D, 2006, 'Our Impoverished View of Educational Research', *Teachers College Record*, 108(6), 949–995.

Comber B, 2001, 'Critical literacies and local action: teacher knowledge and a 'new' research agenda', in B Comber & A Simpson (eds), *Negotiating critical literacies in classrooms*. Lawrence Erlbaum, Malwah, New Jersey, pp 271–282.

Comber B & Nixon H, 2005, 'Children reread and rewrite their local neighbourhoods: critical literacies and identity work', in J Evans (ed.), *Literacy moves on: Using popular culture, new technologies and critical literacy in the primary classroom*. Heinemann, Portsmouth, NH.

Comber B, Nixon H & Reid J (eds), 2007, *Literacies in place: Teaching environmental communication*. Primary English Teaching Association, Newtown.

Cormack P, 2005, 'Place as a starting point for curriculum, pedagogy and assessment in the middle school', presentation to the *Middle School Association of South Australia Term 3 Conference*, Christian Brothers College Conference Centre, Adelaide, 9th September.

Cormack P, Green B & Reid J, 2008, 'River Literacies: discursive constructions of place and environment in children's writing about the Murray-Darling Basin' in F Vanclay, J Malpas, M Higgins & A Blackshaw (eds), *Making Sense of Place: Exploring concepts and expressions of place through different senses and lenses*. National Museum of Australia, Canberra.

Farrell G & McCarthy M, 2002, 'Creating small urban schools: Expeditionary learning as school reform', in L Johnson, ME Finn & R Lewis (eds), *Urban Education with Attitude*. SUNY Press, Washington.

Gruenewald DA, 2003, 'The Best of Both Worlds: A Critical Pedagogy of Place', *Educational Researcher*, 32(4), 3–12.

Haberman M, 1991, 'The Pedagogy of Poverty versus Good Teaching', *Phi Delta Kappan*, 73(4), 290–294.

Hayes D, Mills M, Christie P & Lingard B, 2006, *Teachers & schooling making a difference: Productive pedagogies, assessment and performance*. Allen and Unwin, Crows Nest, NSW.

Homer D (ed.), 2004, *Talk of the Town: Stories and poems written for the course 'Writing the City'*. Lythrum Press, Adelaide.

Johnston K & Hayes D, 2008, '"This is as good as it gets": Classroom lessons and learning in challenging circumstances', *Australian Journal of Language and Literacy*, 31(2), 109–127.

Johnston K & Hayes D, 2007, Supporting student success at school through teacher professional learning: the pedagogy of disrupting the default modes of schooling, *International Journal of Inclusive Education*, 11(3), 371–381.

Pearson M & Somekh B, 2006, 'Learning transformation with technology: a question of sociocultural contexts?', *International Journal of Qualitative Studies in Education*, 19(4), 519–539.

Postman N & Weingartner C, 1969, *Teaching as a Subversive Activity*. Dell, New York.

Smyth J, McInerney P & Hattam R, 2003, 'Tackling school leaving at its source: a case of reform in the middle years of schooling', *British Journal of Sociology of Education*, 24(2), 177–193.

Thomson P, 2002, 'Vicki and Thanh', in *Schooling the rustbelt kids: making the difference in changing times*. Allen and Unwin, Crows Nest, NSW.

Thomson P, 2006, 'Mission possible: making a difference in neighbourhoods made poor', keynote address, AEU Middle Schooling Conference, Adelaide, November 17.

Wheatley N & Rawlins D, 1987, *My Place*. Collins Dove, Melbourne.

Chapter 6

The same but different: researching young people's views of their place in the world

❦❦❦❦

Faye McCallum and Jo Temme

The aspiration

This chapter describes the processes of, and the learnings from, a practitioner inquiry into a pedagogical strategy aimed at improving the academic outcomes of disengaged middle years students from a school servicing an area of disadvantage. The strategy was developed as part of the *Redesigning Pedagogies in The North* (RPiN) project, and was therefore founded on its central premise that student engagement is enhanced by giving precedence to students' life-worlds in the curriculum. Specifically, units of work that acknowledged student youth cultures and enabled middle years students to research their identities were developed in negotiation with students and implemented over a two-year period. The units, designed by Jo with support from Faye, were designed to connect with a number of aspects of the RPiN philosophy.

First, they picked up on literature that emphasises the importance of learning about relationships with place and the environment (e.g., Gruenewald 2003; Smith 2002) and of promoting pedagogies that relate to the life-worlds of students and promote active participation in community life (e.g., Apple & Bean 1995; Ladwig & Gore 1998; Smith 2002; Smyth, Hattam & Lawson 1998). The project was based on the belief that encouraging students to research their life-worlds would lead to greater self-awareness and help them to develop the capabilities that make for more socially sustainable communities (Fielding 2001; McKenzie 2004; Prosser 2006; Sfard & Prusak 2005). At the same time the approach would help to make study relevant and motivating, and so foster higher-order thinking and deeper understandings (Lingard, Mills & Hayes 2002).

Second, the design of the unit was negotiated with the students. It was felt that it would be inconsistent for any approach that sought to focus on the life-worlds of students, not to deeply involve students in choosing the topics and the processes for exploring them, or to use students' prior knowledge as a starting point for curriculum design (e.g., Moll, Amanti, Neff & Gonzalez 1992; Prosser et al. 2008; Thomson 2002).

Third, Jo wanted to 'acknowledge the multiple literacies students encounter both in and outside of the classroom including the Internet, music, television, mobile phones, magazines, e-mail messages, trade books, and advertisements' (Elkins & Luke 1999: 212) and to incorporate this into student learning. She aimed to make formal learning more meaningful by connecting with media and other forms of popular culture, thus blurring the divisions between school, leisure, work and home. More than this, Jo wanted to help students become more discerning about the ways in which commercial interests target youth culture via multimedia. She believed that not to develop these critical sensibilities would, as Atkinson and Nixon (2005: 405) pointed out:

> cut schools off from the dynamic processes that circulate through political life, culture, and the media in capitalist consumer societies and thus renders them and their students less equipped to participate in the development of those spheres through productive and critical interaction.

Finally, Jo wanted to develop an approach to learning that would include rather than exclude students who experience various forms of disadvantage – an approach that would not offer a diluted or softer version of the mainstream curriculum for these students, but would engage and motivate them through rigorous learning experiences. With all of this in mind, Jo and her classes selected study units that focused on identities and youth cultures.

The context

This project was conducted at a large (more than 900 student) co-educational, public school in the northern suburbs of Adelaide. The northern suburbs, referred to by Thomson (2002) as Adelaide's 'rustbelt', now include some of the most socio-economically disadvantaged suburbs in the city, state and nation (Prosser et al. 2008: 19). Some of the students are from generationally unemployed families with a large percentage of students on School Card (the government school measure of poverty), a high incidence of broken and dysfunctional families, and a high frequency of mental health problems. Often, students begin secondary school aiming to do well and gain professional employment, but these aspirations typically get lost as the students move through to the senior years of schooling. Parents also express a desire for their children to do well at school and achieve academically.

Teachers at this school are challenged by the factors that impinge on student aspirations, achievement and satisfaction. Jo had experience of working in this school for over a decade and knew that school success is not related to a lack of ability, but instead to a lack of knowledge and understanding about what is required to achieve success, as well as a lack of role models from preceding generations and current senior students at the school. All of this has an impact on students as they progress through school, making it increasingly difficult for teachers to engage students in educational tasks that not only motivate them, but also result in high academic rigour.

The project
The units were designed for Year 8 and 9 Society and Environment/Integrated Studies classes as a component of a general theme relating to roles and responsibilities in society, with a sub-theme of youth cultures and identities. The focus of each unit was research into the various subcultural youth groups at the school at the Years 8 and 9 levels and was guided by the work of Beach & Finders (1999: 81) who stated that

> once students begin to understand the idea of how social practices serve to construct a social world, they can discuss the kinds of practices typically operating in that world.

It was anticipated that the study would assist students to learn how to better interpret and participate in their world, as well as foster the development of analytical and other academic skills.

In the initial process of negotiating the nature and breadth of the study in the first year of the project, the Year 8 students confirmed the importance of the topic to them. They spoke about their need to establish identities that are separate from parents, teachers and even other peer groups, and yet at the same time they wanted to feel that they are part of a larger whole. They were interested in the complex relationship between the uniqueness of individuals and the concept of inclusion in a larger social entity. As one student, who identified as having an emerging gothic identity, said: 'We are all unique, we like to think and dress differently, but we are all human beings with feelings, we are the same but different'.

During the first year of the project it became clear that the students wanted to explore the bullying and harassment problems in the Middle School as a means to study youth identities. As it happened, the staff of the school had been concerned for some time about this matter. They believed that the bullying and harassment behaviour had its origins in the unwillingness of many students to accept difference in others, and a student culture that devalued education and denigrated those who tried to succeed academically. The staff were looking for ways to help students grow past this blinkered view of the world and to appreciate diversity and academic endeavour. So Jo thought that this project was an ideal opportunity to explore the causes of and look for solutions to the problem.

In the second year of the project, the Year 9 class spent seven weeks looking at youth culture and the various subcultures in it. This involved exploring issues associated with bullying and harassment, identifying the focus of particular teenage subcultures, analysing what is popular for young people, and comparing the views of adults in this environment. Students collated their findings and created a photostory (an incorporation of photos with written and spoken text using a computer program) based on their results. This relatively new and creative technology was chosen because it could extend and improve students' academic ability to write for an audience, as well as enabling students to participate in the celebration that comes with producing work of quality that is shared with others.

The inquiry

Jo wanted to research the effectiveness of the various pedagogies she would use in teaching the units, including the extent to which a focus on students' life-worlds helped to motivate and engage students and what effect this had on student learning. She used the Kemmis and McTaggart (1988) action-research model, where she planned, acted, observed and then reflected before planning the next phase of the research. Jo's inquiry was conducted over two years, with the first year's findings and results being seen as a pilot, the results of which would drive the second year of the inquiry. The research question was: *to what extent does student research into youth cultures engage students in their learning and with what effect on academic outcomes?*

During the action-research cycles, Jo collected qualitative data that included spoken and written data from students, artefacts such as students' assessment pieces, and observations of students' work. These data were used to help ascertain student opinions about their learning. Data collection was conducted in pre- and post-project forms: student opinions were gathered at the beginning of the project via class discussions and through a written survey. They were compared with student opinions expressed in class discussions throughout the project and with the results of a survey completed by students at the end of the project.

Two sample groups were included in the inquiry:

- Group 1 – a Year 8 Integrated Studies class was selected for the first year of the project. Parental permission was sought and given. Of the 28 students, 13 were male and 15 female. From this sample, a focus group volunteered to participate in in-depth discussions about bullying and harassment, and social interactions of their peers.

- Group 2 – a Year 9 Society and Environment class (semester 1) which Jo taught again in an Integrated Studies class (semester 2) was selected for the second year of the project. Parental permission was sought and given. The Year 9 class consisted of 29 students, 18 male and 11 female. Of these, 12 male and eight females were regular attendees, four males and two females did not attend more than one lesson and a further two males and one female attended irregularly.

Four of the students from Group 2 were on a Negotiated Education Plan (NEP). One of these students received regular help from a school services officer at the start of the year due to a brain injury from a car accident. None of the other NEP students received extra help, although each of them had extreme difficulty with literacy tasks. There were four other students who had significant problems with literacy. Five indigenous students attended the class, three male and two female. Of these students, one male never attended, one rarely did, one female was rarely present due to suspensions and an exclusion, and one female and one male were regular attendees. Two of these students received some extra help from the Aboriginal education worker on behavioural issues.

Phase 1

This phase was completed in the first year with Group 1 and showed that students enjoyed studying and researching topics based on their own (youth) culture. They identified significant bullying and harassment issues in the middle years, and their research also offered some insights into the operation of student sub-groups, particularly around issues of power. They found that the groups that had less power were bullied and harassed because of the way they dressed and expressed themselves. Students in the more powerful groups were also more popular and often behaved as though they had more rights than others.

As a teacher of both Society and Environment and Integrated Studies at the middle school level, a main objective for Jo was to help students understand diversity and the need to accept and value differences in others. Phase 1 had revealed a significant topic – bullying and harassment – as a focus for achieving this objective. But while being given a choice in the way they worked was welcomed by the students, Jo did not believe that there had been any obvious improvement in academic learning outcomes in Phase 1. It was clear that students would not progress unless a more explicit learning structure was provided by the teacher. Jo used this knowledge to plan the next phase. Continuing the action-research project from one year to the next allowed time for reflection and learning, and for Jo to explore alternative pedagogies that might contribute to better academic outcomes for students. As a result of the Phase 1 pilot, a further research question was added to inform Phase 2 which was to be conducted in the following year: *what happens to students' understandings of diversity and inclusion when they become researchers of their own and their peers' youth culture?*

Phase 2

This phase began in the second year of the project with Group 2 and it involved the Year 9 class being introduced to their role as researchers of their own culture. Initial discussions focused on students' understandings about friendship groups, as well as issues surrounding bullying and harassment. Discussion broadened to youth culture, with extensive lists being created about the interests of Years 8 and 9 students. The class also identified the extent to which friendship groups changed through the transition years. A discussion was held after watching the movie *Mean Girls,* which supplied a context derived from the youth culture at a typical middle class American high school. The Year 9 class was asked to identify similarities and differences with the youth culture shown in the film and their experiences, including the ways in which groups operated and controlled social situations.

In Phase 2, the qualitative data obtained for the inquiry included verbal accounts such as class discussions recorded on audiotape to gain information about students' views, and observations recorded in Jo's written journal that reflected her impressions of students. Questions that informed the journal were: *how did students perceive the different friendship groups at school?* and, *was there antagonism towards some groups, or were the students inclusive and accepting of all friendship groups?* Journal entries were compared during the project with students' views about friendships and bullying and harassment.

During this phase, students were actively involved in class discussions and could recount numerous examples of incidents in the different friendship groups, including episodes of bullying and harassment. Students could identify with examples shown in the film and further analysis enabled them to list some similarities and differences. As a result of this work, Jo felt they had developed some low-order research skills that could have been a result of her explicit teaching at the beginning of the unit about the roles and responsibilities of student researchers. However, she wanted to develop this further and was quite excited about the prospects of students acquiring new skills, possibly working in groups with less teacher direction, and being able to apply new learning at a practical level.

Phase 3

In a third unit of work, students developed research projects based on topics of interest generated by class discussion and self-selected by the class, with some teacher direction. Each group developed a research question based on a topic related to youth culture. Examples of topics included:
- friendship at school – what is the importance of having friends? what are the qualities of a good friend?
- popular youth music – why is music so important to teenagers?

- healthy and unhealthy eating for students at school – how important is nutrition to Years 8 and 9 students, and do adults eat more healthily?
- gothic culture – what is their identity? How do their interests vary in music, dress, recreational activities etc.?

Student research was conducted using the Internet, magazines and books, film and television, and surveys of students and adults. The purpose was to help students understand and realise that analysing the opinions of others is a valuable tool for understanding their own culture, and that this analysis requires higher-order or critical thinking skills which are critical to high academic learning outcomes. Teacher guidance was really important to ensure that the students experienced a sense of success and satisfaction in their new learning. Each group:

- researched information from external sources. For example the group researching popular music looked at some of the issues in the music industry, and incorporated this knowledge into their research
- researched their peers, either through a survey or through interviews
- presented findings as a photostory. The use of digital technology necessitated learning new technological skills, required thorough planning to create a script, and involved the assistance of a professional journalist who taught script-writing skills which engage and entertain listeners. As a consequence, students' literacies were extended and they were able to use skills other than writing to produce better work than they had previously
- participated in a whole-class viewing of the completed photostory projects and a celebration of quality work.

During this phase Jo collected qualitative data for her inquiry. These included written surveys of students in other classes on topics related to youth culture; an evaluative survey designed to determine student enjoyment and engagement levels; transcripts of interviews and focus group discussions about student experiences that were recorded on audio tape; and student work such as completed research assignments.

An analysis of these data showed that the unit had had mixed success. Technological difficulties delayed the completion of projects and frustrated some students, which meant that a few lost interest. Although most of the students engaged with the professional journalist who came to one of the classes, only two of the more able students felt they could use the skills learnt in this lesson when it came to writing their own photostory scripts. Some students were distracted during the focus groups, so meaningful comments were not always recorded. However, since most of the students enjoyed interviewing others, most surveys were completed. The comments on the surveys surprised some of the students as they found out what others thought about the different groups in the school and how these differences sometimes contributed to bullying and harassment behaviours. Jo felt that the students enjoyed sharing the completed photostories and learnt a great deal from the experience. On the basis on these insights, Jo planned and trialled a final phase in the research.

Phase 4

The final phase involved students participating in lessons based on bullying and harassment, as part of the Integrated Studies curriculum in Semester 2. This was followed by class discussion about students' understandings and perceptions of bullying and harassment at school. Students were asked whether some social groups were more likely to be victims or perpetrators of bullying and harassment. Qualitative data for the teacher inquiry included a written survey of student opinions, verbal recounts from class discussions and observations recorded in Jo's journal.

Jo's pedagogy has always included discussion as a valuable strategy for enabling students to grapple with important issues. However, she had tended to conduct discussions as one-off events. This time the single event became a series of systematic discussions – with one building on the next – and points being recorded. During these discussions Jo focused on the process as well as the content of the discussion, insisting on protocols based on allowing differences in opinion and perspective, respect for others and equality between all members of the class. It was clear from the research data that this enhanced the quality of the learning experience and the learning outcomes for the students.

The insights

In this section we return to the inquiry question: *to what extent does student research into youth cultures engage students in their learning and with what effect on academic outcomes?* Using the data gathered during the four phases of the project, we discuss in more detail some of the insights that emerged from our inquiry.

Insights into engagement and student life-worlds

One of the main findings of our research was the extent to which making students' life-worlds a starting point as well as a focus of student research was a motivating factor in student learning. While some of this related to the fact that students had the freedom to negotiate their own study choices, it was also an outcome of feeling that their lives, cultures and experiences were valued. Indeed, for some students, researching youth cultures more broadly gave them a better understanding of their own identities. For example, a group who researched popular television was able to reflect on an incident that resulted in the eviction of two of the participants of *Big Brother*. The students analysed the event from their own perspectives and discussed how the situation could be used to help teens think about what is acceptable and not acceptable in terms of sexual behaviour. In this way, they felt not only that that their own cultures were being respected, but also that they had a chance to reflect on their attitudes and beliefs in a context where they were not being blamed or accused.

More than this, exploring students' life-worlds – in this case embedding the issue of harassment and bullying in the formal curriculum – resulted in a significant improvement to the culture of the middle school community. Students felt that they both owned the problem and were part of the solution. This was much more productive than lecturing to students about the need to cease practices which were unacceptable to teachers. Clearly the attitudes, skills and understandings developed in this school context can be transferred to other areas of students' lives in the wider community.

An aspect of the project that was connected to students' life-worlds was the opportunity for each student to investigate not only his or her own culture, but also to find out what others thought. The surveys that were developed by each student group and distributed to peers and teachers offered insights into how other members of the school community were thinking, and enabled a comparison with their own thoughts. One of the students in a focus group said this was the section that stood out for him because the task was completely different from anything he had done before. He felt that it was more satisfying and interesting to research what people in the local community thought about the topic under investigation, and to come up with results that he had discovered himself, than simply finding on the Internet what other people had discovered about the topic.

Insights into student understandings of diversity & inclusion

Over the period of the project it became clear that focusing on youth cultures offered a powerful strategy for extending students' understandings of, respect for, and appreciation, of diversity. It thus became an avenue for developing a more inclusive school community.

During the course of the project the ways in which communities can exclude as well as include became obvious. For example, the class discussions on the social construction of stereotypical groups in the school identified student groups like 'gangster wannabes', 'Goths', 'emos', 'plastics', 'sporting heroes' and 'nerds'. The students found that often the norms established by one group would be pitted against another by group members, with little attempt at understanding and respecting difference. Those students with more power established the status quo, and this was sometimes unintentionally enforced by teachers through critical comments about, for example, the appearance of particular student groups.

Jo found that during the course of these discussions many opportunities to explore the nature and cause of bullying and harassment arose, as did ways by which these might be addressed. One example that was recorded in Jo's journal after a whole-class discussion involved a new female student who identified herself as 'gothic' (dark eye makeup, black clothes, chunky jewellery and other distinctive items of dress) and who told of an incident at the local shopping centre which escalated to harassment at school. She commented that the youth culture project gave her a chance to express her philosophy of life and explain her viewpoint to others. She interviewed five of her gothic friends about their philosophies, how they felt about being part of a minority group, how they viewed the rest of humanity, their taste in music and its meaning in their life, and presented her research in a photostory. Her project was not only prolific, but also demonstrated 'intellectual quality, connectedness to the world, and recognition of differences' (Lingard, Mills & Hayes 2000). Jo used this work, and the subsequent whole-class discussion, to help other students understand notions of difference and respect. Initially threatened by the Goths, students began to understand and respect a different sub-culture.

The bullying began to abate. Later, another friend of this girl told the class that from that time on she had felt welcome in the class.

Jo's journal and student surveys confirm that during the course of the project students began to develop new understandings about how they viewed people who dressed differently to themselves, or behaved in ways that initially seemed odd to them. Other students who had at the beginning of the semester been silenced due to their low position on the other students' surrogate social hierarchy, began to speak up and found that they were listened to and their opinions were respected. Once again, it was clear that the new understandings were not only making the class and year group culture more inclusive, but were starting to be used by students as they analysed issues and attitudes in the wider community.

Insights into pedagogy

The project emphasised the importance of not treating a class as a homogenous group, but rather recognising and catering for the huge variation in students' interests and abilities. In the first phase, while some students welcomed the freedom to negotiate their own study and blossomed as independent learners, others floundered with the lack of structure. Jo discovered that if she was to recognise student difference and be inclusive of their needs, she needed to concentrate more on teaching specific skills. Her journal records:

> I have always spent a lot of time doing individual instruction (too much probably), it's just I did even more in this case because it was necessary to complete each stage successfully before beginning the next stage. The teaching change was that I increased the scaffolding and made the steps very specific.

The extreme differences between the abilities of the students did influence the way the project was designed. Students with more academic ability and the capacity to work independently were able to steam ahead. This allowed students who required more help to have individual time with the teacher and to be given more structure and more explicit guidelines for their learning. At the end of the project, Jo decided that next time she would also teach life skills, such as how to listen to instructions and work independently.

Using extended literacies through the use of new technologies in student research undoubtedly increased student engagement. It also made the work academically rigorous. Thus the layering process (photos → music → story or script → audio) not only captured student interest, but also encouraged them to work in different media and to make connections between these. For example, students were challenged by the digital technology photostory as they sought to combine the results of the analysis of their surveys with a series of photos to be presented in a narrative form. As one student explained: 'it was using a bit more of my brain'.

Inevitably there were technological difficulties. Some students who had made significant progress found their files corrupted when they returned to work on them and some groups were forced to rewrite their scripts two or three times. In the evaluation responses there were numerous complaints about the computers, ranging from frustration at their slowness to load, the repeated corruption of files for no apparent reason, and the difficulties associated with finding and importing suitable photos from the Internet. Many popular youth topics and related information and photos had been barred to students by the school. These are practical difficulties that can frustrate the most innovative of pedagogies, and yet despite them, students still had the motivation to finish their work and to give time to polish it.

Finally, Jo reflected on the process of teacher inquiry. She observed that while it was often difficult in a busy teaching week to find the time to gather data and analyse them, the process was invaluable. As each phase of the research progressed she developed new understandings and insights that she was able to employ in the next cycle of the project. It seems that in the challenging teaching contexts in which Jo and her colleagues work, the issue is not whether we research our practice, but rather how we go about doing so. Of course that question cannot be answered without considering the resources needed to support teachers in this crucial work. But it is something that the whole professional education community must work on, especially if we are to address the entrenched inequalities that blight our education systems.

The results of the project written about in this chapter suggest that pedagogies that value the life-worlds of young people and encourage them to explore the issues that confront them, have the potential to motivate and engage students and to enhance learning outcomes. Ongoing work of the sort described here is needed so that we can learn more about such approaches in order to both develop sustainable pedagogies. After all as McKenzie (2004: 18) argued:

> Social sustainability occurs when the formal and informal processes, systems, structures and relationships actively support the capacity of current and future generations to create healthy and liveable communities. Socially sustainable communities are equitable, diverse, connected and democratic and provide a good quality of life.

References

Apple MW & Bean JA, 1995, 'The case for democratic schools', in MW Apple & JA Beane (eds), *Democratic Schools*. Association for Supervision and Curriculum Development, Alexandria, Va, pp 1–25.

Atkinson S & Nixon H, 2005, 'Locating the subject: Teens online@ninemsm', in *Discourse: studies in the cultural politics of education*, 26(3), 387–409.

Beach R & Finders M, 1999, 'Students as Ethnographers: Guiding alternative research projects', *English Journal*, 89(1), 82–90.

Elkins J & Luke A, 1999, 'Redefining adolescent literacies', *Journal of Adolescent & Adult Literacy*, 43, 212–215.

Fielding M, 2001, 'Students as radical agents of change', *Journal of Educational Change,* 2(3), 123–141.

Gruenewald DA, 2003, 'The Best of Both Worlds: A Critical Pedagogy of Place', *Educational Researcher*, 32(4), 3–12.

Kemmis S & McTaggart R (eds), 1988, *The action research planner* (third edn). Deakin University Press, Victoria.

Ladwig J & Gore J, 1998, 'Nurturing Democracy in schools', in J Smyth, R Hattam & M Lawson (eds), *Schooling for a Fair Go*. Federation Press, Leichardt, NSW.

Lingard B, Mills M & Hayes D, 2002, 'Teachers, school reform and social justice: Challenging research and practice', *Australian Educational Researcher*, 27(3), 99–115.

McKenzie S, 2004, 'Social Sustainability: Towards some definitions', *Hawke Research Institute Working Paper Series No.27*. University of South Australia, Magill.

Moll L, Amanti C, Neff D & Gonzalez N, 1992, 'Funds of Knowledge for Teaching: using a qualitative approach to connect homes to classrooms', *Theory into Practice*, 31(2), 132–141.

Prosser B, McCallum F, Milroy P, Comber B & Nixon H, 2008, 'I'm smart and

I'm not joking: aiming high in the middle years of schooling', *Australian Educational Researcher*, 35(2), 15–36.

Prosser B, 2006, *See Red: critical narrative in ADHD Research*. PostPressed, Teneriffe, 51-66

Sfard A & Prusak A, 2005, 'Telling Identities: in search of an analytical investigating learning as a culturally shaped activity', *Educational Researcher,* 25(3), 14–22.

Smith G, 2002, 'Place-based education: Learning to be where we are', *Phi Delta Kappan*, 83(8), 584–594.

Smyth J, Hattam R & Lawson M (eds), 1998, *Schooling for a Fair Go*. Federation Press, Leichardt, NSW.

Thomson P, 2002, 'Vicki and Thanh', in *Schooling the rustbelt kids: making the difference in changing times*. Allen and Unwin, Crows Nest, NSW.

Chapter 7

Exploring teaching through cycles of action research: a story of professional change

❧❧❧❧❧

Sandrine Poissonnier and Kathryn Paige

Kathy introduces

This chapter describes how a classroom practitioner moved from a focus on a teacher-centred classroom to embrace more student-centred learning. The key to the change was participating in a series of action-research projects over a three-year cycle as part of the *Redesigning Pedagogies in the North* (RPiN) project. Each cycle built onto what was learned from the previous cycle. Already an enthusiastic and passionate teacher, through RPiN Sandrine saw the opportunity and was given the time to reflect on socially sustainable practices, resulting in a renewed pedagogy that was informed by research and reflection. Sandrine's journey is one of awakening that all those who are committed to socially just pedagogy have shared. However, by her own admission, she is still taking her first steps as a reflective teacher-researcher. But who of us do not remember our first steps, or wonder at how much further we have to go? It is this shared journey that is the basis of this chapter.

Sandrine's story is that of a teacher who grappled with a new pedagogical approach and in the process became more connected to her school community. It is a story of changing her view of students, families, schools and communities. It tells of a shift from a deficit view to one that values schooling and school communities, and provides informed real-life choices to students. Perhaps most importantly, it is a reflection on what it takes to review one's pedagogical practice in a complex, middle school setting, as well as what it takes to sustain this change for days, weeks, months and even years.

Professional profile

Sandrine has been teaching for 10 years, first in the southern suburbs of Adelaide and now in the suburbs of Adelaide's northern urban fringe. She finds teaching in the North to be exciting and rewarding. Currently working as Middle School and Society and Environment Coordinator of a large secondary school, she is in a position that enables her to help students make the transition from primary to secondary school. This position also offers an opportunity to assist students to explore the world around them during the important, early adolescent years. Sandrine is dedicated to constantly honing her practice and working collectively with her colleagues to explore possibilities for change.

School profile

Students at Sandrine's northern suburbs school predominately come from a lower socio-economic background. There are a number of new-arrival students from countries as diverse as Costa Rica, Cambodia, Laos and Sudan. The school's diverse population also includes a large number of Australian Indigenous students. Ten percent of students are on Negotiated Education Plans. During the time of Sandrine's project the school's priority was to further develop the literacy and numeracy skills of all students. Recently, the school has made a more concerted effort to focus on work quality and behaviour. It is in this context that Sandrine's pedagogical journey and her associated action-research cycles were conducted.

Cycles of change

Sandrine's pedagogy evolved over the three years of the RPiN project. It is fair to say that she started with little knowledge of the term 'pedagogy' or the concept of social justice. What she took from the first cycle of action research in RPiN was a new focus on thinking about teaching, particularly a shift from teacher-centred to student-centred learning. Her research revealed that student-centred learning could not occur without clear structures being in place, so in the second year she sought a tool to help her structure her classroom pedagogy. In the focus of RPiN on student knowledge, skills and interests, she saw a link with the model of multiple intelligences that focused on the abilities of different learners (Gardner 1993). She used this resource to frame lessons and assignments that would suit all learners, while differentiating assessment tasks which impacted positively on student learning and engagement. As she gained further confidence in the third year of RPiN, she realised that imposing external models, while attractive to teachers under pressure, can be limiting, especially if they are used uncritically and without evaluation. Hence, she embraced changing pedagogy as the key to instigating and sustaining the next cycle of research. In the remainder of this chapter, the story of each of these yearly cycles will be explored in more detail.

In order to capture the different perspectives that each of us brought to the project – Sandrine the teacher-researcher engaged in the classroom; Kathy the university researcher fulfilling the role of critical friend – the remainder of the chapter will be constructed as a conversation. Sandrine will explain what happened, and why, during the various stages of the action-research cycles, and Kathy will offer a reflective 'outsider' comment on each of the stages. In this way, we hope to model the possibilities of collaborative inquiry conducted through university–school partnerships; and show how different perspectives and voice can be used to deepen understandings about educational practice.

Sandrine writes about cycle one: moving from teacher-centred to student-centred learning

In the first year of my RPiN classroom research I had time to think about teaching. It was a luxury I had not had before. The process that I followed during this time taught me many things about the students I worked with, including their skills. I had assumed that students were empty vessels that needed to be filled by the teacher. By letting go of my traditional views and assumptions about how students should learn, I was able to see how students had knowledge and skills that they could share with me, and others, in the class.

As part of this, I developed a research question that took into account student learning and teacher change. In essence, the research question was, *how does one go about implementing the change from a teacher-focused classroom to a student-focused one?* To find the answer to this question I needed to change the way I had been teaching and refocus how I delivered the curriculum to meet the learning needs of students.

I started my attempt to consider my students' interests by surveying their attitude to their local area, and found that many of my students had a real disconnection with, and fear of, their local area. This was due largely to negative media reports of violence and crime in the streets in which the students live.

Armed with this information, I went back to the aims of the Society and Environment learning area of the South Australian Curriculum Standards and Accountability Framework (SACSA) framework to develop learning experiences that looked at the local area in a positive way. Some of the students were very proud of their community. I wanted to tap into this and encourage students to teach others about their local area. A unit of work was developed with activities designed to get students talking about their community and how they felt about it. A warm-up activity at the beginning of this topic encouraged students to describe their community using their five senses. So, for example, when asked to explain the smell of their community, they spoke of the local sewerage treatment plant or the Chinese take-away around the corner. After a class discussion, we agreed that community is not only a sense of place, but also people and experiences. In planning these activities, I had been influenced by the place-based learning (Semken & Butler-Freeman 2008) literature whereby students experience learning in their own community by using problem-solving skills.

Following this class-based task, a walking tour was planned. It was met with much enthusiasm, as this extract from my teacher journal illustrates:

> Students are told that they are going on an excursion – excitement whispers through the class until questions burst out: Where are we going? What are we going to do? When do we go? There's a catch; the students have to plan the excursion. They organise themselves into groups and are given a map of the local area. They are then given a list of criteria: this is a walking tour, starting and ending at the school, you have 90 minutes in which to complete the walk, you must include local places of interest. Only one team will have their walk chosen so you need to choose a spokesperson to 'sell' your walk to the rest of the class. Once this is done together we are going to compose a letter home to your parents to gain their permission to go on the walking tour. Students quickly settle to task and begin debating places of interest, how to get there and who should 'sell' their walking tour. The room is abuzz with activity. From this one activity so much is occurring in the classroom amongst students, between students and teacher links are created to learning and the community.

Back in the classroom after the excursion, the students examined the photos that they took along the way. Class discussion centred on both positive (improved school grounds) and negative (vandalised telephone boxes) changes in their local area since they had left primary school. One significant change was the number of older houses being condemned and newer ones being built. Students worked first on their own to complete a series of questions for another student. Then they had to find a partner and together they compared their impressions and discussed their views on their local area. To further develop students' connections to their community, students were given a copy of the local paper and asked to critically examine sections such as the community notice board, editorial, letters to the editor, sports news and advertisements. This assignment was completed quickly as students enjoyed seeing events or notices about what was going on in their local area. My teacher journal recorded their classroom activity in this way:

> They were interested in the articles in the newspaper as they could relate
> to what was in the paper ie 'My mum put in a classified', 'This happened
> a couple of streets over'.

Students were learning that they or their family members had many interactions with their community that were positive and reflected their input to it. As the unit progressed through the various activities, students appeared less fearful of their local area. Learning about their local area was a positive experience for the students. I saw their engagement increase; they were willing to participate in activities and I noted that they were more accepting and acknowledging of others. At the end of my first cycle of action research, I was encouraged to continue to try to use the students' knowledge and their community connections, rather than teacher-centred learning, in the classroom.

Kathy writes: moving from cycle one to cycle two

From our reflections after the first cycle, Sandrine came to see that there was still a lot more to learn about teaching when the students are placed at the centre of learning. While her pedagogy had evolved away from the traditional approach of 'chalk and talk', the outcomes that she hoped to achieve were not as evident as she had anticipated. Why was this?

Drawing from her early experience and working with her research supervisors, she came to realise that giving more control over learning to her students did not mean that she could relinquish her responsibility as a teacher. To improve student engagement and work completion she would need to have a clearer goal in mind. In her review of students' work, it became clear that while she was successful in engaging the students in class activities and received more written work than previously, there was little or no improvement in their grades. On reflection, she realised that she had not provided enough scaffolding to sufficiently equip students to take more responsibility for their learning. Sandrine had assumed that her enthusiasm for the project and the invitation to draw on life outside school would be reflected in the students' desire to complete and hand in work of a higher standard. This was not the case. Sandrine set herself the challenge to better structure student-centred learning, without compromising the student as the centre of learning.

Sandrine writes on cycle two: using multiple intelligences to provide structure

For the second year of the RPiN project I wanted to improve and build on what I had learnt from the previous year. Based on this insight, I spent time reflecting on the available teaching tools that could be used to structure and scaffold students to take more responsibility for their learning.

Based on past discussions with colleagues at various professional development forums, I decided that multiple intelligences (Simmons 2001) could be used in the middle years classroom to provide structure. What was attractive was that the resource for this concept could be used in more than one way: by focusing on certain intelligences and developing them with the whole class; or by using it as a basis for creative approaches to student-inquiry assignments. Multiple intelligences were also chosen because of the diverse composition of the class. I believed that the multiple intelligences learning tool could help the students to recognise that there is a variety of learning styles that could help them to take control of their learning. I saw that this recognition of diversity coincided with the emphasis in the RPiN project on drawing from the life experiences, knowledge and skills of students as resources for planning for learning. Further, I felt this was a model the students could understand and it would scaffold them to take responsibility for more independent inquiry and learning.

The multiple intelligences were introduced to students in early learning so that not only did they become familiar with their own learning style, but they were also able to articulate it to others.

Multiple intelligences were linked to a new topic, 'People and the Law'. The essence of this topic was to learn about Australia's political system and develop respect for the law. The sequence of learning involved class discussion on rights and responsibilities, observations of laws and their effect in the local area, and traditional learning from textbooks to gain background knowledge. The main foci were the role of the local council, what students would like to change, and what they could change.

As students could see purpose in the activities and made connections to events in their lives, this enabled a further shift from a teacher-focused class to a student-focused class. An example of this was students being involved in creating their own class assignment. Clear expectations from simple instructions and student involvement helped the students to quickly begin the assignment. This enabled them to have a say in their learning and involved them in something that excited them, as they clearly understood the needs of the task. This was further evidenced by their enthusiastic participation during class and their willingness to attempt tasks that they may not have in previous topics. The multiple intelligences approach was not limited to assignments; it was also used in other learning experiences. After the first cycle I felt that the multiple intelligences resource was used successfully to structure student-centred learning in the classroom. The students were comfortable using it in a number of activities and in their interactions with others.

The sense of achievement that was felt at the end of these two cycles was evident, first in my journal as I recorded daily improvements in my students' engagement with learning, and second in the surveys conducted at the end of these units that indicated that students felt as if they were able to have more of a say in the classroom and that they felt positive about their learning. There was also some evidence of greater rigour in students' work, but my research and evaluation showed that the extent of this was difficult to ascertain.

Kathy writes: moving from cycle two to cycle three

Sandrine continued to reflect on her practice, knowing that students need to understand the relevance of their learning and how it is going to help them in the future. She realised that a continued focus on the rigour of students' work was also required if students were to access the valued cultural capital available from senior years and higher education. However, on further reflection, Sandrine felt that the focus on multiple intelligences had proved to be limiting, as it was more about the role of different types of brains in learning styles than about the role of students' life-worlds in learning. Sandrine revisited Hayes, Mills, Christie and Lingard (2006) to think again about relevance and rigour, as well as to grapple with ways of developing her pedagogy. Although she was aware of productive pedagogies (with their emphasis on intellectual quality, connectedness, supported classroom environment and working with and valuing difference), Sandrine's reflective practice had up until the end of cycle two focused on one aspect of intellectual quality – learning styles – as a way to improve learning outcomes. Her next research cycle, still in progress, is making another shift in her practice toward more student life-world centred and rigorous learning using a deeper knowledge of Hayes et al. (2006).

The next cycle focuses on the importance of a student-centred classroom by incorporating flexibility in constructing a curriculum that reflects the students' needs and life-worlds in her classroom. By listening and getting to know students and parents much better, Sandrine is able to offer meaningful learning experiences to students in her class. As the following section details, Sandrine wants to know her students better and to use this knowledge to build a coherent and rigorous curriculum that has lead to a socially just classroom.

Sandrine reflects on the cycle: learning about research-informed pedagogy

After completing the two action-research cycles, many themes emerged. In this section I reflect on four key themes.

Rigour in the classroom

Underpinning each of my efforts was a desire to develop greater rigour in the classroom. During my research cycles I came to see that there was a lack of rigour both in my teaching style and in the students' work, which were failing us all in our pursuit of deep learning. In my experience, deep learning has occurred in the classroom when I provide rich, complex tasks that link with students' life-worlds and incorporate authentic assessment, but it has not occurred often enough to affect all the students regularly.

Some students found that when they had an invested interest in the assignment, one in whose creation they had had a say, they wanted to try harder to complete it. By structuring the assignment with a range of options, students were able to choose tasks that they could relate to or that they felt met their interests. As their interest was engaged, they wanted to find or create products that reflected the new knowledge that they had acquired, in this there was more rigour in their work. But this was not enough, I needed to develop ways that would engage all the students in meaningful and intellectually rigorous work.

At first I sought rigour by adapting my pedagogical practices to reflect how students learn, namely multiple intelligence approaches. But this was limited in its support of my pursuit of rigour. It was then that I went back and reread Hayes et al. (2006). I found that, although this text did not provide me with an 'easy solution', the authors did contribute to my understanding of rigorous productive pedagogies and how they could be applied in the classroom. Their discussion on intellectual quality afforded me with the concept of metacognition. They also introduced in a concise manner the concepts of intellectual quality, higher-order thinking skills, deep knowledge, deep understanding, knowledge as problematic, and metalanguage. Using these concepts as a framework, I was able to reflect on my practice and planning and develop a more rigorous approach to my pedagogy in the classroom. I finally had a structure that I could understand and work within and use to analyse my achievements.

However, Hayes et al. (2006) also discussed the need to develop students as the producers of knowledge and that it is the task of the teacher to help students to do this. This was something I still needed to work on. One way is to provide students with opportunities to be more involved in the classroom by acknowledging their connection to the community. It was here that the RPiN notion of rigour through relevant, life-world oriented, connected and socially just teaching appeared promising.

While initially I had focused on one higher-order thinking strategy – multiple intelligences – I came to realise that pre-made models such as these are limiting and could not take me as far as researching my own pedagogy. Further, using the resources provided through RPiN and the discoveries from my inquiry, there was still the potential to meet both the criteria of rigour outlined by Hayes el al. (2006) and those required by the school. I could still map the learning outcomes against the SACSA standards, give the students opportunities to apply the knowledge learnt in different contexts, build on previous capabilities and involve higher-order thinking (such as reflection and critique). Each of these can support greater academic rigour in my Society and Environment classroom.

Student-centred classroom

The shift from teacher-centred pedagogy to a more student-centred classroom was one of great significance to me. This is not only because of the challenge it presented to my pedagogy, but also because of the way I viewed students and how it forced me to confront my unintended deficit views of students. Observing students in a student-centred classroom, where their knowledge is equally legitimate and where they have input into the creation of the curriculum tasks, allows one to appreciate their expertise as learners. It also emphasises that when curriculum is connected to the local community, things that were once seen as deficit can become resources for learning, as seen in Comber and Kamler's (2005) 'Turn-around pedagogies'.

One of the major impacts that these research cycles have had on my pedagogy is that when I am planning tasks for my class I build in a range of strategies. I need to use more research to inform pedagogical change to enhance more rigour. It is an ongoing, life-long process.

Deficit views of adolescents

My view of adolescents was also challenged during this research period. Before this I had felt that I had a good understanding of adolescents, although I was aware of the deficit view of adolescents propagated by the media. In an educational setting I believe we have created the same unintended deficit view of students from poorer communities. My past experience also illustrated my limited assumptions of what students could achieve. Cormack's (1996) article powerfully articulates how we allow this view of young people to affect our interactions with them and unintentionally take a deficit viewpoint. It certainly made me realise that while I pride myself on how I work with young people, I can easily fall into a negative discourse over adolescents. It is a constant battle and I put pressure on myself to find creative solutions. When I find myself speaking negatively, I reflect on what I am doing and use the opportunities available to change my practice. I set high expectations for behaviour and look for ways of managing the learning environment creatively.

Connecting to community- or place-based learning

Enabling students to connect with the place where they live, play and are educated is the focus of the articles written by Smith (2002) and Gruenewald (2003). Smith (2002) stated that the aim of place-based learning was grounding learning in local phenomena and students' lived experiences. He offered a number of examples from American schools that demonstrate how students and their teachers looked at local community issues as a basis for their learning. The advantage of this article is the ease in which I was able to place my own experience and develop a sense of community with students at school. As a teacher and coordinator of Society and Environment, I increasingly work to promote a socially critical perspective and concern for the environment, social justice and equity. But students and their connection to the local area can often be taken for granted by adults. Students need to be given the time, opportunity and a forum in which to think about and discuss their ideas about their local area. My students were pleased to be given a say about their local area. The activities in this unit gave them the means to learn, reflect on and reconnect with their community.

As Student Voice Coordinator I know that middle school students are passionate about influencing their local environment and making a positive change. Last year was committed to connecting students to their community. To build on this I am planning a Go Green Week that will culminate with World Environment Day. Students will be involved in pledging to reduce their environmental footprint. Researching the effect of whole-school projects will be the focus of future studies.

Sandrine looks forward

Despite all the frustrations and daily traumas, the most powerful learning that occurred for me was to realise that I had to change my approach to teaching and learning; I should not expect only the students to change. Over time, I gained confidence that my efforts were making a difference as I saw how students reacted to changes in the classroom. This occurred more when I took the time to listen to students' ideas about curriculum and respond to different learning styles and when I was willing to build stronger learning connections with students' lives in my planning.

I have clearly been informed by being involved in a long-term research project, and think the key to my persistence has been that I have found my own pathway to changing my approach to teaching with the opportunities that RPiN provided. I learned to listen to students and hear what they were saying, and my commitment to these students in this school is stronger than ever.

The research into my pedagogy over the last three years has resulted in me exploring and looking for ways to improve four key aspects: intellectual rigour, student-centred learning, deficit views of adolescents and place-based learning. In doing these things better in the classroom (not perfectly but better), I am working towards establishing a more socially just classroom. Sustaining this over the long term is challenging, but for me the most critical part will be working in a team with like-minded, committed teachers. Having conversations with colleagues about what is working and how to do things differently is what keeps the momentum for pedagogical change going. As a curriculum leader, I want to ensure there is space and time set aside for this.

The change in my thinking and working that has resulted from being part of RPiN has been career changing. I have many more questions to answer but feel empowered by the strategies I now have to help seek answers to them.

Kathy reflects

The project that is the focus of this chapter reflects on a number of characteristics of sustainable pedagogy.

First, it seems that the ability to continue to evolve new forms of pedagogy, at every stage of our teaching career, is vital to giving the best to our students and sustaining ourselves as teachers. This was Sandrine's experience, working firstly with a commitment to socially just schooling and then becoming part of a supportive research community. Sandrine's energy to keep positive with the students, to have high expectations for learning and to keep working with staff to implement change are all indicators of a hope in a fairer future. This sense of a positive future is critical for maintaining socially sustainable education communities. The work Sandrine has been doing is sustainable both in content and process. The process of action research is very important as it creates opportunities for people – staff and students – to investigate and improve shared social practices. It is a cooperative process where they have worked together to find better ways of doing schooling in the north. Each of Sandrine's reflections is a work in progress – unfinished business – but action research allows for ongoing investigation, analysis and reinvention.

Second, there must be scope for change to be effective and not frustrating. While her school had middle school structures in place, Sandrine was still constrained by calendar events (such as sports day and splash day), as well as by senior secondary demands. The importance of co-planning was highlighted, but it was difficult to undertake. Sandrine only working in one discipline, as well as being part of the leadership team, were two factors that inadvertently restricted her opportunities for collaborative team teaching and interdisciplinary approaches. If we are to sustain the socially just educators of today and foster more in the future, we need to look at the conditions, cultures and structures in our schools that present barriers to effective change.

Third, new ways were found to challenge the deficit views of adolescents and improve academic rigour through student-centred learning. Deficit views of students and communities are the antithesis of working towards developing socially sustainable communities. Acknowledging that students have 'funds of knowledge' (Moll, Amanti, Neff & Gonzalez 1992) makes it possible to see the community as a resource and the students as active members of it. Students are not just waiting in the wings to be old enough to vote; we need to recognise that they are already citizens and already helping to produce knowledge. This means that the action research was actually part of the process of creating a 'social' *in* and *for* and *of* the community by focusing on young adolescents. This gives the school a different role in the community, a place to contribute to local social sustainability.

Finally, a key point in the sustainability of teacher innovation is being able to replicate the idea of students' life-worlds, and connection to other school cohorts, in more than one class and with other subjects. This will ensure that a coherent curriculum framework builds up over several years, despite the complexities faced in the middle years of schooling. The challenge each year is to build on what was done in previous years and maintain the momentum, rather than starting from scratch with new staff. This is especially the case with different cohorts of Year 8 students, from different combinations of feeder primary schools, all needing different connections to students' life-worlds to be established. If change is to be sustainable, the challenge for schools is to provide support and incentives for teachers to plan collaboratively, to continue to inquire into their classroom practice and to factor this into their workloads.

I have worked with Sandrine over the last three years, first as associate researcher attached to the school where Sandrine was doing her classroom research and, more recently, as a supervisor for her masters degree. Often I call her to discuss her work and study and at times the story is overwhelming as the day's events are recounted. Hers is a complex school and contributing to better lives in a tough suburb that is caught up in immense socio-economic challenges is not easy. It is not simple work: building social sustainability never can be. But it is the work of all teachers; it is the work of real people, imperfect people doing their best, and people at every different stage of their pedagogical journeys. What I take away from my work with Sandrine is hope for the future.

References

Comber B & Kamler B (eds), 2005, *Turn-around pedagogies: literacy interventions for at-risk students.* Primary English Teaching Association (PETA), Newtown, NSW.

Cormack P, 1996, 'Constructions of the adolescent in newspapers and policy documents: implementations from middle schooling', *South Australian Educational Leader*, 7(6), 1–12.

Department of Education, Training and Employment (DETE), 2001, 'SACSA Society and Environment Curriculum', South Australian Curriculum Standards and Accountability Framework, DETE, Adelaide.

Gardner H, 1993, *Multiple Intelligences: the theory in practice.* Basic Books, New York.

Gruenewald DA, 2003, 'The Best of Both Worlds: A Critical Pedagogy of Place', *Educational Researcher*, 32(4), 3–12.

Hayes D, Mills M, Christie P & Lingard B, 2006, *Teachers & schooling making a difference: Productive pedagogies, assessment and performance.* Allen and Unwin, Crows Nest.

McKenzie S, 2004, *Social Sustainability: Towards some definitions.* Hawke Research

Institute Working Paper Series, University of South Australia, Magill.

Moll L, Amanti C, Neff D & Gonzalez N, 1992, 'Funds of Knowledge for Teaching: using a qualitative approach to connect homes to classrooms', *Theory into Practice*, 31(2), 132–141.

Semken S & Butler Freeman C, 2008, 'Sense of place in the practice and assessment of place-based science teaching' *Science Education*, 92(6), 1042–1057.

Simmons III S, 2001, 'Multiple Intelligences at the Middle Level: Models for learning in Art and across the Disciplines', *Art Education*, 54(3), 18–24.

Smith G, 2002, 'Place-based education: Learning to be where we are', *Phi Delta Kappan*, 83(8), 584–594.

Appendix 1. Data collection and analysis methods implemented in this project

How I collected information	What this looked like in the classroom
Journals	I kept a journal as I taught the unit 'Local Area' and Multiple Intelligences. I reflected almost every lesson on how I went and the how the students responded to what happened in the class.
	Students also kept a journal from the beginning of the year. In first semester the writing was based on personal reflective questions. In second semester the writing was based on questions reflecting their understanding of learning processes.
Survey	I conducted a survey at the beginning of the unit 'Local Area' with some of the questions being designed directly as a result of class conversations about the local area. I ended the topic with another survey to see if I have had made any headway.
Photos	I took photos of the students during both units to capture their engagement in activities such as the design of the multiple intelligences assignment and the local area walk.
Peer evaluation	The Assistant Principal in charge of Curriculum observed me during selected lessons over the two units. She provided feedback in both a verbal and written format about what she observed of my teaching and the students responses.
	Critical conversations with UniSA staff were held on three separate occasions in either group conversations or one to one interviews. This aided in the reflection of my progress and helped me to evaluate what I was doing and how it was going. University staff also interviewed selected students about their thoughts of what was occurring. All of these conversations were recorded and transcribed for analysis
Student work	Completion of their project.

Chapter 8

Making community curricular

in an adult literacy class

<><><><><><>

Peter Voudantas and Robert Hattam

S chooling for a fair go?
In conclusion, we argue from the evidence … that people who are poor
and disadvantaged are victims of a societal confidence trick. They have
been encouraged to believe that a major goal of schooling is to increase
equality while, in reality, schools reflect society's intention to maintain
the present unequal distribution of status and power. Because the myth
of Equal Opportunities has been so widely accepted by Australians,
the nature of unequal outcomes has been largely ignored. Thus failure
to succeed in the competition is generally viewed as being the fault of
the individual rather than the inevitable result of the way our society is
structured. (Fitzgerald 1976: 231)

In this chapter we want to interrupt the claims that are made too easily
about 'schooling for a fair go' in Australia. We agree with Fitzgerald's
enduring quote, that people living in so-called disadvantaged communities are 'victims of a societal confidence trick' – one that is played out
in most public schools in Australia. This myth is perpetuated in part
because the debate about schooling in Australia is conducted as though
we live in a classless society. There is an assumption that all families are
middle class and have the economic, social and cultural resources that
will enable their children to be successful at school. But then the school
system is distorted by a curriculum hierarchy (Teese 1998) that feeds
into credentialing and assessment processes that 'separate the holders of
inherited cultural capital from those who lack it' (Bourdieu 1998: 20).
In this chapter we want to foreground the work of teachers in many

public schools, teachers who are grappling with the reality of inequality and attempting to interrupt the way schooling works to (re)produce social stratification. We are also aiming to contribute to recent debates about the way schooling might contribute to social sustainability, since for us social sustainability is code for social justice through education.

The work we report on in this chapter is an inquiry-based exploration of pedagogies of engagement of students who have historically been disenfranchised by schooling. We describe and reflect on an action-research project in a second-chance high school that serves one of the most disadvantaged regions in Australia. At the time of our inquiry, the school's surrounding community was in the middle of an urban renewal process intended to change the mix of public to private housing, giving rise to increased uncertainty over living arrangements and the displacement of many families in public housing. The school serves a very broad cross-section of the community, from full-time employed people studying specialised subjects at night, and young mothers who make use of the child-care centre and the *Learning Together** program, as well as young students who have either dropped out, drifted off or otherwise been excluded from school (Smyth & Hattam 2004).

Specifically, we report on an action-research investigation conducted by Peter into a program referred to as the *Literacy Package*, which provides opportunities for students with learning difficulties and or disabilities (who may also lack basic skills) to develop literacy, numeracy and ICT skills. The students ranged in age from 16–60, often having left school at an early age with literacy levels equivalent to Years 2–4 (ages 7–9). They enrolled in this program to improve their skills so they could gain meaningful employment or improve their ability to read to their children and complete everyday tasks. Many of the students lacked confidence and found it difficult to ask for assistance, speak to other people and take risks with their learning. This meant that they often did not have independent learning skills. As well, they often were apathetic about their own learning and about issues occurring on their own doorstep. The program had two interacting aspects: one taught by Peter that focused on learning skills applicable to everyday literacy and numeracy;

---

* The school provides a child-care centre for children aged 1 week to 5 years. The *Learning Together* program helps families to develop positive relationships and literacy skills in their children through play and having fun.

the other, taught by a colleague, focused on structured literacy lessons using a phonics program called *Sound Way*.

Peter's action-research project (Kemmis & McTaggart 1990; Lankshear & Knobel 2004; McNiff et al. 1996) focused on the challenge of negotiating learning experiences that will engage adult students fully in the curriculum. The study aimed to explore whether specific classroom activities and practices that involved students in personal and local issues of significance – that is, 'making the community curricular' – would engage and motivate them, while also developing contextualised literacy and communication skills. Associated questions included:

- *What funds of knowledge do students bring to the learning experience?*
- *How well does this knowledge enrich their learning experiences?*
- *How can such funds of knowledge be a resource for curriculum design?*
- *How can students' knowledge and understanding of their own communities be developed and made more relevant to their own learning?*
- *Can this approach raise students' civil and social consciousness and responsibility while improving their skills so that they can have the power to interact with society?*
- *In what ways can a students-as-researchers approach be a catalyst for further learning?*

The project built on Peter's earlier attempts to improve these students' literacy outcomes and involved a typical classroom research project; for example, asking students to use the Internet to research and prepare a report. This approach resulted in reports of varying quality and only rarely motivated students. A further refinement involved opening up the topic to negotiation by the students, with a close link to students' interests and lived experiences. Although this approach addressed the issue of interest and engagement – some students had some very good ideas and research topics – it failed because many students did not have the literacy skills to develop the topics successfully. The intervention we report on here was an attempt to address these issues and was structured in two phases.

In Phase 1, the students were expected to examine the local school community. Their task was to photograph areas, structures and issues that they liked, or disliked and would like to see changed. This concept was used as an opportunity to develop some key literacy skills and processes, such as using digital cameras, file systems and other software. The task was supplemented with some well-timed teaching in the form of mini-lessons to individuals or very small groups. Students were required to present their photos along with a description of where it was taken and why they took it. This gave students an opportunity to commence some structured writing tasks. Some students reported that this was the most they had ever written at school (at least at secondary school). The final product of this exercise was the presentation of their work to the class. Some of the students took this further and developed a proposal, including costing and plans for the changes, which was presented to the appropriate workgroup in the school.

In Phase 2, the students photographed areas in their own communities that they identified as being problematic. They once again said what they liked, disliked and wanted to see changed. They then used these ideas and photos to refine their problem areas and select one they could work with. They were then required to revisit these places and take more photos. Students used a combination of digital and disposable cameras, and uploaded and scanned images for use in their final work and, after being shown how to use Microsoft Photostory, they arranged their photos. The writing task began with students being required to outline their concerns using dot points and match these to photos. This helped to give them a clear direction and purpose. Students were then asked to prepare scripts, using Microsoft Word, that elaborated on each of the dot points, and to narrate and record these. Extra features such as transitions and music could also be included. The final aspect of the program involved using their findings to research an aspect of their work in the hope of formulating a resolution to, or exploring more deeply, the matter of concern.

Rather than report on what happened in each phase, we draw out four of the key themes that emerged from the study, especially those that relate to pedagogy. These are: (1) negotiating the curriculum; (2) widening the audience for assessment; (3) connecting the curriculum to students' life-worlds and (4) students-as-researchers. In the spirit of action research, our comments are couched in the form of critical reflections on practice, pointing to problems and possibilities, rather than attempting to proffer answers. We conclude by exploring the promise of the approach for disrupting the ways in which the curriculum works to reproduce social stratification.

Negotiating the curriculum

Previous attempts by Peter to engage students in negotiating the curriculum involved minimal student input. Given that the main focus was to expose students to literacy tasks, Peter had not placed a strong emphasis on the content, and so incorporating students' personal experiences and background knowledge was not fully considered. Rather, Peter had sought to structure their tasks by introducing them to the genre of report writing, modelling the use of mind maps and brainstorming to develop and expand their ideas. He also reinforced the need to use key terms that emerged from their mind maps to conduct searches on the Internet. Although these strategies had helped students to construct a written report, they did not fully engage or motivate students.

Peter was alerted to the question of student engagement by a student who bred parakeets and had chosen to write a report that used his extensive knowledge of that activity. The student had low literacy skills and demonstrated the sorts of traits expected of a student who had a negative view of school. His engagement and participation up to that point had been minimal. However, this topic engaged him and he actively sought more information from the Internet, took photos of his own birds and identified other rare varieties on the Internet. Peter began to reflect on the power and importance of negotiation. As Cook (1992: 16) pointed out:

> [l]earners will work harder and learn better, and what they will learn
> will mean more to them, if they are discovering their own ideas, asking
> their own questions.

Of course, taking up the challenge of negotiating curriculum involves sharing power in the classroom – not only providing students with the chance to be involved in deciding what they will study, but just as importantly, giving them a say in what they will not do. All too often negotiation is understood as allowing students to choose from a set of options, but not to reject the options outright and select an area of their own (Boomer 1992). The assumption that the teacher is the holder of all the information and that students are there to learn from teachers is a difficult one to disrupt. But then, sharing power can also be resisted by students, especially secondary school students, who 'expect the teacher to wield the power' (Hyde 1992: 71). By contrast, real negotiation involves everyone being a teacher and learner at different times. As Freire (1972: 53) so powerfully observed:

The teacher is no longer merely the-one-who-teaches, but himself is taught, in dialogue with students, who in turn while being taught also teach. They become jointly responsible for a process in which all grow.

Peter's initial unit of work involved negotiating topics drawn from students' life-worlds. Once again, the focus was on the use of research (not specifically web-based), and the development of literacy skills. Such an experiment in negotiation revealed that not all students were interested in their immediate communities, and anyway many did not possess the necessary literacy skills to make sense of their discoveries or to articulate them. In addition, students chose topics they could not manage, and with so much choice it was impossible for Peter to supply the literacy support needed for success. These individual projects also hampered peer discussion across projects and did not encourage students to compare their discoveries. There were no real opportunities for students to support each other and bounce ideas around; nor did students possess the necessary skills to enable them to research successfully in the short time frame allowed. A longer lead-up time is needed to develop these skills and to allow students to gain confidence. Along with these shortcomings, the students were also very reluctant to engage in community research due to a deficit view of their own community. It was clear that more work was required to explore and challenge students' views.

This critical review of what was learnt from the first attempts at negotiation resulted in the design of the *Literacy Package* (outlined earlier), an approach that not only allowed literacy skills to be better developed, but also provided an opportunity to negotiate student-driven content within clearer parameters. In the case of the *Literacy Package* unit, the negotiations were about issues at school (for Phase 1) and then issues in their own communities (for Phase 2). To help students define the selected issue, the first phase allowed negotiation over the photos taken at school, using the four questions suggested by Cook (1992: 21) as the framework for negotiation:

- *What do we know already?*
- *What do we want and need to find out?*
- *How will we go about finding out?*
- *How will we know, and show, that we've found out when we've finished?*

The structure of the *Literacy Package* allowed students to explore what they already knew about the area by asking their own questions and developing a line of inquiry based on their own interests, experiences and curiosity. What they decided to explore, and the outcomes of their research, was based entirely on their own interest. The exchange of ideas by individuals allowed issues to be further clarified and explored. During Phase 2 – researching their community setting – the negotiation became more involved. Group discussions focused on local community issues and this helped to refine students' thoughts as they distilled specific issues from the sometimes very broad issues presented. During this stage, Peter noticed that students had a tendency to see the selected issue as a complaint, rather than engage in a constructive conversation about its causes, effects and possible solutions. Explicit questioning and frequent reference to the purpose and intended audience of their work encouraged students to frame the issues they were considering in a more constructive way.

Our experiences confirmed the power of negotiation. Indeed, we believe that in schools that are struggling to improve learning outcomes for the most disengaged students, the question is not whether to negotiate, but how to manage the negotiation process to make rigorous learning possible. And because the negotiation process cannot be pre-packaged, there is also the challenge of negotiating with each new class. Negotiating the curriculum involves active listening and observation of 'off-task' activities to determine students' interests and find approaches that may achieve successful outcomes. Working within a framework of guiding questions is also very helpful. Our inquiry also revealed that even very reluctant learners can be engaged through negotiation and, on that basis, are open to constructive feedback about their learning. Being open to student input into curriculum design can be an opportunity for what Comber and Kamler (2005) called 'turn-around pedagogy', involving changes in both teaching and student learning.

Providing an audience to whom students can perform their learning

Disinclined students often do not see the purpose or relevance of school and formal education. They recognise the need to develop their reading and writing skills, but school literacy programs often fail to motivate them to achieve this end. Students often ask questions such as: Why do we need to do this? Who cares about this anyway? How will this help me get a job? and if the answers are not convincing, then schoolwork is resisted. Hence providing a convincing purpose for schoolwork is a crucial aspect of engagement. This problem of purpose was partly addressed in the design of the *Literacy Package* by using assessment approaches to provide an authentic audience to whom students could present their learning.

Each phase of the *Literacy Package* had a focus that was directly linked to an audience. Phase 1 focused on issues related to the school, with the audience being the Principal and management group, and the Grounds Committee. Phase 2 was linked to the proposed urban redevelopment of the local community. Students were asked to prepare a presentation to give to members of the local council and the developers to provide input to the project. Although many were very nervous at the prospect of doing this, it acted as a motivational tool and increased the relevance of their work. From the outset, discussions emphasised the audience and the presentation format. The ability to refer to the audience during the preparation of student material was an opportunity to ask questions that would make students think about what they were writing. Peter would often ask: 'Is that the best way of presenting information for …' or 'What information do you think they need to know?' and 'What photo could you take that would best make your point?'[†]

Strong connectedness through researching funds of knowledge

There are many advocates of the view that all learning begins with the integration of students' knowledge into the subject matter being taught (e.g., constructivist learning theory). Crucially, this view is predicated on not trivialising either students' or academic knowledge. Unfortunately, such a view of learning is rarely more than empty rhetoric, especially in high schools. Part of the problem is the paucity of models of teaching that integrate these two knowledges. We believe that what is needed is a 'complicated conversation' (Pinar 2004: 9) to make student life-world knowledges 'pedagogically viable' (Moll 2005: 278).

[†] An afterword: we did not get the opportunity to meet with the council and developers to present the students' work, but we did present to each other and to other teachers. Since completing the semester, a consultancy group has been formed by council, and the students' work was presented to this group.

One promising approach that has been developed by Moll and his colleagues focuses on 'funds of knowledge', by which they mean those 'historically accumulated and culturally developed bodies of knowledge and skills essential for household or individual functioning and well-being', pertaining to 'social, economic, and productive activities of people' (Moll et al. 1992: 139) in local communities. Funds of knowledge include the 'social history of households, their origins and development ... the labour history of families ... how families develop social networks ... including knowledge skills and labour, that enhance the households' ability to survive and thrive' (Moll et al. 1992: 133). Moll and his colleagues proposed a curriculum approach that connects student learning to their life-worlds beyond school by making these funds of knowledge a central learning resource. In this approach, not only is community knowledge valued rather than marginalised or ignored, but students also become teachers as well as learners. Their cultures, backgrounds and experiences are valued and respected. This issue alone – valuing community – was a critical element of the way Peter designed the *Literacy Package*.

The problem for teachers is how this student knowledge is discovered in the first instance. Gonzalez and Moll (2002) described their approach, which involved ethnographic research into communities, as the starting point for curriculum design. In our view, expecting secondary teachers to commit the amount of time required to conduct community-based ethnographic research is unrealistic, involving, as it does, going into students' homes. In addition, adult students tend to be private and reserved about revealing too much about their own lives, and as a result of social pressures and long-term conditioning, many adults who live with poverty and disadvantage fear being judged by teachers or not valued. For many adult students these beliefs may be warranted, given the previous experiences they have had at school. Students take this memory with them into adult life and it becomes a very strong barrier to overcoming learning difficulties. An important part of Peter's inquiry was to explore methods that could be used to address this alienation and to open dialogue about personal and community issues which act as barriers to formal education.

Peter certainly did encounter difficulties in uncovering student knowledge. Some students did not want to engage in any dialogue about their lives, and indeed were disdainful about researching their local community. As Gonzalez and Moll (2002: 638) pointed out, 'the extended networks and social capital of students' may be very difficult to uncover and may, in some cases, be totally absent. And yet the idea of building bridges to funds of knowledge not only relies on discovering this elusive knowledge, but also on giving students the opportunity to share it with others. It is central to the idea of 'making community curricular' and of developing student confidence. In the *Literacy Package*, Peter's response to this dilemma was to begin by exploring the local community, with the students playing the role of guides, rather than individualising the process by visiting houses.

In Phase 2, Peter's use of neighbourhood visits offered vivid insights into the lives of his students and was an opportunity for students to share their own experiences. When Peter drove the bus through the areas in which they lived, students gained in confidence as they talked about their neighbourhoods. This was not only a great opportunity to develop close relationships and trust with students, but it also offered some very powerful insights into some of the serious difficulties faced by the students. They used this opportunity to talk about the photos they had taken and the matters they had identified in class. By the end of the program, what was most evident was the willingness of students to discuss issues constructively. They had shifted from complaining or whingeing, to identifying a problem and coming up with a solution. Our research clearly demonstrated how students' social and civic consciousness could be developed. Students brought a wealth of knowledge about their community into the work we did in class. This information was shared and became the conduit through which rich literacy tasks and the development of associated skills could be explored. The students' knowledge and associated discussions, rather than their low literacy skills base, became the focus, thus enhancing the learning of new skills.

Students as researchers of their own knowledge

Pedagogies based on the teacher as the font of all knowledge assume that 'learning becomes something gained through reading texts, listening to lecturers, or viewing videos' (Smith 2002: 586) and that student research is simply another assessment tool which reinforces knowledge presented by teachers. In this model, the classroom research task is not student generated and the outcomes involve, in most cases, a regurgitation of someone else's knowledge.

Our experience with this project suggests a more powerful model. It confirms the findings of other research that designing the curriculum around funds of knowledge so that students research their life-worlds and community problems, means that students become knowledge producers as well as knowledge receivers (Atweh & Burton 1995; Bland & Atweh 2007; Egan-Robertson & Bloom 1998; Thomson & Comber 2003; Thomson & Gunter 2007). In this approach, teachers support students to do their own research, which involves research training, gathering data, making meaning and devising representations of their findings. Such an approach requires a pedagogical emphasis that encourages student-centred learning by valuing student opinion, incorporating student views into action and giving students a valued and recognised role within their community.

The approach changes the curriculum from being a process that is teacher-centred, to one that is student-generated and democratic. Smith (2002: 589) described it as real-world problem solving where students play '... a pivotal role in identifying problems, selecting one as a class focus, studying its characteristics and dynamics, developing potential solutions and then organising and participating in efforts to solve the problem'. To support these elements in a democratic classroom involves a move from being teacher-centred to one which places the teacher in the position of facilitator, linking problems to the required curriculum and providing appropriate resources and support (Smith 2002). This approach to teaching validates the culture and experience of students' families by building on their existing knowledge. Students have the opportunity to connect with local people by sharing their results (Smith 2002).

The *Literacy Package* demonstrated many benefits of the student-as-researcher approach. Students engaged in ethnographic work during Phase 2 – identifying problems, photographing them and preparing dialogue to explain both the issues and possible solutions to them – and in the process began to develop a genuine interest in community issues and solutions to them. They shared discoveries with each other and willingly compared notes they had prepared on their own findings. Students also appreciated the potential for extending what they had found out by exploring other aspects of the topic. For example, as a direct result of her concern that the local council was not spending enough on parks and roads, one student extended her research to an examination of the budgets of different councils in order to examine how different organisations spent their budgets. She discovered that council revenue varied markedly between councils in very different socio-economic regions and she began to develop an appreciation of the unequal distribution of community resources and the reasons for this. During this process the student was developing her very limited skills in formal literacy, numeracy and the use of ICT for research purposes, as well as a greater appreciation of the importance of obtaining these skills.

Concluding comments

In this action-research project we explored the problematic nature of working with adult students to develop their literacy skills. The main barrier to engagement is external factors that distract students from continuing with their studies. Developing resilience can only be attempted when students are motivated by a desire to challenge their own behaviours. This project managed to engage and motivate the students. Two students in particular who initially failed to see the relevance of community research, eventually engaged in alternative projects during the second phase, attending on a very regular basis and improving their literacy skills.

The aim of the research was to improve students' learning outcomes. The most important outcome for this group of students was the development of literacy skills, and the confidence to take risks and understand that there is no shame in making mistakes and not knowing how to do something. Using a very structured approach to research and modelling, this approach to negotiating the curriculum proved successful for all students in Phase 1. There were high levels of engagement, peer mentoring and support. The usual slow start to the year was avoided by jumping straight into taking photos and doing the real work. This was enhanced by the display of competent IT skills by the younger students. As a consequence, Peter was able to provide one-on-one support to other students. The real strength of Phase 1 was the opportunity this new approach gave students to get out of the classroom and get to know the school. In addition, Phase 1 also gave Peter an excellent opportunity to work with individual students and get to know them. The interactive dialogue was usually very positive, and was an opportunity for all students to produce a well-formatted and well-written piece of work.

During an interview at the end of the semester some students indicated that they had initially found the task of critically talking about the school daunting. Many felt uncomfortable doing this, mainly due to uncertainty about what Peter would say and how he would react to their criticism. They also had an opportunity to begin to explore the idea of providing critically constructive feedback that was not directed to an individual. Many appeared ambivalent about their ability to provide constructive feedback.

Phase 2 saw students exploring beyond the school gates. This proved to be far more complex and demanding. It required detailed negotiation with students to get them to feel comfortable doing the work. However, following this negotiation, the students did improve their literacy and communication skills, along with gaining an increased awareness of their own community. One significant outcome was the development of the confidence to take risks with their learning and a desire to pursue further learning. For those students who participated in Phase 2, there was a clearly demonstrated link between their on-task engagement and literacy outcomes. Students commented positively on how the project influenced their literacy development. The project was a means through which students could have a voice on matters that they considered important.

In the opening of this chapter, we highlighted the problem of interrupting the way schooling works to (re)produce social stratification. Unfortunately this problem has either fallen from the policy agenda in recent years, or else is being dealt with through policies of devolution and 'cruel accounting' (Thomson 1998). We think that ignoring the problem of educational inequality, or treating it with therapies that devalue the public school sector and damage teachers' work, will fail to bring about any substantial changes in what is an obstinate problem. What Peter's work highlights though, is the possibility of making a difference to the educational future of historically disadvantaged groups of young people. When all is said and done, the solution to educational inequality must involve the work of teachers and students in classrooms; it is a curriculum and pedagogical problem. We think that the project of disrupting the socially (re)productive function of schooling needs to be described in terms of a positive project that brings the curriculum and pedagogical work of teachers to the fore. In this regard, Peter's work offers a few lines of flight that require further research and development. These include:

- negotiating the curriculum, with a key issue being how to negotiate in ways that enable rigorous learning
- providing more authentic purpose and audience for student learning, with a key issue being how students can be assisted to see the purpose of their learning
- providing learning that is strongly connected to student life-worlds, with a key issue being how to make student life-world knowledge pedagogically viable
- offering students opportunities to produce their own knowledge.

References

Atweh W & Burton L, 1995, 'Students as Researchers: rationale and critique', *British Educational Research Journal*, 21(5), 561–575.

Bland D & Atweh B, 2007, 'Students as researchers: engaging students' voices in PAR', *Educational Action Research*, 15(3), 337–349.

Boomer G, 1992, 'Negotiating the curriculum', in G Boomer, N Lester, C Onore & J Cook (eds), *Negotiating the Curriculum: Educating for the 21st Century*. Falmer, London, pp 4–15.

Bourdieu P, 1998, *Practical Reason: On the Theory of Action*. Polity, Cambridge, UK.

Comber B & Kamler B, (eds) 2005, *Turn-around pedagogies: literacy interventions for at-risk students*. Primary English Teaching Association (PETA), Newtown, NSW.

Cook J, 1992, 'Negotiating the Curriculum: Programming for Learning', in G Boomer, N Lester, C Onore & J Cook (eds), *Negotiating the Curriculum: Educating for the 21st Century*. Falmer, London, pp 15–31.

Egan-Robertson A & Bloom D (eds), 1998, *Students as Researchers of Culture in Their Own Communities*. Hampton Press, Cresskill, New Jersey.

Fitzgerald RT, 1976, *Poverty and Education in Australia: Commission of Inquiry into Poverty*. 5th Main Report, Australian Government Publishing Service (AGPS), Canberra.

Freire P, 1972, *Pedagogy of the Oppressed*. Penguin, London.

Gonzalez N & Moll L, 2002, 'Cruzando el Puente: Building bridges to funds of knowledge', *Educational Policy*, 16(4), 623–641.

Hyde S, 1992, 'Sharing power in the Classroom', in G Boomer, N Lester, C Onore & J Cook (eds), *Negotiating the Curriculum: educating for the 21st Century*. Falmer, London.

Kamler B & Comber B (eds), 2005, *Turn-around Pedagogies: literacy interventions for at-risk students.* Primary English Teaching Association (PETA), Sydney.

Kemmis S & McTaggart R (eds), 1988, *The action research planner* (3rd edn). Deakin University Press, Victoria.

Lankshear C & Knobel M, 2004, *A handbook for teacher research: from design to implementation.* Open University Press, Buckingham.

McNiff J, Lomax P & Whitehead J (eds), 1996, *You and your action research project.* Routledge, London.

Moll L, 2005, 'Reflection and Possibilities', in N Gonzalez, L Moll & C Amanti (eds), *Funds of Knowledge: Theorizing Practices in Households, Communities and Classrooms.* Lawrence Erlbaum, Mahwah, New Jersey.

Moll L, Amanti C, Neff D & Gonzalez N, 1992, 'Funds of Knowledge for Teaching: using a qualitative approach to connect homes to classrooms', *Theory into Practice*, 31(2), 132–141.

Pinar W, 2004, *What is Curriculum Theory?* Lawrence Erlbaum Associates, Mahwah, New Jersey.

Smith G, 2002, 'Place-based education: Learning to be where we are', *Phi Delta Kappan*, 83(8), 584–594.

Smyth J & Hattam R, 2004, 'Dropping Out', *Drifting Off, being Excluded: Becoming Somebody Without School.* Peter Lang, New York.

Teese R, 1998, 'Curriculum hierarchy, private schooling and the segmentation of Australian Secondary schooling, 1947–1985', *British Journal of Sociology of Education*, 19(3), 401–417.

Thomson P, 1998, 'Thoroughly Modern Management and a Cruel Accounting: The Effects of Public Sector Reform on Public Education', in *Going Public: Education Policy and Public Education in Australia.* Australian Curriculum Studies Assoc, Canberra, pp 9–17.

Thomson P & Comber B, 2003, 'Deficient 'disadvantaged students' or media-savvy meaning makers? Engaging new metaphors for redesigning classrooms and pedagogies', *McGill Journal of Education*, 38(2), 305–328.

Thomson P & Gunter H, 2007, 'The methodology of students-as-researchers: valuing and using experience to develop methods', *Discourse: studies in the cultural politics of education*, 28(3), 327–342.

Chapter 9

The RPiN challenge for principals:
achieving a 'pragmatic-radical' balance

❦❦❦❦

Lew Zipin, Marie Brennan and Brendyn Semmens

The RPiN context

The school, as a key common institution for our society, has been under contestation since its inception as part of the public realm. In contemporary times, struggles over the purposes of schools continue, with strong emphases on the roles of education in shaping learners as 'human capital' for 'workforces of the future', and mere glimpses that education is also for other purposes, such as citizenship. Secondary schools situated in Indigenous, rural/remote and/or high-poverty communities are under most stress. Adding to this stress are populist assaults from political sources, interest groups and media. Rather than recognise the complexities of conditions in which these schools operate, such populism derides them for alleged failures in staff competence to produce student achievements in literacy, mathematics, science and computing (Nelson 2004; see also Snyder 2008) and other 'competencies' which make learners 'work ready'.

The 10 secondary schools that were partners in the *Redesigning Pedagogies in the North* (RPiN) project are situated in just such a region, where resources for building social and economic sustainability are meagre. Principals in those schools are subject to multiple claims on their efforts: to meet student and family needs; to support staff and ensure their continuing professional development; to position the school to gain enrolments; to comply with the state policies and procedures; to address the community more broadly; and to build school capacity to develop education that challenges learners in ways suited to the times.

In this chapter, our working definition of 'social sustainability' is the creation of democratic workplace contexts for both staff and students, with particular emphasis on building curriculum that connects student lives beyond school to their school learning. We explore challenges to the work of the principal – both systemic, and those posed by RPiN – including resource shortages; differences (sometimes conflicting) between teacher and leader standpoints on how to teach adolescents; and the difficult yet vitally needed creation of sustainable professional learning communities. Our perspectives as authors emerge from differing standpoints in the equation of educational practice: a former principal of one of the RPiN schools, and two members of the university-based research team. However, we share commitment to building strong social justice through schooling, particularly in forming democratic communities in schools and across to their surrounding social contexts.

Current times, especially in contexts of poverty and other limiting conditions, pose acute dilemmas for leadership, often difficult to address, let alone resolve. We begin by placing RPiN principals in their context before moving to consider the nature of the kinds of pressures and challenges that the RPiN project itself brings to schools and their principals. These challenges can be seen to express vexed issues of our time; but they also present opportunities to re-think towards an alternative politics of leadership. In pursuing such re-thinking, we deploy Boomer's (1999: 53) conception of 'pragmatic radical' educators, defined as 'people who can read their world critically and with subtlety, who can act individually and collectively to defend themselves and change things, and who have a highly developed drive to bring about higher levels of justice and democracy in the society'. We consider how aspirations to be a 'pragmatic radical' leader run into pressures that can jeopardise both terms of this challenging synthesis: that is, mere 'realism' that accepts limiting constraints, rather than *pragmatism* that explores what works to expand possibilities; and mere complaint about contextual limits that does not hold to '*root*' (i.e. '*radical*') values that can sustain pragmatic efforts over time to change educational contexts in the direction of those values. We finish with reflections on the role of educational leaders in new times, with suggestions for future efforts to connect lives and learning.

The principals' context

RPiN engaged all 10 secondary schools in the three districts that comprise Adelaide's northern suburbs. The initial impetus for the project came from conversations between some of the university researchers and some principals from these schools. Eventual project partners included the state government's Social Inclusion Unit (SIU) of Premier and Cabinet, and the Australian Education Union (AEU) SA; but, along with the practising teachers, the key *organisational* partner to the university researchers was the Northern Adelaide Secondary Schools Principals Network (NASSPN). Having formed prior to RPiN, NASSPN comprised all 10 northern suburb principals, who sought to create an association through which they could work together to understand and negotiate the challenges they shared.

This cooperative move was a significant achievement in a policy climate driven by 'student/family choice' and other neoliberal premises that incite competition between schools to win students, provoking quests to establish superiority of market image and community reputation, compared to rival schools. Within this atmosphere of policy-induced competitiveness, the NASSPN group of course was not without its internal conflicts, as competition between schools was necessary for school survival: principals struggled with how best to attract students, and how best to work with community expectations. Still, NASSPN brought a track record of coordinated efforts in many initiatives contributing to northern suburbs educational improvement, addressing a wide range of issues identified as endemic to the region: high levels of unemployment, poor infrastructure, low levels of qualifications and other social problems (Cappo 2009). The region drew strong focus from federal and state governments, parallel with the RPiN project, including a federal 'sustainable regions' program focused on employment and infrastructure, housing redevelopment and action on health and education as priority areas. For schools in the area, retention levels to the end of school were among the lowest in the state and significantly under the national average. Two RPiN secondary schools were in the top category of 'disadvantaged schools' and several others appeared in the next two categories.

While such targeting meant that there was a level of additional funding provided, most of the schools were working in physical plant that was run down, with comparatively low levels of resources, including IT access. Perhaps more importantly, teaching staff turnover was substantial, often

40% per annum. Replacement was usually from newly graduated teachers who needed induction to, and professional experience with, the school, the community and the region. Moreover, during the three years of the project there was a 70% changeover among the principals (including the third author of this chapter).

Such conditions make it difficult for schools to maintain constructive future-oriented momentum. The burden of building towards sustainable democratic classroom contexts for teachers and students – including a level of cohesion and shared purposes between school and community – is disproportionately difficult in this group of schools, which are asked to do more with less, under conditions almost designed for failure. The principal's position is thus a critical one in developing both a climate of support and challenge for staff, and the conditions of orderly routines within which staff and students can carry out their work – a framework within which it is then possible to make alterations, experiments and researchful interventions.

NASSPN principals all recognised that the middle years is a transitional pivot point when alienation often sets in and can set up a trajectory toward early school leaving – and thus the importance of reinvigorating the design of middle years teaching-and-learning. All the schools had histories prior to RPiN in developing middle schooling approaches – involving curriculum, pedagogy, assessment and organisational redesigns – to create stronger student engagement in learning. Middle schooling approaches have evolved, first and foremost, as efforts to meet learning needs of students whose embodiments, in poverty-associated life conditions, present challenges to mainstream educational approaches. RPiN aimed to work with small groups of teachers from each school to develop curriculum and pedagogies that link student work to 'funds of knowledge' from their lives outside of school; and to scaffold from these learning engagements with knowledge that has familiarity in their lives outside school, to learning success in mainstream academic knowledge.

Yet in putting alternative approaches into practice, schools uncover systemic and institutional (or school–cultural) obstacles to their best efforts to meet students' learning needs, requiring further program redesigns. The principals helped to pinpoint some of these obstacles in reflective feedback provided through yearly interviews as well as formal and informal meetings with the University team. The sections that follow are all based on principal observations, from their standpoints in school system governance, in school leadership and in the RPiN project.

Principal perspectives on teachers struggling to work with students from high poverty backgrounds

Principals, along with the project teacher-researchers, were quick to observe significant teaching and learning problems associated with students from an area of high poverty. Principals noted in particular that there was disjuncture between views among their staff about what this implied about needs to adapt their teaching, and obstacles to changing the culture of the school to accommodate those views about teaching differently. They recognised the conservative force of accumulated institutional habits and how hard it was to change such habits, which are often reinforced by student and parent expectations about what school is supposed to achieve. For example, principals noted that, while many teachers share an ethic of care for students, and recognise the importance of supportive relationships, critical reflexivity is not as strong an ethos as needed in the professional culture of teaching staff. As such, an ethos of 'caring relations' often stays limited to a focus on building student 'self-esteem' through non-educative kinds of 'caring', without analysing how inherently intelligent learners are held back by systemic obstacles that could be worked around through innovative educational efforts.

Without blaming staff, principals could see that, in struggling with the challenges of students who do not embody the cultural capital for success in mainstream academic work, some teachers build up *deficit* views of these students (as if they lack capacities for schooling that are inborn and cannot be taught and learned in school). Although teaching predominantly working class students, some teachers hold onto the norm of a middle class learner, which can lead to value clashes with students and inhibit openness to potential learning assets in their cultural life-worlds. When facing difficult student 'behaviours', some teachers too readily fall back on institutional habits such as worksheets, rather than work on building stronger learning relations and more effective pedagogical strategies.

Principals suggested many reasons why it was difficult to tackle teachers' divergent, sometimes contradictory, and sometimes 'deficit' views of teaching northern suburb learners. Long-term staff, closer to retirement, sometimes become set in their ways, resisting new approaches which might suit changing times and contexts; while new staff often needed support to survive their first year or two of teaching before they are ready to integrate into, and contribute to, a school-wide approach. High staff turnover; demands of marketing, meetings and other 'non-teaching' activities; the traditional subject-oriented specialisms of the secondary school, and more, all worked against middle years alternative approaches such as integrated curriculum, fewer teachers per year covering more areas, or taking up literacy and numeracy needs across subject areas. Secondary teacher tendencies to focus largely on mastering subject content, and not as much on whole-school organisation, building professional identity, or understanding of diverse students as culturally distinctive learners. More than this, they tend not to engage in development of crucial pedagogical innovation strategies.

Such insights were common among principals, but they often felt hamstrung in working proactively to build a different school ethos or culture. Without a substantial team of experienced staff, professional orientation to the routines of school life needed constantly to be under construction. In schools from areas of high poverty, there is a larger than usual need to cope with events that disrupt working-day patterns of schooling, for example sickness, industrial action, student suspension, misunderstandings between organisers, fights, damage to equipment, or even double room bookings (Thomson 2002). Such factors have a deleterious impact on trying to sequence and support change in a structured way. They get in the way of building overall staff capacity to talk and think together, to develop shared perspectives on whole-school approaches for working with students from diverse high-poverty backgrounds, and so on.

Perceived systemic obstacles to widespread reform

Northern area principals and their teachers reported the experience of 'reform fatigue' (Lingard et al. 2003), having had many reforms externally imposed, abandoned and newly imposed – usually without consulting school staff. Constant urgencies to improve and reform usually appear as small initiatives that unsettle school plans without making constructive differences. In consequence, some schools are now fairly resistant to seeing possible virtues of new teaching and learning approaches. Under the pressure of systemic factors such as workload, managerial surveillance and the need to be continually accountable for small rafts of initiatives, teachers can become inclined to operate behind closed doors.

> For a couple of years now we've tried, as an admin I suppose, to create more of an open-door culture within the school, constantly talking to people about 'Why is your door shut?' … and the ability for all of us, like a colleague walking past, and so on, to move in and out of each other's environment … The way I remember it … back there in the early '80s … it was a collaborative experience … [whereas now] for some people it's 'We've had the door open, but it's the noise coming from the other classrooms' … There's one wing downstairs where there's a sense of 'We're a bit of a team down there and this is how we go about doing it', but then you get five classrooms upstairs where, you know, it's like five Balkan states, and 'This is how we operate, and this is the demarcation line'. (Principal 9)

Such 'balkanisation' inhibits cultural development of substantial and trusting staff relations, professional community and an ethos of collaborative innovation. This meant that many teachers would perceive RPiN as one more demand, even if the school was formally a partner in the project, and some colleagues enthusiastic about their work in it. And for principals, difficulties in finding regular relief teachers to cover teacher absences also made it hard to release staff for RPiN project roundtables and other functions, or to increase the size of participating teacher teams.

> It's a sad fact that, somewhere along the development of South Australian secondary schools … the embracing of the positives derived from … professional critical self-reflection has evaporated and there are I think some valid reasons for that, but let's not get into that. The point about that is that [School 5], like a lot of other places, has not had a culture of professional dialogue, a culture of talking to another about how I'm going and how I could grow professionally, you know, all of those things are part of the means by which you, you know, move the RPiN agenda along. (Principal 5)

A significant systemic obstacle to middle school curriculum and pedagogical redesigns – especially along RPiN project lines – was formal disjuncture between middle and senior years curriculum and assessment regimes. The latter is dominated by pressures on students to achieve a certificate that selectively privileges university-oriented criteria, inducing narrow conceptions of 'rigour', and divorced from relevance to students' lives.

There is a difference in the middle years between the focus on kids constructing their own learning and the very different and more prescriptive syllabus that you inevitably get in [senior secondary programs], which is still very heavily dominated by the universities ... so teachers are constantly juggling that. (Principal 3)

[There is] the age-old problem I suppose of, or challenge, or the debate between middle schooling pedagogy, if you like, and the demand for rigour in the senior school? You know, that's the criticism of [middle years experiments]. (Principal 2)

Staff in some of the RPiN schools tended to specialise in one or other level, making it harder to develop a whole-school approach. Fears of poor results in impending senior-year regimes would often seep down into the subjectivities of both teachers and students in middle years classrooms, inhibiting receptiveness to alternative organisational and educational approaches that might more readily engage learners making the transition from primary to secondary schooling. Further, as schools cannot themselves employ staff, there is a difficulty in retaining teachers who show promising middle schooling dispositions and capacities.

Despite the 'trickle-down' of senior certificate pressures that privilege university-oriented criteria, many northern suburb students tend to cluster in 'vocational' subjects, in preference to 'academic' pathways. However, vocational curricula on offer are often limited to a narrow 'skills' focus that does not challenge students, further alienating rather than engaging them. This is exacerbated by limited job opportunities in northern suburb areas, and lack of infrastructure such as public transport, such that vocational offerings were even more limited than in schools elsewhere. Orientation around 'vocationalism' can reinforce deficit views of students among teachers, and among students as well, feeling themselves 'on the lesser path' yet not capable of the 'higher' academic path. In this way, the sense of being a 'lesser' school can accumulate, affecting staff and students with weakened morale. This is not helped by sensationalist media coverage – a constant feature of work in Northern schools, interrupting teachers' sense of worth, and often unsettling the community. Several schools bore negative media scrutiny over long periods, which made it hard to sustain readiness to take innovative risks.

Principals also identified various work 'intensification' factors that reduce time for professional dialogue among staff about how to improve teaching and learning. For example, even as teaching workloads intensify due to understaffing, workloads increase in administrative and other dimensions of school operation as well. Increased competition with private schools, and federal introduction of a new Australian Technology College in the area, induced schools to widen their zones of enrolment, involving staff in competitive marketing and liaisons with primary schools, all adding to work intensification. Increasing complexity of school organisation and timetables (for example to allow schools to share teachers, students to travel to other schools, or introduction of vocational subjects) also reduce the time available for staff to share collective professional development and meetings. Particularly, principals note decline in the sort of professional development that is neither 'individual' (for which the school system allocates 37.5 hours per year) nor system-determined, but staff-owned, purposeful and cohesive, working to generate whole-school ethos and strategies.

Principals noted increased competing demands for resource use to achieve long-term goals, as a larger number of long-term goals come to require attention: both those school staff would endorse, and unwelcome but system-imposed accountabilities. Even more troubling is that some of these relate to plans of past principals and governing councils which may no longer be seen as realistic or even desirable by current incumbents.

In contemplating all these factors of school complexity in 'new times', principals reflected on changes in their own work profile, including the debilitation of their capacities to *lead* rather than merely *manage*. They commented how 'new managerialism' imposes a 'CEO model' that pulls the work time of principals and other school leaders into addressing accountability and marketing demands, thereby lessening their presence in the school and their capacity to lead in developing curriculum and pedagogy, and in mentoring staff – especially early career staff – in these core educational dimensions of their work. As well, changing governance structures meant less autonomy at the school level in core educational determinations, reinforcing declines in collegiality and collaboration.

> It's just that there is a really difficult culture … I mean, most of us who are principals of the schools in the RPiN project have come from teaching in the late '70s, early '80s … and here we are going through the experience 'It used to be this way, and now it's this way'… And whether

> it's stated or left unstated, one of the issues is DECS' style change, and the sense of as a profession where we've been taken and how we're being attended to, and whether our needs are met ... is really a complex issue ... [W]hen we shifted to the Chief Executive model, and basically political appointments, it really has changed, I reckon, possibly irretrievably, the nature of public education, because we're forever going like this, you know ... the government of the day needs this ... 'Here's the agendas, these are the targets, go away and meet them', not 'What are you doing well, how can we build on it?' (Principal 9)

Witnessing these shifts in the work of being a principal, younger staff are then less drawn toward career moves into positions such as coordinators, weakening school leadership at middle levels, which is urgently needed to build and sustain revitalised middle years programs. Principals testify to the squeezes of '*middle* manager' positioning: that is, in system terms, they sit at the 'top' of the school, but 'below' the Education Department, in an era of governance through increased centralised power that effects itself through policy steering from 'above' while devolving responsibilities 'down below' (Taylor et al. 1997) – including demands that are often ideo-politically motivated, out of touch with grounded conditions, and so impossible to meet in any real sense. Principals nonetheless must work in a tense 'middle', functioning as both managers and colleagues, mediating between downward demands to which they must be account-able, and lateral or upward needs of teachers, students and surrounding communities to which they feel duties of care.

How principals fielded the RPiN challenges

The array of institutional and broadly systemic obstacles to changes in meaningful social-justice directions can easily induce principals and teachers into overly 'realistic' – rather than *pragmatic* – responses. Such 'realism' thwarts Boomer's (1999: 58) vision of 'pragmatic radical' educa-tors because, as against a serious pragmatism, it focuses on 'the chronicle of failure' rather than 'on the achieved and achievable'. Even more significantly, against a serious *radicalism*, it dissipates sense and conviction about values and aspirations that speak to deep-rooted purposes of educa-tion: at best, it tinkers with 'outcomes' in systemic terms, but denies 'the power of imagination and dreaming of better worlds' (Boomer 1999: 58).

Still, multiple initiatives and demands, competing for scarce resources of leadership (and teacher) time and attention, characterised the context into which the RPiN project entered principals' considerations. In ambivalent and sometimes anxious ways, principals both recognised and deflected – they both greeted and resisted – the more radical promises and expectations for curricular and pedagogical change that RPiN brought into their purview within their schools. In crucial ways, the principals saw their own and their schools' involvement with RPiN through the sober prism of difficult squeeze-plays with which they coped as middle managers. That RPiN posed a radical form of curriculum and pedagogy – working against the grain of 'business as usual' – carried both positives and negatives from principals' perspectives. Most principals could see the potential for RPiN to help them grow professional learning communities in at least small groups inside their school. A stunning testimony was offered by a principal who, in an interview two years into the project, comments on how pedagogies of participating teachers in his school were affected by RPiN:

> I remember being involved in the RPiN project, you know, last year, and one of the pieces of excitement that seems to have come out each year is the giving of permission to teachers to explore kids' environment and learning, and the teachers learning something … The whole business of teaching … is much more doable when the teacher is consciously saying 'I can learn something valuable from you students', and I can remember one of the teachers going out and filming spots … Out in the physical community, spots that were important to the students … social points, congregations points, … and from that you get a little story, a little anecdotal description of the context … and that gave the teacher the chance to learn something about the kids' environment, so the kids got to say, to perform their learning … and that [gave] capacity to know, the teacher's wanting to know that as a basis to say 'Well, what learning can I do in maths, or music, knowing this about the kids' environment?' … The sheer learning of that environment was the most valuable thing they [teachers] will do in terms of a tool of intimacy and relationship building, and purpose to the teaching. So that's the type of PD that's there … the sort of nice conceptual basis, is that the teachers celebrated learning from the students, which is all about power too … it's about sharing power, and sharing the role of the teacher … [A]nd it's not necessarily the information that's important; it's the honouring of the

[life]world by the teacher ... you can understand the role of the teacher,

honouring the learning or the world of the young person. (Principal 6)

This lyrical and passionate articulation, by a busy principal who could chronicle all the internal and contextual factors that made RPiN a difficult challenge, suggests that, within his positional consciousness, the evidence of his senses does sustain images of deeply alternative ways to practise teaching and learning. In a context of highly complex socio-political-economic environments that work against such sustainability, RPiN has supported his professional identification with radical leadership possibilities. Yet, in other moments of the same interview, this very principal protested that RPiN was merely one project among many and could not be given priority in the school.

We are doing a whole lot of other things that are on the board, and the RPiN one is not getting the air play and the PD it needs to make it ... So I think one of the things that has to come out is that you're either doing RPiN or nothing else, because the demography of schools is so demanding that you can only really take one focus, big focus, at a time ... and the focus that this school is taking at the moment is international accreditation, and I don't know whether you're aware of that or not ... But if I wasn't doing international accreditation then, in fact, where would my focus be? ... It would be the middle school, because that's where the greatest need is at the moment, it really is. (Principal 6)

Such protestation, in a 'realist' voice, dampens the sense of radical potential to achieve significant and long-term change. Not only does the school juggle many initiatives, but they are not commensurate in quality or focus, ranging from those stemming from Departmental instructions (e.g., an inquiry into how to improve maths and science test scores); those ensuing from school improvement efforts (e.g., roundtable assessments); those following market-competition impulses (e.g., instituting a middle years International Baccalaureate), and so on. We think it fair to say that, in all the 10 secondary schools, RPiN could not claim precedence over such other initiatives and agendas, many preceding RPiN in time, and many more mainstream than RPiN's orientations – which then can start to seem 'off the deep end' rather than getting to a radical heart of educational matters. Sometimes these initiatives could connect to RPiN – but thinning its radical impulse – and sometimes they were greatly contradictory to RPiN vectors of educational experiment. The principals 'heard' the promotion of RPiN through these prior and multi-agenda filters; and, in the interviews, they needed the university team to understand their sense of limits, from where they stood.

> The striking thing for me … is that this is an organisation that is … not crumbling, but I mean we are doing so much … The Council of International Schools stuff, the RPiN stuff, the roundtable assessment stuff that connects with RPiN; we're involved in a Learning to Learn project … you know, we're just so bloody busy doing that, the professional learning aspect [from RPiN] is more implicit than explicit at the moment. (Principal 9)

In some interview moments, principals were almost apologetic and confessional in tone, acknowledging that they had not given RPiN deep attention.

> It's been potentially a very useful device. I don't think we've exploited it enough in terms of giving the people that are doing it enough kudos in front of the staff … I'm a bit remiss … for whatever reasons, probably a lack of time, I don't think we've done that very well with staff here. (Principal 4)

Some acknowledged that they had neglected conversing about RPiN, and supporting its developments, even among the few teachers from their school who participated in the project. All the more marginal was building broader professional development around RPiN.

> What I have not, what we haven't done very successfully … is adopt an agenda that says 'How do we instil this stuff in others?' … I'll be honest, we haven't by design set an agenda that says, um, you know, what these guys are doing is going to drive some really critical stuff about what we're going to do across the board. (Principal 5)

Making RPiN a whole-school project to realise its social justice potential was perhaps too large a step – as suggested by the principal who, quoted above, had so lyrically appreciated 'the type of PD that's there', and how it had made the whole 'business of teaching … much more doable' among his RPiN teachers.

> I'll be blunt, and – it's making a difference for individuals, and the issue I know how is that translating into leadership capacity, or leadership inclination, or leadership pedagogy, so at the moment we have had two teachers last year involved in the project, and two teachers this year, and … that has tended to be what the project is about. And so really it has

been good for the immediate people around them … but in terms as a major strategy in the school for redefining what middle schooling is, we're not there yet. (Principal 6)

To make RPiN initiatives sustainable required developmental effort and time. First the participating teachers had to learn together, through RPiN roundtables, how to design curriculum and pedagogies that connected learning to students' life-world funds of knowledge. Then these teachers, and university researchers, needed to communicate with school leaders and share in developing broader professional development. Both the RPiN principals and their university partners expressed desire to build such sustainability. However, they did not find time or resources to undertake the difficult pragmatic challenges of building conditions under which teacher professional learning communities – given momentum in RPiN roundtables – could develop and expand over time within the schools (especially given problems of staff and principal turnover).

In terms of social justice, the most radical commitment expressed by principals was to a vision of middle years change in curriculum and pedagogy, seen as vitally important for retaining students who otherwise typically leave school in Year 10. In pre-RPiN conversations, this was the key impetus that had led them into a partnership project with the university researchers. Across the interviews, principals indicated frustrations over persuading teaching staff towards this purpose. One principal, speaking about his efforts to institute a middle years roundtable portfolio assessment, accompanied by critical reflection about curriculum and pedagogy among teachers, made the following observation:

[I]t was really interesting watching [teachers'] responses because, there we are, reliant on teachers engaging in thinking about the lives of the kids with whom they work … and almost half of them are bailing out, and that goes back to … the inevitable tension between middle years and the senior years, and … *en masse* teachers spoke with their feet. It doesn't matter how they get to our school, they invariably want to end up in the senior years; and what we're hearing from our primary colleagues is it doesn't matter how they get to the primary school, they invariably want to go down to 3–4, maybe 5, and steer clear of the 6–7 situation, and so what we've got in the north … is an absence of interest and commitment around working with kids in the middle years. (Principal 9)

Another principal suggested that, given the institutional trajectories of teachers, such a situation is not surprising:

> Teachers all went to university, all went to uni, right, really value the degree and the profession, would really like to teach students who would be going to uni. They all talk about, even though the middle school teachers love their middle school, they all want to teach senior school because this is like you're not a real secondary teacher until you've actually taught ... your special subject ... Thank goodness [SACE] is changing because ... the recommendations will definitely meet more of the needs of our students ... but the specialist subject teachers still tend to have the content headset. (Principal 10)

The above are just a few citations from many interview passages in which all 10 RPiN principals struggled with challenging dilemmas of making the middle years work. However, they generally articulated a moderately progressive, rather than radical, approach to middle schooling – for example, 'constructivism', 'integrated curriculum', and so on – while noting how institutionalised norms and statuses tend to work against it, for example, 'subject specialism', a 'content headset' and university selectivity. Despite their recognition that Years 8 and 9 are transitionally pivotal for engaging and retaining students who do not embody 'winning' cultural capital for mainstream academic success, they also indicated ambivalences and doubts about how deeply middle years schooling could be shifted. Our interpretation is that 'progressive' methodologies struck a 'safer' register, in relation to what they sensed that 'the system' would bear given the stalwartly mainstream 'rigours' of syllabi for senior secondary certification. The principals all signalled hope, with sensible scepticism, that an impending review of the secondary certificate would attenuate its constraining forces. Some crucial questions, then, are:

- How can the middle years provide *engagingly* 'rigorous' (or – our preferred word – *vigorous*) curriculum for students?
- How can/should senior years curriculum expectations be accommodated, finessed and/or resisted?
- Can experiments with middle years redesign push beyond a middling 'constructivism', in social justice directions that shift from a deficit to an *asset* view (Comber & Kamler 2005) of northern area students' innate intelligence and cultural knowledge?

RPiN was thus often taken up by principals more as a helpful bit of professional development than as a deeply aspiring social justice project. To the degree that principals took RPiN on, they tended to adapt it to more mainstream initiatives within the school that adulterated the strong social justice logic of substantial curriculum and pedagogy redesign. Our reading is that the principals all sincerely saw worth, for their schools, in the social justice logic of RPiN. However, this was superseded by doubtfulness as to how far a radical logic could be worked into school agendas. For the take-up to *work* in strong social justice terms, it had to be central to the school's overall goals; but such centrality did not fit the less radical orientations of most school-based agendas.

Balancing *pragmatic* with *radical* practicalities

Although sporadic, we have shown interview moments in which principals let institutionally habituated guards down and revealed appreciation of the social justice import of life-world based learning redesign. Current historical conditions are pervaded with neoliberal-*cum*-managerial times constraints upon principals (and students and teachers), which also limit educational projects such as RPiN. Within schools, such projects need pragmatic-radical leaders who find ways to incorporate deeper approaches to curriculum and pedagogy within the professional development of their staff (Hayes et al. 2006). Yet readiness to articulate, let alone enact, such a vision is more often than not repressed within the climate of pressures and limits that principals inhabit. Moments of radical imagination are hard-won amidst the impossible tasks of trying to resolve unresolvable tensions. The tense problematics we have drawn out from the principal interviews exist within a changing educational context, both broadly in terms of policy and governance structures, and locally in terms of the shifting challenges facing secondary schools in high-poverty locales. For those pursuing socially just reform against such systemic and institutional grains, 'pessimism of the intellect', as Gramsci (1971) puts it, is indeed warranted. But to balance this intellectual scepticism (not cynicism), as Gramsci also puts it, 'optimism of the will' is also a necessary attitude for sustaining the vitalities of hope.

Boomer's concept of 'pragmatic radical' educators and leaders has perhaps never been more urgently needed than now for exploring connections between leadership, democracy and sustainability. The concept also carries rich suggestion of leadership dispositions and strategies by which public secondary school principals could lead in creating professional environments that sustain innovative curriculum design and teaching practice beyond the tenure of any individual principal. Leadership needs the willing creation and nurturing of an environment of personal and professional trust, the transparency of consultation and decision-making, an equitable flow of information, responsiveness to the ideas and suggestions of others so they are able to influence directions taken by the group, and the courage of all participants to reflect upon their practice and work together to grow further.

The RPiN project offered opportunities for some of these elements to flower. The challenge for teachers to learn together and construct new and sustainable forms of pedagogy was taken up in RPiN roundtables, and within all schools, each in different ways. Some groups of RPiN teachers have influenced some colleagues in seeking to sustain curriculum and pedagogical redesign beyond the life of the project; and some principals have expressed ambitions to build professional development that extends RPiN concepts and methods to more staff. RPiN thus helped to strengthen capacities of educators to reflect on their practices and relations, as teachers and leaders.

Principals embody pivotal positions in the life of the school. Aspiration to both *pragmatic* and *radical* professional environments is thus crucial; and we argue that there is a reciprocal relationship between sustainable democratic schools and the style, strategies and approaches embodied in being a principal. In elaborating his idea of the 'pragmatic radical educator', Boomer noted the danger of the term being misunderstood, demonised and trivialised. However, he also underscored the concept's potential to provoke new thinking about the role of educators, and to motivate enrichments in professional identities, relations and practices. Principals in the RPiN gave testimony to struggles at the fine line between a self-limiting 'realism' that does not risk reaching for what might bring 'failure' or sanction, and a self-expanding *pragmatic radicalism* that seeks institutional shift and re-building such that schools can live up to more socially just purposes. If it is hard for principals to give the full vigour of professional pro-action to the latter, it is also hard for them to accept the self-limitation of the former. Into this tense matrix, RPiN brought its challenges – challenges which had implications for principals' own professional identities and opportunities for reflection on them.

References

Boomer G, 1999, 'Pragmatic radical teaching and the disadvantaged schools program', in B Green (ed.), *Designs on Learning: Essays on Curriculum and Teaching*. Australian Curriculum Studies Association, Canberra, 49–58.

Cappo D, 2009, *People and Community at the Heart of Systems and Bureaucracy*. Social Inclusion Unit, Government of South Australia, viewed 25 February 2009, <www.socialinclusion.sa.gov.au/files/DPC%20SASII%20book_final%20approval.pdf>

Comber B & Kamler B (eds), 2005, *Turn-around pedagogies: literacy interventions for at-risk students*. Primary English Teaching Association (PETA), Newtown, NSW.

Farrington F, nd, *Social Exclusion in South Australia: Analysing the South Australian Labor Party's Social Inclusion Initiative*, viewed 3 February 2009, <unijobs.holon.net/socialexclusion/farringtonsocialexclusionsapolicy.pdf>.

Gramsci A, 1971, *Selections from the Prison Notebooks*. International Publishers, New York.

Hayes D, Mills M, Christie P & Lingard B, 2006, *Teachers & schooling making a difference: Productive pedagogies, assessment and performance*. Allen and Unwin, Crows Nest, NSW.

Lingard B, Mills M, Christie P & Hayes D, 2003, *Leading learning: making hope practical in schools*. Open University Press, Buckingham, England.

Nelson B, 2004, *Strengthening the Teaching Profession: launch of the National Institute for Quality Teaching and School Leadership*, Media release, viewed 1 April 2009, <www.dest.gov.au/minimas/live/nelson/2004/06/n721030604.asp>.

Newman L, Biedrzycki K, Patterson J & Baum F, 2007, A *Rapid Appraisal Case Study of South Australia's Social Inclusion Initiative*, viewed 3 February 2009, <www.socialinclusion.sa.gov.au/files/SEKN_SA_Case_Study_Final_Report.pdf>

Snyder I, 2008, *The literacy wars: Why teaching children to read and write is a battleground in Australia*. Allen & Unwin, Sydney.

Taylor S, Rizvi F, Lingard B & Henry M, 1997, *Educational policy and the politics of change*. Routledge, London, New York.

Thomson P, 2002, *Schooling the rustbelt kids: making the difference in changing times*. Allen & Unwin, Crows Nest, NSW.

Chapter 10

Promoting a culture of inquiry

in schools and education systems

◇◇◇◇◇◇

Alan Reid and Bill Lucas

Introduction: community-based schooling & the importance of inquiry

There are two broad themes that recur throughout this book. The first relates to the power of organising the curriculum about and through the life-worlds of young people by drawing on the funds of knowledge that they bring from these life-worlds into the classroom. The second relates to the pedagogical challenges that such an approach produces and how these can be addressed through practitioner inquiry. In each chapter, the authors describe the ways in which they tried to systematically investigate problems, issues, dilemmas and puzzles as they arose in classroom contexts.

It is clear that the relationship between community-based pedagogies and practitioner inquiry is not serendipitous, but symbiotic. A curriculum which starts from the life-worlds of students is, by definition, a curriculum which is located in the specificity of context. It is one about which it is difficult to generalise. The issues that arise in its practice are usually idiosyncratic, not only to the classroom and community environments, but also to the individuals involved. This means that teachers need to have the wherewithal to respond to issues as they arise, in a thoughtful and systematic way, using data, theorising and strategising – sometimes on the run, sometimes over longer periods of time. In short, inquiry must be central to their professional being.

The educators in this book all demonstrated practitioner inquiry in action, albeit using different methods to deal with very different problems.

At the same time as they grappled with community-based pedagogies, the teachers monitored the processes and outcomes and identified emerging challenges, always in a spirit of exploration, always tentative about their new insights and ready to subject these to critical scrutiny. This is not to romanticise what happened. The stories they tell have not been sanitised – they are 'warts and all' accounts of the demands and difficulties, indeed the struggles, of working in this way. But it is to say that powerful pedagogies of the kind outlined in this book need to be nurtured by educators with inquiring sensibilities. That of course, is easier said than done.

In this chapter we want to conduct an inquiry into inquiry. We will argue that if inquiry is to become an established part of professional life, strategies are needed for embedding it into the educational life of schools and systems of education. We will draw on the sorts of approaches described in this book to suggest some possible strategies. However, first we need to explore the obstacles to practitioner inquiry, particularly as they relate to curriculum work, and it is to that task we now turn.

The dominant model of curriculum development & change*

The dominant model of the official curriculum understands teachers as being central to the processes of implementation, but not to those of conceptualisation and development. That is, in many, even most, education systems, teachers are treated as classroom technicians whose task it is to put in place the ideas and plans of 'experts' in education bureaucracies, rather than as professionals with important knowledge and insights. This approach is institutionalised in the structures and processes of education systems.

> The extent to which the curriculum development process marginalises teachers varies depending on the system. In some education systems there is a history of widespread consultation; in other jurisdictions consultation is limited and there is a high level of central prescription. Nevertheless, in both cases consultation about a curriculum document is invariably about the detail – it rarely involves input into the process of conceptualisation. (Smyth et al. 2000)

There are a number of problems with this dominant model. First, the model impoverishes the knowledge base of educational policy making.

---

* Parts of this chapter are based on a paper written for the South Australian Department of Education and Children's Services (DECS) in 2004 (see Reid 2004).

By foregrounding bureaucratic knowledge, the model marginalises arguably the most consequential knowledge in an education system: school-based knowledge-in-action, that is, the curriculum knowledge produced by educators in the context of working with children and young people.

Second, the model promotes a facade of change. All that has been discovered about educational change over the past 20 years tells us that change occurs when those whose practice is the focus of the change are involved in the process of challenging and rethinking the assumptions and theories on which their practice is based (e.g., Fullan 1999, 2001, 2003). Unless this happens, imposed change in the form of a new curriculum 'product' is simply filtered through the lens of established beliefs and practices, and is colonised by that practice. The same things are done, but with new labels.

Third, the model limits the possibilities for real improvement, because it does not encourage educators to focus on deepening their understanding of teaching and learning. Indeed the model promotes superficial forms of external accountability. It understands accountability to mean closing the gap between what is developed (or aspired to) centrally and the outcomes in schools. When the gap refuses to close, the fault is invariably located with schools and/or the students and families who inhabit them. This is a spurious form of accountability, because it encourages educators to hide issues and problems, rather than discuss them openly. In so doing it contributes to the privatisation of professional practice. Real accountability is transparent because it is based on genuine attempts to deepen understandings about teaching and learning through inquiry and research, discussion and debate, in an atmosphere of collaboration and trust. By contrast, imposed accountability encourages educators to generate smokescreens to hide problems.

Finally, the model fails to recognise the rapidly changing contexts in which schools operate and for which they are preparing students. Contemporary times have been labelled as the end of certainty (e.g., Kelly 1992). That is, the confident 20th century belief that scientific rationality can solve all our social and environmental problems has been replaced by a recognition of the greater complexity and ambiguity of late modern times. In all countries, economic, political and cultural globalisation, accompanied by new communication technologies, are affecting every aspect of our lives, including work, family, communities, citizenship and identities. The nature and speed of this change has significant implications for education because it redefines the capabilities that are needed to live in the 21st century.

Kress (2000), for example, maintained that the scale of change calls for an 'education for instability', by which he meant that education for the stabilities of well-defined citizenship or participation in stable economies must be replaced by education for creativity, innovativeness, adaptability and ease with difference and change. This form of education would seek to promote in children and young people the capabilities to generate new ideas, insights and explanations to meet the challenges of the changing contexts in which they live.

In the 21st century educators must have the capacity to question their routine practices and assumptions and to investigate the effects of their teaching on student learning. Many of the issues facing educators today are bound by context: they are not amenable to universal solutions. That is, educators face the considerable challenge of designing curricula for local contexts that are flexible enough to address the rapid growth of knowledge, and that recognise the increasing religious, cultural and ethnic diversity in their student populations (Hattam & Prosser 2008; Hattam & Zipin 2009). Educators must have the capacity to be always deepening their understandings of teaching and learning through reflection and inquiry. After all, if the task of educators is to develop in children and young people the learning dispositions and capacities to think critically, flexibly and creatively, then educators too must possess and model these capacities.

This argument suggests that the dominant model of curriculum change, where educators are excluded from the development process and expected simply to implement programs developed by others, is no longer tenable. From this perspective, educators are professionals who are able to theorise systematically and rigorously in different learning contexts about their professional practices – including the problems, concerns, dilemmas, contradictions and interesting situations that confront them in their daily professional lives; and can develop, implement and evaluate strategies to address these. That is, educators are understood as people who learn *from* teaching rather than as people who have finished learning how to teach (Darling-Hammond 2000).

If being an educator in the 21st century centrally involves the capacity to inquire into professional practice, then the notion of inquiry is not a project or the latest fad. *It is a way of professional being.* The question that needs to be asked is not whether educators should be inquirers into professional practice, but how they can become more so and how they can continue to build their inquiry capacities throughout their professional lives.

Unfortunately, the dominant model of educational change creates its own logic and dynamic and entrenches the view of educators as technicians whose job it is to implement policy and curriculum products designed by others. Ironically, one of the responses to the speed of change has been to strengthen this view. Thus, often the reaction to the challenges of the new environment has been to devise and implement more curriculum packages and construct more accountability mechanisms. It is an old response to a new challenge. What is an alternative?

Rethinking the role of teachers in curriculum decision-making: an inquiry-based approach

The various examples given in this book suggest a viable alternative to the dominant approach – one that addresses the kinds of issues outlined above by establishing a system that organises its practices on and around inquiry and research. Such an approach would mean moving from the well-worn path of producing and imposing more curriculum products as a response to new challenges, to an approach that focuses on the strengthening of professional capacity and agency. This does not mean that an official curriculum and educational resources are not needed. Rather, it suggests that these should be more responsive to the insights and issues that emerge from a process of inquiry and research. That is a very different dynamic. But before explaining how this might work, it is important to briefly sketch out what we mean by inquiry.

There is a wealth of research and professional literature that focuses on inquiry, also referred to as reflective practice. Its beginnings can be traced back to the work of John Dewey (1933, 1958), but it is in the last 20 years that the literature has burgeoned through the writing of scholars such as Cochran-Smith and Lytle (1993), Farrell (2004), Goodman (1984), Lankshear and Knobel (2004), Schon (1983, 1990) and Zeichner and Liston (1996). Elsewhere, one of us has defined inquiry as a 'process of systematic, rigorous and critical reflection about professional practice, and the contexts in which it occurs, in ways that question taken-for-granted assumptions' (Reid 2004: 4). It involves educators pursuing their 'wonderings' (Hubbard & Power 1993), seeking answers to questions or puzzles that come from real-world observations and dilemmas. Its purpose is to inform decision-making for action.

The case studies in the preceding chapters suggest that there are a number of aspects to inquiry. First, it is not just a technical activity with just a focus on how to make existing practices more efficient. It has two other important dimensions. There is a conceptual dimension which involves educators analysing the reasons for actions taken, such as examining the theory behind their practices and exploring alternatives; and there is a critical dimension which involves justifying what is done in relation to the moral, ethical and socio-political issues associated with practice, and looking at the external forces and broader social conditions that frame it, in order to gain greater understanding (Farrell 2004). Critical forms of inquiry such as those described in this book are centred on a commitment to equity and social justice which seeks to further our understandings of the complex notion of pedagogical justice (Hattam & Zipin 2009). The sorts of reflective questions asked recursively by the authors in relation to their curriculum projects authors were:

- What are we doing in relation to this practice, issue, question, puzzle?
- Why are we doing this? (e.g., What theories are expressed in our practices, and whose interests do these represent?)
- What are the effects of these practices? Who is most and least advantaged?
- What alternatives are there to our current practice? Are these likely to result in fairer outcomes? What will we do? How will we monitor these changes in order to assess their outcomes?

Second, inquiry can be undertaken individually, but it is often more powerful when it is conducted with invited others – perhaps other teachers who are interested in the same puzzle, or people outside the school. Students can be involved as inquirers, learning about their learning, and about inquiry, as they explore an inquiry question with their teacher. Reflection is best conducted as a social rather than a solitary practice, and our ideas can be better clarified when we talk with others about them. As Osterman and Kottkamp argued:

> Because of the deeply ingrained nature of our behavioural patterns, it is sometimes difficult to develop a critical perspective on our own behaviour. For that reason alone, analysis occurring in a collaborative and cooperative environment is likely to lead to greater learning. (Osterman & Kottkamp 1993: 25, quoted in Zeichner & Lister 1996: 18)

The wider the question, the wider the scope for involvement of others. An inquiry question that relates to a whole institution demands a much broader involvement. Of course there might be a small number of staff members who lead the inquiry, but they will find ways of involving those who are affected by the issue – such as other staff, students, parents and community members – both in the process of reflection as well as data gathering.

Third, it is important to look outside the classroom or school for ideas and inspiration for exploring the inquiry process. Inquiry can be an exercise in navel gazing, or it can offer a powerful means to look outwards, engaging with the ideas, innovations and research that are circulating in the wider society. Looking at what others do in similar situations, or what the research says, are all ways to expand the possibilities of inquiry.

Fourth, inquiry is not simply series of steps or procedures. While it involves logical problem-solving processes, it also involves intuition, passion and emotion (Prosser 2008). It is a holistic way of working and responding to the many issues and dilemmas that emerge in any school. Teachers who are inquirers will never announce that they 'do' inquiry, thus separating the activity from their professional being. Rather they might describe how they work – that is, the ways in which they inquire into their professional practice and how they are always striving to develop and expand their capacity to inquire.

Fifth, there are a number of ways in which a process of inquiry or reflection can be facilitated. Over the course of their professional careers, educators might develop a suite of inquiry approaches and techniques, a sort of inquiry toolbox. The key characteristic of each approach is that it is designed to facilitate critical reflection. Inquirers will continue to work to sharpen these through practical experience and reflection, and to add to the toolbox by exploring new approaches. A number of the approaches are outlined in the case study chapters and include action research, critical dialogue and systematic observation and reflection.

It is crucial to recognise that each of these approaches to inquiry has a body of research literature behind it. This suggests that a teacher's inquiry toolbox needs to be built slowly. It might involve selecting an approach, reading about it, talking with people who have used it, experimenting with it and documenting experiences, and reflecting on the approach itself as well as on the focus of the inquiry in which it has been used. No education system or single institution should simply exhort people to engage in inquiry without an acknowledgement that inquiry skills need to be built thoughtfully and systematically.

Finally, inquiry will only flourish in conditions that promote it. Since the basis of inquiry involves critical self and collaborative reflection on established practices and routines, it presumes an institutional and system-wide environment of *trust*. That is, educators must feel that they can reveal aspects of their practice about which they have concerns and explore these without it counting against them. A culture of inquiry would also be one that celebrates discussion and debate. However, such an environment demands a number of characteristics, not the least of which is that such debate is civil and respectful, where people are not put down or demeaned for holding different viewpoints, where there is a genuine attempt to listen to all, not just the most powerful, and where there is a plentiful supply of good humour. It also demands that participants are open-minded and willing to subject their beliefs, assumptions and practices to critical scrutiny.

For decades now across the world, many teachers, individually and collaboratively, have engaged in practitioner inquiry, exploring their teaching systematically and critically. And yet, as is demonstrated in this book, despite the power of the learning from such practices, inquiry is still not something that is at the centre of professional practice. It is still a struggle. Why is this? In our view it is because the focus has tended to stay on the teacher, without a consideration of the wider context in which they operate. It is clear from the chapters in this book that educational institutions as a whole (such as schools) and the central and regional offices of education systems, must model and support inquiry if it is to flourish. Unless this happens, inquiry approaches are destined to be constrained at best and fail at worst. Wells (1994) argued that inquiry and research should focus on whole-school improvement, not just individual classroom improvement, and that the policies, artefacts and processes of the school should be consistent with inquiry. This is an important step, but in our view going beyond individual educators to the whole-school level is still not sufficient.

The operations of education bureaucracies are also fundamental to inquiry and research. Unless they are consistent with inquiry, they can actually work against it.

This means more than just supporting schools. It also means developing policies and processes for such areas as planning and reporting, curriculum and human resources in ways that both model and sustain inquiry and research. In another context, Fullan (2003) called this a 'tri-level reform' model where the interaction between the layers of the system mutually reinforces the reform aspirations. This may seem obvious, and yet despite plentiful rhetoric, to our knowledge there are no education systems in the world that have consciously organised their policies and practices such that they are consistent with inquiry and research. It is time to challenge the dominant model of educational change, based as it is on understanding educators to be passive implementers of policy, rather than active agents in policy development. But, the question remains, what is the alternative?

Teachers & processes of educational change: an alternative approach

We propose an alternative model based on a system-wide culture of inquiry and research where teachers are engaged in inquiry and research into the problems, puzzles and dilemmas associated with their educational practice; and where the new knowledge and the issues that emerge from this process are fed back into classrooms and schools, deepening learning and reinvigorating professional discussion and debate. But more than this, an alternative model would ensure that there are structures and processes in place that enable the insights and issues from inquiry to be aggregated and responded to at the various bureaucratic levels such as Regional and Central Office levels.

It is important to understand that this model is not a 'bottom-up' approach. Rather, it is constructed on an understanding that there is an iterative dynamic between the various layers of the system. The government will of course continue to express priorities, although these may be affected by the knowledge that schools produce and the issues that they identify. But much of the work of Central and Regional Offices will involve responding to the implications of what is emerging from inquiry and research in relation to these priorities – meeting the needs identified by schools for learning and professional development resources, providing arenas in which the new professional knowledge can be shared and debated, altering policies to reflect new insights, and so on.

It is also important to understand that the model does not suggest that the only worthwhile knowledge is that produced in schools. Far from it. The sort of inquiry being argued for here will draw on innovative ideas and the latest research produced in other contexts and other countries. For example, there would be a close relationship with university researchers, with a constant and interactive flow of people and ideas. But the difference is that these ideas would not be imposed. They would be treated as part of an inquiry mix, examined systematically by those engaged in the business of educating.

It will be apparent that the dynamic here is very different from that of the dominant approach. Rather than responding to the challenges of contemporary times by mandating policies developed in places removed from classrooms, this model focuses on the processes of inquiry and research, and the development of professional capacity through a dynamic relationship between schools, communities, regions and the Head Office. The products and policies follow. Put another way, the sorts of questions that schools ask in this model are: Where is our current practice in relation to this priority? What are the issues? What do we need to know about these and how will we get the information? What support do we need? What should we aim to achieve? How will we know if we get there?

In our view there are a number of advantages of this approach. The model has the potential to:

- lead to genuine forms of accountability that are based on collaborative efforts to identify problems and their causes
- make the policy, plans and products of the bureaucracy more responsive to the needs of schools
- lead to genuine change because it is consistent with what is known about the factors that promote change

- provide a much richer source of information for education policy-making.

But just as there are many advantages, so too are there dangers. A key one of these is the danger of superficiality, where the concept of inquiry is embraced enthusiastically, but applied uncritically to many activities and issues without a deep understanding of the processes and the conditions that are needed for it to flourish. Other dangers involve loading on the expectation that teachers engage in practitioner inquiry, without providing the time and resources for it to occur; the imposition of centre agendas under the guise of inquiry; or failing to identify and remove the dominant or institutionalised practices that are inconsistent with, and so work against, a genuine culture of inquiry.

It is crucial that education systems move gradually, thoughtfully and systematically to build a culture of inquiry. So what needs to change if an education system is to move to this approach? What would be the characteristics of a system that was organised around inquiry and research? For us, an education system that has institutionalised inquiry and research as a way of being would have at least three characteristics that would be apparent at every layer of the organisation.

First, all staff in the education system would possess, and continue to develop, the skills and dispositions for inquiry and research. This would need to happen in a coherent and systematic way. For example, education systems might take stock of the resources and programs supporting the development of inquiry capabilities, and explore additional ways to refine and expand inquiry capabilities (Dana, Gimbert & Silva 2001). The latter might include working with the universities and their pre-service teacher education students to explore approaches to linking students to inquiry projects, thus providing an inquiry resource to schools and a valuable learning experience for students (e.g., Reid & O'Donoghue 2004).

Second, there would be structures and processes that model and support inquiry and research. An education system that was organised on a culture of inquiry would ensure that its structures and processes at every level, from the classroom to central office, are consistent with, and promote, inquiry. These would facilitate knowledge exchange, encourage discussion and debate, and promote evidence-based policy.

Third, the culture of an inquiry-based system would be one that consciously builds an environment that nurtures the conditions within which inquiry and research can flourish and grow (Smith-Maddox 1999). These conditions need to be a common denominator across the system. They include the nature of relationships and the conduct of professional conversations, and they need to be explicit and never taken for granted. The sorts of conditions that foster deep and transparent critical inquiry include ones that encourage discussion and debate involving the widest range of voices possible; reject certainty and dogmatism; are based on trust, where people feel free to talk about difficulties and concerns in their teaching; model inquiry at all layers of the system; and are respectful, tolerant and civil.

Concluding comments

Moving to a culture of inquiry will not happen overnight (Hargreaves & Goodson 2006). It will have to be built thoughtfully and systematically, and it needs to be sustainable. Hargreaves and Fink (2003) described this as moving beyond the notion of implementation of change towards the *institutionalisation* of change. For them, sustainable change involves building long-term capacity for improvement, not squandering resources on glamorous pilot projects that burn brightly for a time and then vanish without a trace. Sustainable change cultivates and recreates an 'educational ecosystem' that promotes diversity and creativity, not standardisation. In short, sustainable change:

> is enduring, not evanescent. It does not put its investment dollars into the high profile launch of an initiative and then withdraw them when the glamour has gone. Sustainable improvement demands committed relationships, not fleeting infatuation. It is change for keeps and change for good. Sustainable improvement contributes to the growth and good of everyone, instead of fostering the fortunes of the few at the expense of the rest. (Hargreaves & Fink 2003: 694)

This book documents the exciting pedagogical possibilities that are presented when the curriculum focuses on the life-worlds of students by bringing the community into the school and contributing to community building. In this chapter we have argued that such approaches, if they are to be sustainable, must be accompanied by systematic and critical practitioner inquiry that enables teachers to grapple with issues and dilemmas as they arise in local contexts. But inquiry is so fundamental to pedagogical change and innovation that it cannot be understood as only the responsibility of teachers. In our view, the challenge for contemporary times is for education jurisdictions to promote system-wide cultures of inquiry. Such systematic support would foster the conditions for practitioner inquiry to grow and flourish rather than mandate policies that ignore the vitality of local schools and their communities.

References

Cochran-Smith M & Lytle SL, 1993, *Inside/Outside: Teacher Research and Knowledge*. Teachers College Press, New York.

Dana N, Gimbert B & Silva D, 2001, 'Teacher inquiry as professional development for the 21st century in the United States', *Change: Transformations in Education*, 4(2), 51–59.

Darling-Hammond L, 2000, 'How teacher education matters', *Journal of Teacher Education*, 51(3), 166–173.

Dewy J, 1933, *How we Think*. Henry Regnery, Chicago.

Dewy J, 1958, 'How we think', in W Kolesnick (ed.), *Mental Discipline in Modern Education*. University of Wisconsin Press, Madison. (Original work published in 1933.)

Farrell T, 2004, *Reflective Practice in Action*. Corwin Press, Thousand Oaks, California.

Fullan M, 1999, *Change Forces: The Sequel*. RoutledgeFalmer, London.

Fullan M, 2001, *The New Meaning of Educational Change* (3rd edn). Teachers College Press, New York.

Fullan M, 2003, *Change Forces with a Vengeance*. Routledge Falmer, London.

Goodman J, 1984, 'Reflection and teacher education: a case study and theoretical analysis', *Interchange*, 15, 19–27.

Hargreaves A & Fink D, 2003, 'Sustaining leadership', *Phi Delta Kappan*, 84(9), 693–700.

Hargreaves A & Goodson I, 2006, 'Educational change over time? The sustainability and nonsustainability of three decades of secondary school change and continuity', *Educational Administration Quarterly*, 42(1), 3–41.

Hattam R & Prosser B, 2008, 'Unsettling deficit views of students and their communities', *Australian Educational Researcher*, 35(2), 15–36.

Hattam R & Zipin L, 2009, 'Towards pedagogical justice', *Discourse*, 30(3), 297–301.

Hubbard R & Power B, 1993, *The Art of Classroom Inquiry*. Heinemann, Portsmouth, New Hampshire.

Kelly P, 1992, *The End of Certainty*. Allen and Unwin, St. Leonards, NSW.

Kress G, 2000, 'A curriculum for the future', *Cambridge Journal of Education*, 30(1), 133–145.

Lankshear C & Knobel M, 2004, *A handbook for teacher research: from design to implementation*. Open University Press, Buckingham.

Osterman K & Kottkamp R, 1993, *Reflective Practice for Educators*. Corwin Press, Newbury Park, CA.

Prosser B, 2008, 'Critical pedagogy and the mythopoetic; a case study from Adelaide's northern urban fringe', in T Leonard & P Willis (eds), *Pedagogies of the imagination: mythopoetic curriculum in educational practice*. Springer Press, Dordrecht, pp 203–222.

Reid A, 2004, 'Towards a culture of inquiry in DECS' Occasional Paper Series, No. 1, South Australian Department of Education and Children's Services, Adelaide, pp 1–19.

Reid A & O'Donoghue M, 2004, 'Revisiting enquiry-based teacher education in neo-liberal times', *Teaching and Teacher Education*, 20(6), 559–570.

Schon D, 1983, *The Reflective Practitioner*. Basic Books, New York.

Schon D, 1990, *Educating the Reflective Practitioner: Towards a New Design for Teaching and Learning*. Jossey-Bass, San Francisco.

Smith-Maddox R, 1999, 'An inquiry-based reform effort: Creating the conditions for reculturing and restructuring schools', *The Urban Review*, 31(3), 283–304.

Smyth J, Dow A, Hattam R, Reid A & Shacklock G, 2000, *Teachers' work in a globalizing economy*. Falmer, London.

Wells G, 1994, *Changing Schools from Within: Creating Communities of Inquiry*. OISE Press, Toronto.

Zeichner K & Liston D, 1996, *Reflective Teaching: An Introduction*. Lawrence Erlbaum, Mahwah, New Jersey.

References

Aikenhead G, 2006, *Science education for everyday life*. Teachers' College Press, New York.

Anyon J, 2005, *Radical possibilities. Public policy, urban education and a new social movement*. Routledge, New York.

Apple MW & Bean JA, 1995, 'The case for democratic schools', in MW Apple & JA Beane (eds), *Democratic Schools*. Association for Supervision and Curriculum Development, Alexandria, Va.

Atkinson S & Nixon H, 2005, 'Locating the subject: Teens online@ninemsm', in *Discourse: studies in the cultural politics of education*, 26(3), 387–409.

Atweh W & Burton L, 1995, 'Students as Researchers: rationale and critique', *British Educational Research Journal*, 21(5), 561–575.

Australian Bureau of Statistics, 2005, *Schools Australia 2005 (ABS cat. no. 4221.0)*. Australian Bureau of Statistics, Canberra.

Australian Council of Deans of Education, 2003, 'The Role of the Teacher: Coming of Age', <www.acde.edu.au/publications.html> accessed 27/04/2009.

Baker J, 2002, *Window*. Walker Books, NSW.

Baker J, 2004, *Belonging*. Walker Books, NSW.

Balsiger PW, 2004, 'Supradisciplinary research practices: History, objectives and rationale', *Futures*, 36(4), 407–421.

Barratt R, 1998, 'Shaping Middle Schooling in Australia: A report of the National Middle Schooling Project', Australian Curriculum Studies Association, Deakin West.

Bauman Z, 1998, *Work, Consumerism and the New Poor*. Open University Press, Buckingham.

Beach R & Finders M, 1999, 'Students as Ethnographers: Guiding alternative research projects', *English Journal*, 89(1), 82–90.

Beane J, 1991, 'The Middle School: natural home of integrated curriculum', *Educational Leadership*, 49(2), 9–13.

Beane J, 1995, 'Curriculum Integrations and the disciplines of knowledge', *Phi Delta Kappan*, 76(April), 616–622.

Beane J, 1997, *Curriculum integration: Designing the core of democratic education*. Teachers College Press, New York.

Bennett K, Beynon H & Hudson R, 2000, *Coalfields regeneration: Dealing with the consequences of industrial decline*. The Policy Press, Bristol.

Berliner D, 2006, 'Our Impoverished View of Educational Research', *Teachers College Record*, 108(6), 949–995.

Berry T, 1999, *The great work: Our way into the future.* Bell Tower, New York.

Bland D & Atweh B, 2007, 'Students as researchers: engaging students' voices in PAR', *Educational Action Research*, 15(3), 337–349.

Boomer G, 1992, 'Negotiating the curriculum', in G Boomer, N Lester, C Onore & J Cook (eds), *Negotiating the Curriculum: Educating for the 21st Century.* Falmer, London, pp 4–15.

Boomer G, 1999, 'Pragmatic radical teaching and the disadvantaged schools program', in B Green (ed.), *Designs on Learning: Essays on Curriculum and Teaching.* Australian Curriculum Studies Association, Canberra, 49–58.

Bourdieu P, 1984, *Distinction: A Social Critique of the Judgement of Taste.* Routledge & Kegan Paul, London.

Bourdieu P, 1998, *Practical Reason: On the Theory of Action.* Polity, Cambridge, UK.

Bourdieu P & Passeron JC, 1990, *Reproduction in Education, Society and Culture (2nd edn).* Sage Publications, CA.

Bowers CA, 2005, *The false promises of constructivist theories of learning. A global and ecological critique.* Peter Lang, New York.

Brown ER, 2005, 'Introduction', in ER Brown & KJ Saltman (eds), *The Critical Middle School Reader.* Routledge, New York, pp 1–13.

Cameron S, 2003, 'Gentrification, housing redifferentiation and urban regeneration: "Going for growth" in Newcastle upon Tyne', *Urban Studies,* 40(12), 2367–2382.

Cappo D, 2009, People and Community at the Heart of Systems and Bureaucracy. Social Inclusion Unit, Government of South Australia, viewed 25 February 2009, <www.socialinclusion.sa.gov.au/files/DPC%20SASII%20book_final%20approval.pdf>

Carrington V, 2006, *Rethinking the Middle Years: early adolescents, schooling and digital culture.* Allen & Unwin, Crows Nest.

Centre for Labour Research, 2002, *Living and Learning: a profile of young people, employment, education and training in northern Adelaide.* University of Adelaide, Adelaide.

Childress H, 2000, *Landscapes of betrayal, landscapes of joy. Curtisville in the lives of its teenagers.* State University of New York Press, New York.

Chin J, 2001, *All of a place: Connecting community schools, youth, and community.* Bay Area Reform Collaborative, San Francisco, CA.

City of Playford, 2006, *City of Playford Wellbeing Plan 2006–2011.* City of Playford, Adelaide.

Cochran-Smith M & Lytle SL, 1993, *Inside/Outside: Teacher Research and Knowledge.* Teachers College Press, New York.

Cochran-Smith M & Lytle SL, 1999, 'The teacher research movement: a decade later', *Educational Researcher*, 28(7), 15–25.

Comber B, 2001, 'Critical literacies and local action: teacher knowledge and a 'new' research agenda', in B Comber & A Simpson (eds), *Negotiating critical literacies in classrooms*. Lawrence Erlbaum, Malwah, New Jersey, pp 271–282.

Comber B & Kamler B (eds), 2005, *Turn-around pedagogies: literacy interventions for at-risk students*. Primary English Teaching Association (PETA), Newtown, NSW.

Comber B & Nixon H, 2005, 'Children reread and rewrite their local neighbourhoods: critical literacies and identity work', in J Evans (ed.), *Literacy moves on: Using popular culture, new technologies and critical literacy in the primary classroom*. Heinemann, Portsmouth, NH.

Comber B & Nixon H, 2009, 'Teachers' work and pedagogy in an era of accountability', *Discourse*, 30(3), 333–345.

Comber B, Nixon H & Reid J (eds), 2007, *Literacies in place: Teaching environmental communication*. Primary English Teaching Association, Newtown.

Comber B, Thomson P & Wells M, 2001, 'Critical literacy finds a 'place': Writing and social action in a low-income Australian Grade 2/3 classroom', *The Elementary School Journal*, 101(4), 451–64.

Connell RW, 1993, *Schools and Social Justice*. Pluto Press, Melbourne.

Cook J, 1992, 'Negotiating the Curriculum: Programming for Learning', in G Boomer, N Lester, C Onore & J Cook (eds), *Negotiating the Curriculum: Educating for the 21st Century*. Falmer, London, pp 15–31.

Cormack P, 1996, 'Constructions of the adolescent in newspapers and policy documents: implementations from middle schooling', *South Australian Educational Leader*, 7(6), 1–12.

Cormack P, 2005, 'Place as a starting point for curriculum, pedagogy and assessment in the middle school', presentation to the *Middle School Association of South Australia Term 3 Conference*, Christian Brothers College Conference Centre, Adelaide, 9th September.

Cormack P, Green B & Reid J, 2008, 'River Literacies: discursive constructions of place and environment in children's writing about the Murray-Darling Basin' in F Vanclay, J Malpas, M Higgins & A Blackshaw (eds), *Making Sense of Place: Exploring concepts and expressions of place through different senses and lenses*. National Museum of Australia, Canberra.

Costanza R, 2003, 'A vision of the future of science: Reintegrating the study of humans and the rest of nature', *Futures*, 35(6), 651–671.

Cross R & Price R, 2002, 'Teaching controversial science for social responsibility:

The case of food production', in W-M Roth & JD Desautels (eds), *Science education as/for sociopolitical action*. Peter Lang, New York, pp 99–123.

Cumming J, 1993, *Middle Schooling for the 21st Century*. Incorporated Association of Registered Teachers of Victoria (IARTV), Jolimont, Victoria.

Dana N, Gimbert B & Silva D, 2001, 'Teacher inquiry as professional development for the 21st century in the United States', *Change: Transformations in Education*, 4(2), 51–59.

Darling-Hammond L, 2000, 'How teacher education matters', *Journal of Teacher Education*, 51(3), 166–173.

Davies B, 2000, *(In)Scribing body/landscape relations*. Alta Mira Press, Walnut Creek, CA.

Delpit L, 1993, 'The 'silenced dialogue': Power and pedagogy in educating other people's children', in L Weis & M Fine (eds), *Beyond Silenced Voices: Class, Race and Gender in United States Schools*. State University of New York Press, Albany, NY, pp 119–39.

Department of Education, Training and Employment (DETE), 2001, 'SACSA Society and Environment Curriculum', *South Australian Curriculum Standards and Accountability Framework*, DETE, Adelaide.

Després C, Brais N & Avellan S, 2004, 'Collaborative planning for retrofitting suburbs: Transdisciplinarity and intersubjectivity in action', *Futures*, 36(4), 471–486.

Dewy J, 1933, *How we Think*. Henry Regnery, Chicago.

Dewy J, 1958, 'How we think', in W Kolesnick (ed.), *Mental Discipline in Modern Education*. University of Wisconsin Press, Madison. (Original work published in 1933.)

Egan-Robertson A & Bloom D (eds), 1998, *Students as Researchers of Culture in Their Own Communities*. Hampton Press, Cresskill, New Jersey.

Elkins J & Luke A, 1999, 'Redefining adolescent literacies', *Journal of Adolescent & Adult Literacy*, 43, 212–215.

Elliott M, Sandeman P & Winchester H, 2005, 'Embedding Community Engagement: Northern Adelaide and the University of South Australia', in proceedings of *Engaging Communities*, the 4th Australian Universities Quality Forum, Sydney, 6–8 July, 55–61.

Esbjörn-Hargens S & Zimmerman M, 2009, *Integral ecology: Uniting multiple perspectives on the natural world*. Integral Books, Boston, MA.

Eyres V, Cormack P & Barratt R, 1993, '*The education of young adolescents in South Australian government schools: Report of the Junior Secondary Review*', Education Department of South Australia, Adelaide.

Farrell G & McCarthy M, 2002, 'Creating small urban schools: Expeditionary learning as school reform', in L Johnson, ME Finn & R Lewis (eds), *Urban Education with Attitude*. SUNY Press, Washington.

Farrell T, 2004, *Reflective Practice in Action*. Corwin Press, Thousand Oaks, California.

Farrington F, nd, *Social Exclusion in South Australia: Analysing the South Australian Labor Party's Social Inclusion Initiative*, viewed 3 February 2009, <unijobs. holon.net/socialexclusion/farringtonsocialexclusionsapolicy.pdf>.

Fensham PJ, 2003, 'What do the "All" need in science education?' in D Fisher & T Marsh (eds), *Proceedings of the Third Conference on Science, Mathematics and Technology Education*. Key Centre for School Science and Mathematics, Curtin University of Technology, Perth, Western Australia, pp 1–20.

Fensham PJ, 2004, 'Engagement with science: An international issue that goes beyond knowledge', paper presented at the *Science and Mathematics Education Conference (SMEC)*, Dublin City University, Ireland, 23–24 September.

Fensham PJ & Harlen W, 1999, 'School science and public understanding of science', *International Journal of Science Education*, 21(7), 755–763.

Feyerabend P, 1988, *Against method*. Verso, London.

Fielding M, 2001, 'Students as radical agents of change', *Journal of Educational Change,* 2(3), 123–141.

Fitzgerald RT, 1976, *Poverty and Education in Australia: Commission of Inquiry into Poverty*. 5th Main Report, Australian Government Publishing Service (AGPS), Canberra.

Freire P, 1972, *Pedagogy of the Oppressed*. Penguin, London.

Fullan M, 1999, *Change Forces: The Sequel*. RoutledgeFalmer, London.

Fullan M, 2001, *The New Meaning of Educational Change* (3rd edn). Teachers College Press, New York.

Fullan M, 2003, *Change Forces with a Vengeance*. Routledge Falmer, London.

Gardner H, 1993, *Multiple Intelligences: the theory in practice*. Basic Books, New York.

Gell-Mann M, 1994, *The quark and the jaguar: Adventures in the simple and the complex*. Freeman, New York.

Gidley J, 2002, 'Global youth culture: A transdisciplinary perspective', in J Gidley & S Inayatulla (eds), *Youth futures: Comparative research and transformative visions*. Praeger, Westport, CA, pp 3–18.

Gold E, Simon E & Brown C, 2005, 'A new conception of parent engagement. Community organising for school reform', in F English (ed.), *The SAGE handbook of educational leadership: Advances in theory, research and practice*.

Sage, Thousand Oaks, CA, pp 237–268.

Gonzalez N & Moll L, 2002, 'Cruzando el Puente: Building bridges to funds of knowledge', *Educational Policy*, 16(4), 623–641.

Gonzalez N, Moll L & Amanti C (eds), 2005, *Funds of knowledge: Theorizing Practices in Households, Communities and Classrooms.* Lawrence Erlbaum, Mahwah, New Jersey.

Goodman J, 1984, 'Reflection and teacher education: a case study and theoretical analysis', *Interchange*, 15, 19–27.

Goodrum D, 2006, *Inquiry in science classrooms: Rhetoric or reality?* <www.acer. edu.au/research_conferences/2006.html> accessed 27 November 2007.

Goodrum D, Hackling M & Rennie L, 2001, *The status and quality of teaching and learning of science in Australian Schools.* Department of Education, Training and Youth Affairs, Canberra.

Goodrum D & Rennie L, 2007, *Australian School Science Education National Action Plan*, 2008–2012, <www.dest.gov.au/sectors/school_education/publications_ resources/profiles/Australian_School_Education_Plan_2008_2012.htm> accessed 17 September 2007.

Gramsci A, 1971, *Selections from the Prison Notebooks.* International Publishers, New York.

Groundwater-Smith S, Mitchell J & Mockler N, 2007, *Learning in the middle years: More than a transition.* Thompson, South Melbourne, Victoria.

Gruenewald DA, 2003, 'The Best of Both Worlds: A Critical Pedagogy of Place', *Educational Researcher*, 32(4), 3–12.

Gruenewald DA & Smith G, 2008, 'Making room for the local', in DA Gruenewald & G Smith (eds), *Place-based education in the global age: Local diversity.* Lawrence Erlbaum, Mahwah, New Jersey, pp xiii-xxiii.

Haberman M, 1991, 'The Pedagogy of Poverty versus Good Teaching', *Phi Delta Kappan*, 73(4), 290–294.

Habermas J, 1984, *The theory of communicative action: Reason and the rationalization of society* (T. McCarthy trans.). Polity Press, Oxford, UK.

Hargreaves A & Fink D, 2003, 'Sustaining leadership', *Phi Delta Kappan*, 84(9), 693–700.

Hargreaves A & Goodson I, 2006, 'Educational change over time? The sustainability and nonsustainability of three decades of secondary school change and continuity', *Educational Administration Quarterly*, 42(1), 3–41.

Hattam R, 2005, 'The (im)possibility of listening to early school leavers: implications for middle schooling', paper presented at the *Australian Guidance & Counselling Association Annual Conference*, Adelaide, 29 September.

Hattam R, Brennan M, Zipin L & Comber B, 2009, 'Researching for social justice: contextual, conceptual and methodological challenges', *Discourse: Studies in the Cultural Politics of Education*, 30(3), 303–316.

Hattam R & Howard N, 2003, 'Engaging Lifeworlds: public curriculum and community building', in A Reid & P Thomson (eds), *Rethinking Public Education*. Post Pressed, Flaxton, Qld.

Hattam R, McInerney P, Smyth J & Lawson M, 1999, *Enhancing School-Community Dialogue*. Teachers' Learning Project Investigation Series, Flinders Institute for the Study of Teaching, Adelaide.

Hattam R & Prosser B, 2008, 'Unsettling deficit views of students and their communities', *Australian Educational Researcher*, 35(2), 15–36.

Hattam R & Zipin L, 2009, 'Towards pedagogical justice', *Discourse*, 30(3), 297–301.

Hayes D, Mills M, Christie P & Lingard B, 2006, *Teachers & schooling making a difference: Productive pedagogies, assessment and performance.* Allen and Unwin, Crows Nest, NSW.

Hodson D, 2003, 'Time for action: Science education for an alternative future', *International Journal of Science Education*, 25(6), 645–670

Homer D (ed.), 2004, *Talk of the Town: Stories and poems written for the course 'Writing the City'.* Lythrum Press, Adelaide.

Horlick-Jones T & Sime J, 2004, 'Living on the border: Knowledge, risk and transdisciplinarity', *Futures*, 36(4), 407–421.

Hubbard R & Power B, 1993, *The Art of Classroom Inquiry*. Heinemann, Portsmouth, New Hampshire.

Hyde S, 1992, 'Sharing power in the Classroom', in G Boomer, N Lester, C Onore & J Cook (eds), *Negotiating the Curriculum: educating for the 21st Century.* Falmer, London.

Irwin A & Wynne B (eds), 1996, *Misunderstanding science? The public reconstruction of science and technology.* Cambridge University Press, Cambridge.

Jenkins EW & Pell RG, 2006, *The relevance of science education project (ROSE) in England: A summary of findings.* Centre for Studies in Science and Mathematics Education, University of Leeds, Leeds.

Johnston K & Hayes D, 2007, Supporting student success at school through teacher professional learning: the pedagogy of disrupting the default modes of schooling, *International Journal of Inclusive Education*, 11(3), 371–381.

Johnston K & Hayes D, 2008, '"This is as good as it gets": Classroom lessons and learning in challenging circumstances', *Australian Journal of Language and Literacy*, 31(2), 109–127.

Jones D, Melville W & Bartley A, 2007, 'Science, inquiry and professional learning', *Professional Educator*, 6(2), 18–21.

Jones S, 2004, 'Living poverty and literacy learning: Sanctioning topics of students' lives', *Language Arts*, 8(16), 461–9.

Kamler B & Comber B (eds), 2005, *Turn-around Pedagogies: literacy interventions for at-risk students*. Primary English Teaching Association (PETA), Sydney.

Kelly P, 1992, *The End of Certainty*. Allen and Unwin, St. Leonards, NSW.

Kemmis S & McTaggart R (eds), 1988, *The action research planner* (third edn). Deakin University Press, Victoria.

Klein JT, 2004, 'Prospects for transdisciplinarity', *Futures*, 36(4), 515–526.

Knobel M & Lankshear C, 2003, 'Planning Pedagogy for i-mode: from flogging to blogging via wi-fi', *English in Australia – Literacy Learning: the middle years*, 139 (Summer 2003-04), 78–102.

Kress G, 2000, 'A curriculum for the future', *Cambridge Journal of Education*, 30(1), 133–145.

Ladwig J & Gore J, 1998, 'Nurturing Democracy in schools', in J Smyth, R Hattam & M Lawson (eds), *Schooling for a Fair Go*. Federation Press, Leichardt, NSW.

Lankshear C & Knobel M, 2004, *A handbook for teacher research: from design to implementation*. Open University Press, Buckingham.

Lawrence RJ & Despres C, 2004, 'Futures of transdisciplinarity', *Futures*, 36(4), 397–405.

Lee S & Roth W-M, 2002, 'Learning Science in the community', in W-M. Roth & J Désautels (eds), *Science education as/for sociopolitical action*. Peter Lang, New York, pp 37–66.

Lemke JL, 2001, 'Articulating communities: Sociocultural perspectives on science education', *Journal of Research in Science Teaching*, 38(3), 296–316.

Lingard B, 2007, 'Pedagogies of indifference', *International Journal of Inclusive Education*, 11(3), 245–266.

Lingard B, Mills M, Christie P & Hayes D, 2003, *Leading learning: making hope practical in schools*. Open University Press, Buckingham, England.

Lingard B, Mills M & Hayes D, 2002, 'Teachers, school reform and social justice: Challenging research and practice', *Australian Educational Researcher*, 27(3), 99–115.

Lowe I, 2009, *A big fix: Radical solutions for Australia's environmental crisis* (2nd edn). Black Inc, Melbourne, Australia.

Luke A, 1997, 'New narratives of human capital: Recent redirections in Australian Educational Policy', *Australian Educational Researcher*, 24(2), 1–22.

Luke A, Elkins J, Weir K, Land R, Carrington V, Dole S, Pendergast D, Kapitzke C, van Kraayenoord C, Moni K, McIntosh A, Mayer D, Bahr M, Hunter L, Chadbourne R, Bean T, Alverman D & Stevens L, 2003, *Beyond the Middle – A report about Literacy and Numeracy Development of Target Group Students in the Middle Years of Schooling*. Department of Education, Science and Training (DEST) and The University of Queensland, Australia.

Lusted D, 1986, 'Why Pedagogy?' *Screen*, 27(5), 2–14.

McDougall J, 2002, 'Teaching the visual generation: Teachers' responses to art, media and the visual literacy challenge', paper presented at *AARE Annual Conference 2002*, University of Queensland, Brisbane, viewed 18 March 2007, <www.aare.edu.au/02pap/mcd02235.htm>.

McInerney P, Hattam R & Smyth J, 2002, *Improving Numeracy Outcomes: A review of the Literature*. Flinders Institute for the Study of Teaching, Adelaide.

McKenzie S, 2004, 'Social Sustainability: Towards some definitions', *Hawke Research Institute Working Paper Series No.27*. University of South Australia, Magill.

McKnight J, 1995, *The careless society. Community and its counterfeits*. Basic Books, New York.

McNiff J, Lomax P & Whitehead J (eds), 1996, *You and your action research project*. Routledge, London.

McNiff J, Lomax P & Whitehead J, 1996, 'Living educational action research, in J McNiff, P Lomax & J Whitehead (eds), *You and your action research project*. Routledge, London, pp 7–28.

McWilliam E, Lather P & Morgan W, 1997, *Headwork, field work, textwork: A text shop in new feminist research*. The Centre for Policy and Leadership Studies, Brisbane.

Main K & Bryer F, 2007, 'A framework for research into Australian middle school practice', *Australian Educational Researcher*, 34(2), 91–106.

Maney B, 2005, 'Re-positioning the reluctant high-school reader', in B Comber & B Kamler (eds), *Turn-around pedagogies: Literacy interventions for at-risk students*. Primary English Teaching Association (PETA), Sydney.

Manning A, 1996, 'Look before you Leap' (Plenary Address), *Literacy: getting insights from classroom research conference*, Balyana, South Australia.

Marks GN & McKenzie P, 2000, 'Early School Leaving and 'non-completion' in Australia', *LSAY Briefing Paper No. 2*. Australian Council for Educational Research, Canberra.

Massey D, 1994, *Space, place and gender*. University of Minnesota Press, Minneapolis.

Meegan R & Mitchell A, 2001, '"It's not community round here, it's neighbourhood": Neighbourhood and cohesion in urban regeneration projects', *Urban Studies,* 38(12), 2167–2194.

Megalogenis G, 2006, *The Longest Decade.* Scribe Books, Carlton North.

Moll L, 2005, 'Reflection and Possibilities', in N Gonzalez, L Moll & C Amanti (eds), *Funds of Knowledge: Theorizing Practices in Households, Communities and Classrooms.* Lawrence Erlbaum, Mahwah, New Jersey.

Moll L, Amanti C, Neff D & Gonzalez N, 1992, 'Funds of Knowledge for Teaching: using a qualitative approach to connect homes to classrooms', *Theory into Practice,* 31(2), 132–141.

Nelson B, 2004, *Strengthening the Teaching Profession: launch of the National Institute for Quality Teaching and School Leadership*, Media release, viewed 1 April 2009, <www.dest.gov.au/minimas/live/nelson/2004/06/n721030604.asp>.

Newman L, Biedrzycki K, Patterson J & Baum F, 2007, A *Rapid Appraisal Case Study of South Australia's Social Inclusion Initiative*, viewed 3 February 2009, <www.socialinclusion.sa.gov.au/files/SEKN_SA_Case_Study_Final_Report.pdf>

Noakes M & Clifton P, 2005, *The CSIRO total wellbeing diet.* Penguin, Victoria.

O'Brien D, 2001, *'At-Risk' adolescents: Redefining competence through the multiliteracies of intermediality, visual arts, and representation*, International Reading Association, Inc, Australia, viewed 18 March 2007, <www.readingonline.org/newliteracies/obrien/index.html>.

Office of Employment 2003, *Regional Profile: Northern Adelaide Statistical Subdivision*, Department of Further Education, Employment, Science and Technology, Adelaide.

Oldfather P, 1995, 'Songs "come back to most of them": Students' experience as researchers', *Theory into Practice,* 43(2), 131–7.

Osborne J & Collins S, 2001, 'Pupils' views of the role and value of the science curriculum: A focus group study', *International Journal of Science Education,* 23(5), 441–467.

Osborne J, Simon S & Collins S, 2003, 'Attitudes towards science: A review of the literature and its implications', *International Journal of Science Education,* 25(9), 1049–1079.

Osterman K & Kottkamp R, 1993, *Reflective Practice for Educators.* Corwin Press, Newbury Park, CA.

Ovsienko H & Zipin L, 2007, 'Making social justice curricular: Exploring ambivalences within teacher professional identity', in P Jeffrey (ed.), *Proceedings of the Australian Association for Research in Education Annual Conference*. Adelaide, 2006.

Paige K, Lloyd D & Chartres M, 2008, 'Moving towards transdisciplinarity: An ecological sustainable focus for science and mathematics pre-service education in the primary/middle years', *Asia-Pacific Journal of Teacher Education*, 36(1), 19–33.

Pearson M & Somekh B, 2006, 'Learning transformation with technology: a question of sociocultural contexts?', *International Journal of Qualitative Studies in Education*, 19(4), 519–539.

Peel M, 1995, *Good Times, Hard Times: the past and the future in Elizabeth*. Melbourne University Press, Carlton.

Pendergast D & Bahr N, 2005, *Teaching Middle Years: Rethinking Curriculum, Pedagogy and assessment*. Allen & Unwin, Crows Nest, NSW.

Pinar W, 2004, *What is Curriculum Theory?* Lawrence Erlbaum Associates, Mahwah, New Jersey.

Pocock B, 2003, *Work/Life Collision*. Federation Press, Annandale, NSW.

Postman N & Weingartner C, 1969, *Teaching as a Subversive Activity*. Dell, New York.

Prosser B, 2006, *See Red: critical narrative in ADHD Research*. PostPressed, Teneriffe, 51-66

Prosser B, 2008, 'Critical pedagogy and the mythopoetic; a case study from Adelaide's northern urban fringe', in T Leonard & P Willis (eds), *Pedagogies of the imagination: mythopoetic curriculum in educational practice*. Springer Press, Dordrecht, pp 203–222.

Prosser B, 2008, 'Unfinished but not exhausted: a review of Australian middle schooling', *Australian Journal of Education*, 52(2), 151–167.

Prosser B, McCallum F, Milroy P, Comber B & Nixon H, 2008, 'I'm smart and I'm not joking: aiming high in the middle years of schooling', *Australian Educational Researcher*, 35(2), 15–36.

Pusey M, 1998, 'Australia: Once the lighthouse social democracy of the world. The impact of recent economic reforms', *Thesis Eleven*, 55 (November), 41–59.

Reid A, 2004, 'Towards a culture of inquiry in DECS' Occasional Paper Series, No. 1, South Australian Department of Education and Children's Services, Adelaide, pp 1–19.

Reid A & O'Donoghue M, 2004, 'Revisiting enquiry-based teacher education in neo-liberal times', *Teaching and Teacher Education*, 20(6), 559–570.

Rennie L, 2006, 'The community's contribution to science learning: Making it count', presentation to ACER Research Conference, *Boosting Science Learning:*

What Will It Take? August 14, 2006, ACER Press, Camberwell, Victoria.

Rose N, 1996, 'The death of the social? Re-figuring the territory of government', *Economy & Society*, 25, 327–356.

Schon D, 1983, *The Reflective Practitioner*. Basic Books, New York.

Schon D, 1990, *Educating the Reflective Practitioner: Towards a New Design for Teaching and Learning*. Jossey-Bass, San Francisco.

Sefton-Green J (ed), 1998, *Digital Diversions: Youth Culture in the Age of Multimedia*. University College London Press, London.

Sellar S, 2009, 'The responsible uncertainity of pedagogy', *Discourse*, 30(3), 347–360.

Sellar S & Cormack P, 2009, 'Redesigning pedagogies in middle years classrooms; challenges for teachers working with disadvantaged students', *Pedagogy, Culture & Society*, 17(2), 123–139.

Semken S & Butler Freeman C, 2008, 'Sense of place in the practice and assessment of place-based science teaching' *Science Education*, 92(6), 1042–1057.

Sfard A & Prusak A, 2005, 'Telling Identities: in search of an analytical investigating learning as a culturally shaped activity', *Educational Researcher*, 25(3), 14–22.

Simmons III S, 2001, 'Multiple Intelligences at the Middle Level: Models for learning in Art and across the Disciplines', *Art Education*, 54(3), 18–24.

Skamp K & Logan M, 2005, 'Students' interest in science across the middle school years', *Teaching Science*, 52(4), 8–15.

Smith G, 2002, 'Place-based education: Learning to be where we are', *Phi Delta Kappan*, 83(8), 584–594.

Smith-Maddox R, 1999, 'An inquiry-based reform effort: Creating the conditions for reculturing and restructuring schools', *The Urban Review*, 31(3), 283–304.

Smyth J, Dow A, Hattam R, Reid A & Shacklock G, 2000, *Teachers' work in a globalizing economy*. Falmer, London.

Smyth J & Hattam R, 2004, *'Dropping Out', Drifting Off, being Excluded: Becoming Somebody Without School*. Peter Lang, New York.

Smyth J, Hattam R & Lawson M (eds), 1998, *Schooling for a Fair Go*. Federation Press, Leichardt, NSW.

Smyth J, McInerney P & Hattam R, 2003, 'Tackling school leaving at its source: a case of reform in the middle years of schooling', *British Journal of Sociology of Education*, 24(2), 177–193.

Snyder I, 2008, *The literacy wars: Why teaching children to read and write is a battleground in Australia*. Allen & Unwin, Sydney.

Sobel D, 2004, *Place-based education: connecting classrooms and communities*. The Orion Society, Greater Barrington, MA.

Sorenson M, 2008, 'STAR. Service to all relations' in DA Gruenewald & G Smith (eds), *Place-based education in the global age: Local Diversity.* Lawrence Erlbaum, Majwah, New Jersey, pp 49–64.

Sousa D, 2006, *How the brain learns* (3rd edn). Hawker Brownlow Education, Heatherton, Victoria.

Starnes B, 1999, *The Foxfire approach to teaching and learning: John Dewey, experiential learning and the core practices.* ERIC Clearinghouse on Rural Education and Small Schools, Charleston.

Suzuki D & McConnell A, 1997, *The sacred balance: rediscovering our place in nature.* Allen & Unwin, St Leonards, NSW.

Taylor M, 2000, 'Maintaining community involvement in regeneration: what are the issues?', *Local Economy,* 15(3), 251–255.

Taylor S, Rizvi F, Lingard B & Henry M, 1997, *Educational policy and the politics of change.* Routledge, London, New York.

Teese R, 1998, 'Curriculum hierarchy, private schooling and the segmentation of Australian Secondary schooling, 1947–1985', *British Journal of Sociology of Education,* 19(3), 401–417.

Thomson P, 1998, 'Thoroughly Modern Management and a Cruel Accounting: The Effects of Public Sector Reform on Public Education', in *Going Public: Education Policy and Public Education in Australia.* Australian Curriculum Studies Assoc, Canberra, pp 9–17.

Thomson P, 2002, 'Vicki and Thanh', in *Schooling the rustbelt kids: making the difference in changing times.* Allen and Unwin, Crows Nest, NSW.

Thomson P, 2006, 'Mission possible: making a difference in neighbourhoods made poor', keynote address, AEU Middle Schooling Conference, Adelaide, November 17.

Thomson P & Comber B, 2003, 'Deficient 'disadvantaged students' or media-savvy meaning makers? Engaging new metaphors for redesigning classrooms and pedagogies', *McGill Journal of Education,* 38(2), 305–328.

Thomson P & Gunter H, 2007, 'The methodology of students-as-researchers: valuing and using experience to develop methods', *Discourse: studies in the cultural politics of education,* 28(3), 327–342.

Tytler R, 2007, *Re-imagining Science Education: Engaging students in science for Australia's future.* ACER Press, Camberwell, Victoria.

Tytler R & Symington D, 2006a, 'Boosting science learning and engagement: what will it take?' proceedings of the ACER Research Conference, *Boosting science learning – what will it take?* 13–15 August, Canberra, www<research.acer.edu.au/research_conference_2006/1> Accessed 22 July 2009.

Tytler R & Symington D, 2006b, 'Science in school and society', *Teaching Science*, 52(3), 10–15.

Vacca R, Vacca J & Bruneau B, 1997, 'Teachers Reflecting on Practice', in J Flood, S Brice-Heath & D Lapp (eds), *Handbook of research on teaching literacy through the communicative and visual arts*. Macmillan Library Reference USA, New York.

Valencia R (ed), 1997, *The evolution of deficit thinking. Educational thought and practice*. Falmer, London.

Van de Walle J, 2007, *Elementary and Middle School Mathematics: Teaching Developmentally*, 6th edn. Pearson Education, Boston USA.

Venville G, Wallace J, Rennie L & Malone J, 2002, 'Curriculum integration: Eroding the high ground of science as a school subject?' *Studies in Science Education*, 37, 43–84.

Webb J, 2000, 'Action research and the classroom teacher', *Practically Primary*, 5(1), 16–24.

Wells G, 1994, *Changing Schools from Within: Creating Communities of Inquiry*. OISE Press, Toronto.

Wheatley N & Rawlins D, 1987, *My Place*. Collins Dove, Melbourne.

Wood G, 1992, 'The school and the community'. In G Wood (ed.), *Schools That Work: America's Most Innovative Public Education Programs*. Plume, New York.

Zeichner K & Liston D, 1996, *Reflective Teaching: An Introduction*. Lawrence Erlbaum, Mahwah, New Jersey.

Ziman J, 1994, 'The rationale of STS education is in the approach', in J Solomon & G Aikenhead (eds), *STS Education International Perspectives on Reform*. Teachers College Press, New York, pp 21–31.

Zipin L, 2009, 'Dark funds of knowledge, deep funds of pedagogy; exploring boundaries between lifeworlds and schools', *Discourse*, 30(3), 317–331.

Zipin L & Reid A, 2008, 'A justice-oriented citizenship education: Making community curricular', in J Arthur, I Davies & C Hahn (eds), *SAGE Handbook of Education for Citizenship and Democracy*, SAGE, Los Angeles, 533–544.